Long-Distance Pigeon Racing

JOHN CLEMENTS

FOREWORD BY ALEX RANS,

SECRETARY OF THE CUREGHEM CENTRE, BRUSSELS

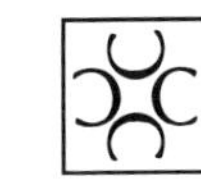

THE CROWOOD PRESS

First published in 2007 by
The Crowood Press Ltd
Ramsbury, Marlborough
Wiltshire SN8 2HR

www.crowood.com

British Library Cataloguing-in-Publication Data
A catalogue record for this book is available from the British Library.

ISBN 978 1 86126 944 7

Typeset by Phoenix Typesetting, Auldgirth, Dumfriesshire

Printed and bound in Singapore by Craft Print International Ltd

Contents

Foreword

Alex Rans

(Secretary of the Cureghem Centre, Belgium, organizers of the International Barcelona)

I am pleased to be asked to write a foreword to this book because it confirms what I have been thinking and trying to do for many years. The book tries to get behind many modern techniques and take our thinking back to the pigeon itself. A return to the central role of the pigeon is long overdue. John Clements has done this by seeking out the views of successful fanciers who have, in their various ways, accepted the challenge of long-distance racing regardless of the circumstances in which they find themselves. Some have lasted longer than their contemporaries, some have achieved top results with limited financial resources, while others have succeeded in getting their pigeons to distances that not long ago were thought impossible. The one thing they have in common is that they have all accepted the challenge of breeding better pigeons to fly and compete in long-distance events.

Alex Rans seated at the desk from where he plans the Barcelona International.

If there is one message from this book it is that long-distance pigeon racing is essentially about the pigeon. It is from within the natural resources and unique ability of special pigeons that the sport will not only thrive but flourish. We must all begin to look from the pigeon outwards. The greatest improvement we can all make in our own lofts is for the pigeons under our care to breed a higher percentage of really good birds. Improved breeding will always improve everyone's performance by the greatest amount. This book confirms this message by providing examples of those that have accepted the challenge.

Its central message leaves me more confident than ever that the sport has a brighter future than has seemed possible for many years. This will be achieved through improved breeding and the critical study of results. This book will become a part of all our futures and perhaps even the future of the sport itself.

Acknowledgements

I would like to thank all the fanciers I have interviewed for this book, not only for their valuable and honest contributions, but also for the excellent meat and drink I have enjoyed during my visits. I would particularly like to thank two fanciers and their wives, Russell Bradford and his wife Clare, and Geoff Cooper and his wife Catherine, who not only fed me but showed extra hospitality by allowing me to sleep overnight, followed by a hearty breakfast the next morning. I really wish to thank Alan Darragh and his wife for picking me up at Belfast airport and delivering me back after my work was done – this was more than helpful. The many times I have visited Herman Brinkman, Jelle Outhuyse, Ad Hagens and Bernard Deweerdt have always given great pleasure. You can easily see why they are all such good fanciers – choosing a wife in the first instance must be a part of it. I cannot forget to mention Nigel Lane and his wife Judith. It was Nigel who took me to France to interview Robert Ben in Calais. Unfortunately I was delayed by road works on my way to meet Nigel. Not only did he turn around when half way to the Channel Tunnel, but not once did he complain about having done so. I thank him enormously.

Lastly, may I thank Alex Rans, the Secretary of the Cureghem Centre, for writing the foreword. Alex has always been more than helpful in so many ways. I appreciate it more than I can say.

John Clements
Stockport, 2006

Photography Acknowledgements

The author and the publisher would like to thank the following individuals and organizations for providing photographs and for granting permission for them to be reproduced in this book:

The Bath Chronicle
Peter Bennett, Darlington
Anthony Bolton, Broadstairs
Sid Collins, Doagh, Co. Antrim
Catherine Cooper, Peasedown St John, Bath
Henk Kuijlaars, Gravenzandweg 20, 2671 JR Naaldwijk, The Netherlands
Martin Kwarkernaat, De Vredenburg 20, 3291 GC Strijen, The Netherlands
Keith Mott, Esher, Surrey
Northern Ireland Provincial Amalgamation (F. C. Russell, Secretary)
Peter van Raamsdonk, Kerklaan 45, 2291 CD Wateringen, The Netherlands
Bryan Siggers, Pigeon Photographer, Ash Vale, Surrey GU12 5LE
Jelle Outhuyse, Harlingen, The Netherlands
Foto Sinaeve, Stationsstraat 23, 8110 Kortemark, Belgium
Els de Weyn, Steenakker 212, 9000 Ghent, Belgium
Jan Van Wonterghem, Kortinghse Straat 14, 8520 Kuurne, Belgium

CHAPTER 1

Herman Brinkman

Tuk, Steenwijk, The Netherlands

BACKGROUND

Herman Brinkman lives in Tuk, a small suburb of Steenwijk in the province of Overijssel. Quiet and unassuming, he is a languages teacher by profession, his speciality being German; his English is also excellent. He is fully committed to pigeon racing at extreme distances. It is his life's work. You know he believes in what he is doing from the way he smiles and his eyes twinkle when the subject is mentioned. Anxious for his advice, you are obliged to wait, for this quiet, capable man is inclined to let you talk first while he listens. He then says much less than you would like, but that is his nature.

Performances from Barcelona since 2000
International positions in the top 2%
2001
14th International (25,760 birds)
424th International (25,760 birds)

2004
78th International (24,913 birds) (this pigeon flew Barcelona again in 2005)

John Clements and Herman Brinkman.

The distance from Barcelona to the Brinkman loft is 1,306km (816 miles)

He has of course won many other awards, including championships. From 1994 to 1997 he was champion of the National 'Fondspiegel' competition in different categories. Seventy-six times he has had pigeons in the top thirty in national races. Many other fanciers have done well with his pigeons. Even Alex Rans, the Secretary of the Cureghem Centre and the organizer of the

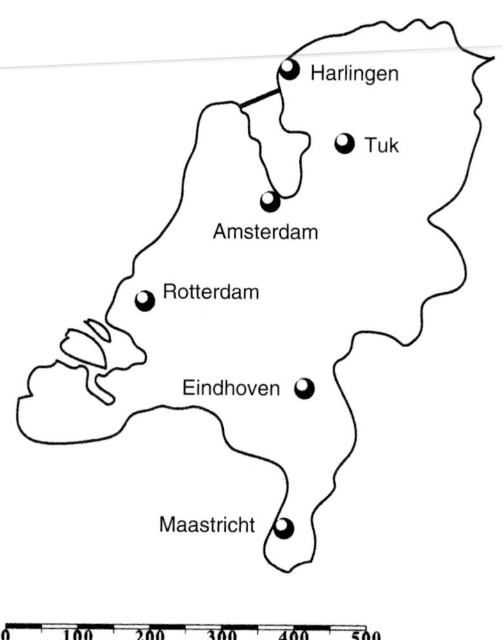

The Netherlands showing the Northerly location in the Netherlands of the Outhuyse and Brinkman lofts, both flying more than 800 miles from Barcelona.

Map of the five original Race Points (four in France and one in Spain) used for international events organized by Belgian Clubs. The countries that usually take part in these races are Germany, Luxembourg, France, Belgium, the Netherlands and Great Britain, but Poland, Hungary and Czechoslovakia also enter from time to time. Barcelona is the longest race and generally considered the premier race of the series. Barcelona re-started in 1951 after World War II with an entry of only 2,039 pigeons. It has grown over the years to well over 25,000 pigeons.

The Brinkman loft in winter.

International Barcelona, has Brinkman birds and has done well with them. Jan and Hanne Sas from Vorselaar (Belgium), Bennie Homma from Balk (Netherlands) and Beullens and son of Heverlee (Belgium) won 9th, 27th, 74th and 111th National Barcelona. As recently as 2004 a pigeon of W. Derksen of Almelo in the Netherlands, with half 'Brinkie Boy' blood and flying over 1,200km (750 miles), was 72nd International Barcelona, beating Herman himself (78th) in the same race.

THE INTERVIEW

The Start

How old are you, when did you first start with pigeons and when did you move up to long-distance pigeons?

I am now fifty-six years old. I started with pigeons while I was still at school, probably about twelve or fourteen years of age. My father had the pigeons. I was only allowed to clean them – I was not given the luxury of making decisions.

I was eighteen years old when I first came into contact with a long-distance pigeon. I was at University at Groningen at the time. A neighbour gave me a very good hen that was first in the National from Ruffec in an overnight flight. Later on, in October I think it was, I came home from Groningen and went in the loft. The hen was missing. I asked my father where the pigeon was and he told me, 'This pigeon was not a good pigeon for it only won one prize, so I put it out.' My father was not a long-distance man; his requirement was for pigeons to fly every week and win many prizes each season. This is an example of the difference between long-distance thinking and middle-distance thinking.

What stock did you first buy for the long distance and do you still have some of these pigeons in your present colony?

Later on I persuaded my father to have some long-distance pigeons. My father and I went to Ko Nipius for some Jan Aarden pigeons. He was a top long-distance man at that time.

That was the start with long-distance pigeons. Almost nothing is left of those pigeons now, but one of my early great pigeons, 'Fijne Zwarte', has contributed greatly to my colony and some of this blood is still present in the family today.

By the time I was twenty-seven and thinking of getting married and setting up on my own, I was firmly convinced that long-distance racing was what I wanted to do. You could say I was sold on the idea. Because I would need furniture for my new house, I decided to combine the two ambitions. I went to buy furniture from Hans Eijerkamp, who was and still is one of the biggest furniture dealers in Holland. Hans is also a pigeon fancier.

In those days if you bought furniture from Hans Eijerkamp, as part of the deal you got some pigeons for free. I asked him for some of the best long-distance pigeons he had. He promised me four from the best of the Van der Wegen strain. These pigeons were of impeccable pedigree, the best he had. They came from such illustrious ancestry as 'De Lamme', 'De Barcelona' and 'Oud Doffertje', all foundation pigeons of the Van der Wegen family. Of course I was anxious to see what such pigeons off such a good strain would look like. When they arrived at my house in Tuk, I was so disappointed with them I thought of sending them back. They looked so small and insignificant, not at all what I expected.

I telephoned Hans and he told me that of course he would change them, but if I were wise I should hang on to them and wait to see how they developed. Reluctantly I agreed and I'm glad I did. These four original Van der Wegen pigeons are now famous: three of the birds turned out to be champion breeders. I learnt a valuable lesson from this. Long-distance pigeons do not always look the part. Indeed, long-distance pigeons are not always beautiful. What is absolutely necessary in long-distance pigeons is for them to be of good racing ancestry. Good looks are secondary. Even today, and in spite of the experience I had with the original Van der Wegen birds, I am still inclined to select young pigeons by looking and handling, but I have learned to curb this tendency a bit. Every year I write down the ring numbers of what I consider to be future good prospects, but these selections almost always turn out to be wrong when subsequently tested in actual races. My son makes fun of me for being so wrong. Where I am possibly a little bit clever is that I admit I do not know how to select pigeons accurately before they have flown, even though I still do it. Over the years I have learnt to leave a lot to the pigeons to prove themselves. It is they who have to do it, they who have to fly the races and decide how to get home. I should have more confidence in the pigeons and less in my ability to select. The only thing I can do is to try to breed ability into the flock as a whole and hope super ability comes out from time to time in individual pigeons.

A current 'Champion': 'Barca Boy' – 78th International Barcelona 2004.

The First Cross

When did this happen?

In 1990 I bought pigeons from Vertelman and son of Hoogkarspel. I thought my present colony was getting too inbred. These Vertelman pigeons were based on the strains of Jan Theelen, Martha Van Geel and Van der Wegen. I think I bought twelve pigeons from Vertelman. One of these was a pigeon that turned out to be one I later called the 'Golden Breeder'. He produced good pigeons from the very start. Among the first pigeons he produced were 'Brinkie Boy' and the 'Drie Barcelona', both very good pigeons. 'Brinkie Boy' won first National Limoges. The 'Golden Breeder' was mated with '633', which as a yearling was 20th National Bergerac. This pigeon had the old original Ko Nipius blood in it from 'Fijn Zwarte' and some of the Van der Wegen blood going back to 'De Lamme'.

Again, as so often happens in long-distance pigeon racing, not everything was a success. At the time I bought the Vertelman pigeons there were also two full brothers of the 'Golden Breeder' in the same kit of pigeons. These two brothers produced nothing worth mentioning. This is an example of something you find time and time again in long-distance pigeons. Only a few individuals have that vital ingredient to be champions. Even fewer can pass this vital ingredient on to their offspring.

What influences you when you import stock into your loft? Must they be bred from sons and daughters of good birds, and do you have a preference for either cocks or hens?

First of all I study results from the National and International races. I also take note of the distance flown and the numbers taking part in these races. In 1990 I spotted the name Vertelman and sons of Hoogkarspel, here in the Netherlands. They were doing really well and were on top form at the time.

Brinkie Boy, a first cross that went on to produce winners. Brinkie Boy is a favourite of Herman Brinkman. Photo: © Copyright Peter van Raamsdonk

Territory – each cock owns its nest box.

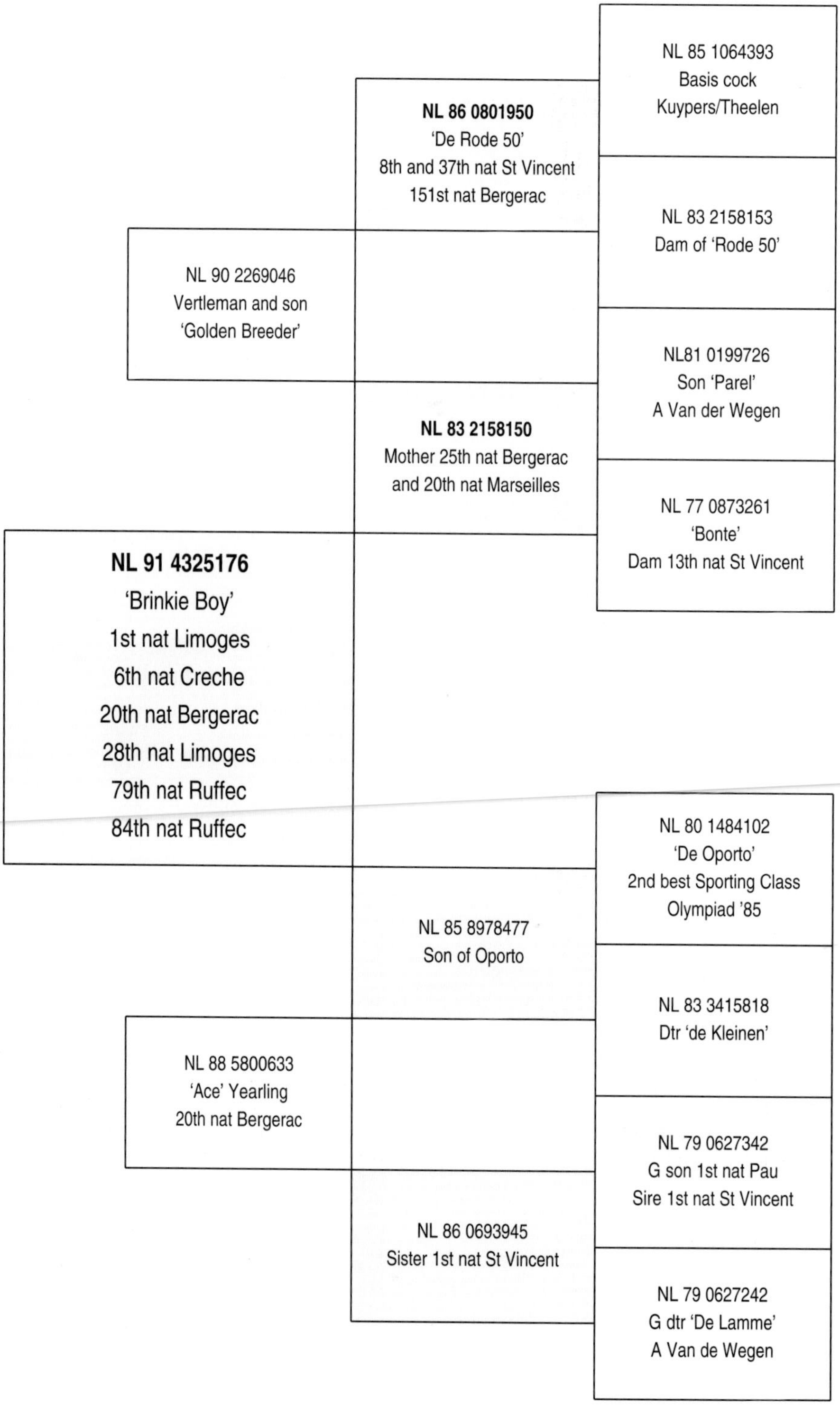

NL 91 4325176
'Brinkie Boy'
1st nat Limoges
6th nat Creche
20th nat Bergerac
28th nat Limoges
79th nat Ruffec
84th nat Ruffec

NL 90 2269046
Vertleman and son
'Golden Breeder'

NL 86 0801950
'De Rode 50'
8th and 37th nat St Vincent
151st nat Bergerac

NL 85 1064393
Basis cock
Kuypers/Theelen

NL 83 2158153
Dam of 'Rode 50'

NL 83 2158150
Mother 25th nat Bergerac
and 20th nat Marseilles

NL81 0199726
Son 'Parel'
A Van der Wegen

NL 77 0873261
'Bonte'
Dam 13th nat St Vincent

NL 88 5800633
'Ace' Yearling
20th nat Bergerac

NL 85 8978477
Son of Oporto

NL 80 1484102
'De Oporto'
2nd best Sporting Class
Olympiad '85

NL 83 3415818
Dtr 'de Kleinen'

NL 86 0693945
Sister 1st nat St Vincent

NL 79 0627342
G son 1st nat Pau
Sire 1st nat St Vincent

NL 79 0627242
G dtr 'De Lamme'
A Van de Wegen

Pedigree of Brinkie Boy.

Their results were fantastic. I noted that Vertelman was 9th National from Barcelona, a distance of 1,277km (800 miles). I thought 9th National at this distance was so good I must visit him and see the man and the pigeons for myself. I didn't know him personally, so I telephoned and arranged to visit him.

I always think anything you use for a cross must be off good top-quality birds that are performing well at a similar distance to your own and are raced in similar circumstances. Both cocks and hens are important, but I think as a general rule the good cocks come from good hens and good hens from good cocks. Occasionally a super breeder will produce both good cocks and good hens, but it is very rare. In fact good breeders are very rare themselves. You must always be on the look out for good breeders in your own loft; they are the future.

I will give an example. This year I bought a pigeon from the 1st National Brive. I will probably breed twenty pigeons from him. If the pigeons as a team are not up to standard and fail to live up to the criteria I need, then the whole lot must be disposed of. I must make up my mind quite quickly. I do not allow more than two or three years at the maximum. I can't afford to wait about with new pigeons, considering the space I have and the number of birds I can keep. They have to be better or at least as good as my own.

Have you made any mistakes?

Oh, yes. I can't name names, of course, but I have bought pigeons with exactly the right pedigree and performance and still they have failed. The whole business of breeding pigeons for long distances is fraught with difficulty. Some that I have bought with great expectations did not do any good at all. It is a gamble, I think. There is one thing, though. When you visit someone with the intention of buying birds from him, you must feel the man wants to help you. If you feel this then it is likely you will get pigeons off some of his best birds, and then you have a chance. If they are not off the best, and are not backed by good performance, then you have little chance. Here in the Netherlands we are lucky that we are able to compete in top races of undisputed quality. My position here in Tuk is not ideal, however, because I am one of the longer flying fanciers. I am mostly at a disadvantage in international races because of the distance, but it would be a huge mistake to avoid competing at the top level because of this reason. You must always compete against the best, regardless of your position, if only to test your breeding against the best birds and in the best races available.

The Race Team from Year to Year

How do you treat young birds in the year of their birth? Do you race young birds? What do you expect of them? Do you breed late breds?

I race them but I don't expect anything from them. If I can, I try to race them to 400km (250 miles), but I go on holiday in late summer so it is not always possible. The pigeons always fit in with my life style and family commitments. I do rear a few late-bred youngsters off the best birds after they have finished racing for the year.

How are the late breds treated and are they, as is generally perceived, a lot of trouble?

When I visit my father, who lives some kilometres away in Raalte, I take them with me and release them there. I do this all through the winter months regardless of the conditions. This year I bred twelve; I lost two of them, not in training but taken by hawks.

No, I do not think they are a lot of trouble providing you are patient. Late pigeons, because they are born in the summer in good weather, have the best conditions to grow. Late pigeons are generally bred from better parents. For all these reasons I think they can be better birds than others, but you must be patient and wait for them. Generally they are healthier. Some of my best pigeons have been hatched late in the year. I think they are worth waiting for.

How do you treat yearlings? How do you evaluate them and what do you expect of them?

If it can be arranged they fly in a race from 800km (500 miles), though that is not always possible. They are not expected to win a prize: all they are expected to do is to get home in reasonable time. They are introduced to widowhood and raced on widowhood as yearlings.

Do you evaluate them in the hand?

I do, I can't resist it, but most times I am wrong. The basket is a much better selector. I make many mistakes. I don't think there is one fancier in the whole world who knows which pigeons are better before they are tested by the basket. I don't think it is possible to know this sort of thing. You can look at muscles, eyes, bones and all these things, but the basket is still by far the best guide simply because we can't see inside their heads.

Is there any physical attribute you particularly look for in a mature pigeon? Are you looking at the wing, the throat, the head, a particular shape of the body or what?

I do like good feather, but for the rest, the basket is best. Good pigeons come in all shapes and sizes.

Immunity

Do you consider a high degree of immunity to illness essential for a long-distance loft to perform well?

Dirty lofts that have not been cleaned out clinically are good since they cultivate high immunity. Over time such lofts build up a sound constitution that helps race birds contend with confinement in the basket during races. Often the healthy pigeon you have sent to the race sits next to a sick pigeon for four or five days in the race pannier. In conditions like this they should not easily fall to ailments of any kind; indeed, while some pigeons that lack a good immunity are losing form, yours should thrive and possibly gain form. There is something else to consider. During preparations for a really long race it is essential that things go well in the races leading up to the big one. Any kind of sickness interrupts smooth preparation. A good immunity helps to achieve protection in the build-up phase so that form increases, rather than decreases, on the run up to the important race.

Do you also think that quite dirty lofts, like yours, help the pigeons to be more content?

Yes, I think it is important that the pigeons feel at home in the loft. If you are interfering all the time by constantly scraping and cleaning, contentment suffers. You have to realize the loft is their home; you have to recognize and respect this. To further help contentment I have an aviary in front of each loft where the pigeons can go out all through the winter. The aviary has a wire bottom through which the droppings can fall. Most of the time they prefer to sit outside. This is also good. It is good to allow the pigeons to have a choice but in some things you cannot allow choice. The pigeons have to be vaccinated every year for instance. This you must do. My pigeons are vaccinated for paramyxo and pigeon pox in one combined dose.

If illness, such as a respiratory condition, were to arise spontaneously, would you immediately suppress the individual or its offspring without attempting to treat the pigeon, or would you allow it to persist and wait for the pigeons to get over it?

If the loft is well built and has good ventilation then you have no problem, but if something persists you have to do something about it and treat each pigeon individually. In my experience, if the loft is well designed with good ventilation then you usually don't have a problem.

But three weeks before Barcelona I do treat with Linco Spectrin, which is a mild antibiotic for the breathing, and for trichomoniasis (canker).

Do you think that these treatments affect the form of the pigeons?

Yes, I think they can. It's not always good and form can suffer, but if everything is given three weeks before Barcelona they have time to build up form in time for the race.

Do you use anything like garlic or extra amino acids on their food, something for form like oil, or even peanuts?

No, I have tried all these things and they do not help, especially in long races. The only extras I use are some small seeds I give them prior to the long races. But perhaps I am old-fashioned. I know supplements help racing cyclists. Perhaps I should take another look and see if I can improve things a bit, but at the moment I don't have any plans.

Advice for the Novice

What advice would you give a novice attempting to build a team of long-distance pigeons, and what stage should he have reached after three years?

A novice should start with ordinary healthy pigeons and use them as feeders. He must then go to two very good fanciers who have good results at the distance you require and buy eggs off their best birds. The two fanciers must have different strains of birds.

After three years he should be racing very well – not international races, at extreme distances, but National and overnight races.

To be truthful I really don't think you have allowed enough time for him to evaluate himself. The first thing is, he must have a very good loft. A dry, well-ventilated loft is essential, and such a loft, with good ventilation and conditions, and where the birds are happy, can only be achieved by trial and error. If he is to be a good fancier he must be motivated and patient at the same time.

Before and After the Race

Do you fly widowhood, on the nest, both systems or something else?

Most of the time on widowhood, but this year I had twelve couples on nest. The nest hens were coupled with twelve stock pigeons so the cocks were always there when they returned from races.

Are the yearlings on widowhood and how much exercise do they take?

Yes, I have a total of fifty cocks on widowhood,

including the yearlings. I encourage them to exercise freely around the loft. It is very, very important, perhaps the most important thing of all. They must exercise around the loft twice a day for 90 minutes each time. I have a ball that I throw at them to start them off. They perhaps begin with as little as 20 minutes, but gradually I build them up to 90 minutes twice a day. Exercise around the loft is very important – if they don't exercise then you can't hope to get a prize.

Can you give me some idea of how you would treat a three- or four-year-old widowhood pigeon being prepared for big races such as Barcelona or Perpignan?

This year I didn't breed from the older pigeons, those that are three or four years old or more. It is important to forego breeding in order to delay the wing moult. When they are racing from Perpignan in August I want a good wing. I want two or three moulted flights only. If you do not breed in the early part of the year this is then possible. If you breed and rear youngsters early the breeding kick starts the moult sooner than you would like. The yearlings that are only going to 700 or 800km (430 or 500 miles) are bred from, but the older pigeons are not.

Do the Perpignan pigeons also go to Barcelona or, should I say, do the Barcelona pigeons go on to Perpignan in the same year?

That is the intention, but it's not always possible if it is a hard race from Barcelona. It's too much to ask of the pigeon in such conditions at this distance. If it is an easy race from Barcelona then it is possible, but not every year is easy. If you push them beyond their limit you can lose too many good pigeons. They may look all right on the outside but inside they are not so good. You can't ask a pigeon to give everything twice in one season. A pigeon must always have reserves it can call on.

This year, before Barcelona, I raced the pigeons from Ruffec, a distance of 866km (540 miles). After this race they rested for three or four weeks prior to Barcelona. They need to conserve energy and stamina for such a race, but every week I give them the hen to keep their interest and train them for 50km by car. The hen is always waiting. Apart from that I do nothing.

Regarding the hens that are raced to the nest, what condition are they sent in and how are they trained?

The best condition is for the hen to be sent sitting on a three- or four-day-old youngster. Some hens are good on eggs, but most of the time sitting on a such a youngster is the best. I do not train them by car or anything like; they must exercise at the loft in the early afternoon while the cocks are sitting on the eggs. I don't know if that is good enough, but my circumstances dictate that I do it this way. If I were at home, instead of working, it would be possible to exercise the hens twice a day, but when you have a job that's not possible. With pigeons there is always a compromise to be made. I think with more time I could do better with hens.

What do you do in the final three or four days before basketing for an important international race and what do you do after they come home?

I give them some small seeds with their food – nothing special. I don't give peanuts or anything like that; maybe it is good, but at the moment I don't do it. After the race they are allowed to rest. I don't allow the hen on the first day they return, so I lock them up alone and feed them in their box, since the box that's their territory is their reward for the effort they have put in. Cocks are prepared to suffer a long flight just to return to their box. They have the hen on the second day, then after a day or two they are allowed to go outside. I don't want them to have to fight for their box immediately they return owing to the condition they're in. A tired pigeon forced to fight when it is not in top condition would have its morale destroyed for a whole season, and possibly for the whole of its career.

I'll give you a good example of how territory works and how you can take advantage of this trait in a pigeon's character. In 2001 I won the 5th National and 14th International from Barcelona. That year a yearling was lost, so the pigeon that was to fly Barcelona ended up occupying two boxes, his own and that of the lost yearling. When he

Hermanator – 14th International Barcelona 2001 against 25,760 pigeons. Photo: © Copyright Peter van Raamsdonk

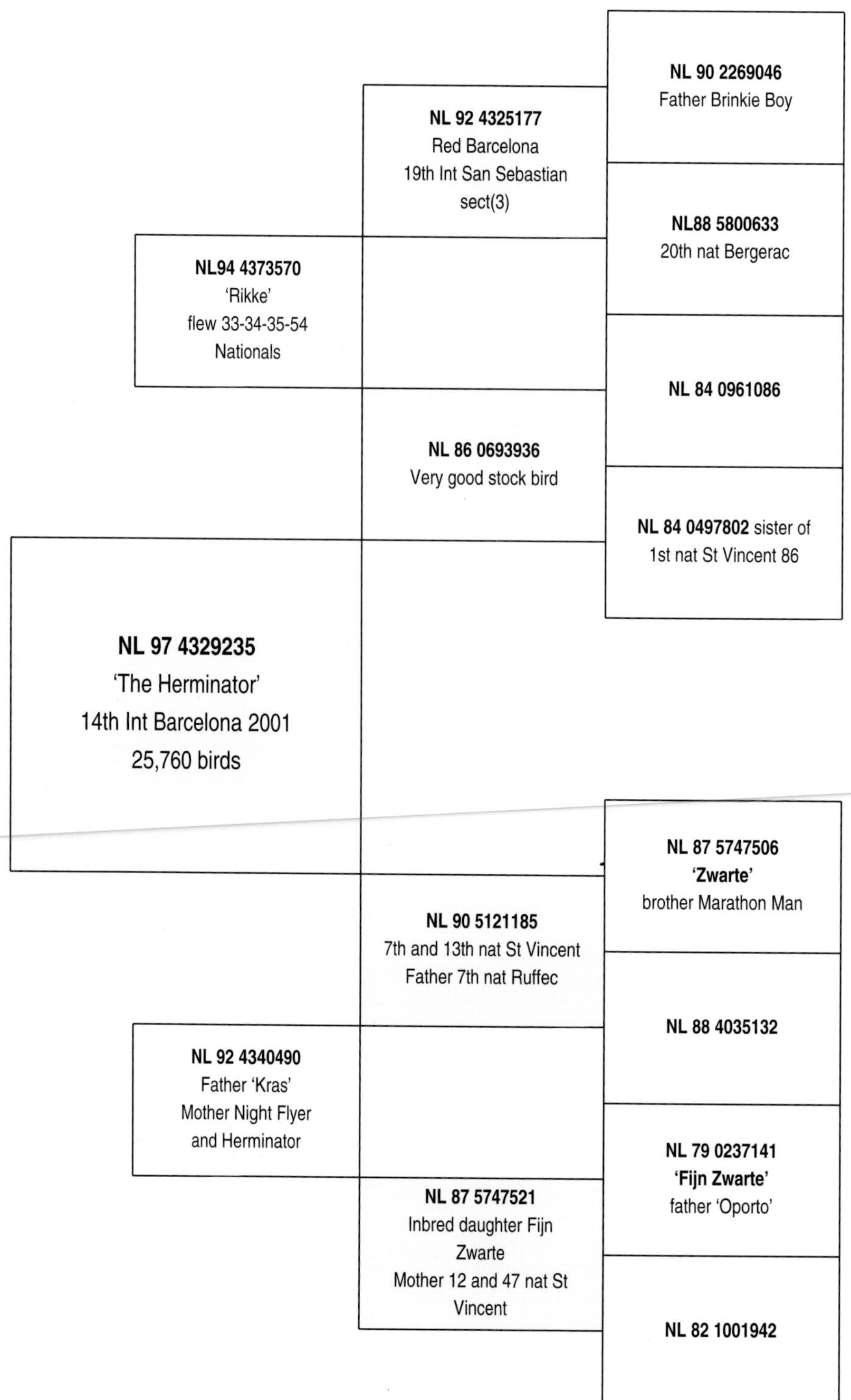

Pedigree of Herminator, a pigeon that goes back to '046', the 'Golden Breeder'.

Brinkie Girl, a daughter of Brinkie Boy.
Photo: © Copyright Martin Kwakernaat

came back from Barcelona everything was closed – it was so early in the morning I didn't expect to see anything so soon, certainly not from Barcelona. I opened the section where he normally was, but he didn't want that and went over to the yearling's box on the other side. That year he raced and was competitive for extra territory, the yearling box as well as his own. This pigeon cultivated his own motivation. As events turned out it worked very well and he flew a magnificent race.

Motivation originated by the pigeon itself is very important – I think motivation turns an ordinary pigeon into a special pigeon on the day. But he must want to do it himself. Motivation is best when the pigeon learns at its own speed, not when its learning is imposed by a time-scale to suit its owner. The pigeon in question, the one that motivated himself, I called Hermanator. He is now a top breeding pigeon of the loft.

Red Barcelona, the grandfather of 'Hermanator' and himself a top-class Brinkman pigeon.
Photo: © Copyright Peter van Raamsdonk

The Moult and Winter Treatment

Are the pigeons separated for the winter and, if so, when? Do they get any special treatment?

After racing they are allowed to rear a youngster. They are then separated. They are given plenty of baths at this time and good moulting food, but nothing extra special. Separation improves the moult and in my opinion improves the quality of the feather. Silky feathers that come from a good moult indicate health.

Pairing up the Birds

When do you pair the race birds and the stock birds?

I pair the race birds about 25 March and the stock birds in December. For the stock birds I keep the lights on in the loft a little after dark in an attempt to simulate longer daylight.

What physical characteristics do you look for when pairing up the birds? Do you compensate for size or colour of the eye, etc?

Every year we go to Texel, one of the West Frisian islands off the northern coast, for an autumn break. Cars are not allowed on the island, so in the long quiet evenings I make a 'couple list' and pair the birds on paper. When I get back to the loft this sometimes changes, but the last few years I have followed a rule that if a pigeon has a light eye I always couple it with one with a dark eye. I don't know if this really matters but I do it. The feather colour does not matter – if they are good at racing then anything goes.

The Loft

What do you consider important for the construction and ventilation of the racing loft?

Ventilation is very important. If the cocks live for a whole year in a loft without good ventilation, you win nothing. After a loft has first been built you need to make adjustments in order to refine the ventilation so that it is as near perfect as possible. Buildings and other nearby features can have an effect on the ventilation, as can trees and the direction the loft is orientated. The loft must also be absolutely dry: you can smell a loft without good ventilation. Of course, you must not overcrowd the pigeons.

Numbers

How many birds do you have in your race team?

I have fifty widowhood pigeons, including yearlings. There are also twelve pairs of breeders and I breed approximately eighty young birds each year.

At the end of the year do you expect to have eighty left?

No, definitely not. Most years about fifty or so are left. This means I have twenty-five yearling cocks for widowhood the following year.

Would you like to have more pigeons?

Even if I were a very wealthy man with unlimited resources I would not want to have any more. I have too many already. The clever fancier is the man who has few pigeons. If you have too many, breeding and racing can get out of control – you can become less efficient, you notice less and the pigeons do not perform as well.

Do you consider a certain number of breeding pigeons an essential minimum for maintaining the quality of your colony?

Yes, I think twelve breeding pairs are absolutely necessary, including a number of experimental pairings.

As regards racing, in order to compete in overnight races and the international programme you need at least fifty pigeons, but quality must always come first. If necessary you should enter fewer races with top-quality pigeons rather than more races with average pigeons, but always enter races where the standard is high as soon as you are able. If you do well in events of a high standard you will have a good idea of the quality of your family of pigeons and how your breeding is coming along.

S417
PVR NOS-TT 417 ma 09 jul 22:40:20
DUIVENSPORT 1/13

Voorlopige uitslag Int.Meerd.Fondvlucht
ZLU 9 juli 2001

BARCELONA

1	S.Heijmann	Beesel	1307m
2	J.H.C.Crombach	Kerkrade	1251m
3	P.Janssen	Millingen a.Rijn	1203m
4	H.Wijnands & Zn	Maastricht	1170m
5	H.Brinkman	Tuk	1159m
6	J.Vorselen	Thorn	1128m
7	Weststrate-Martens	Kapelle	1127m
8	W.Verbaal	Valkenswaard	1084m
9	R & B Gardien	Maasdijk	1073m
10	A.Huynen	Heerlen	1071m

Duiven gelost 8 juli om 09.10 uur
Aantal Ned. duiven in concours:7.567

Teletext record of the Herminator performance from Barcelona in 2001, when he was 14th International and beat many pigeons flying a lesser distance.

The Main Birds

Which individual stock birds were essential to the development of your colony?

The 'Fijn Zwarte', the 'Golden Breeder', the original Van der Wegen pigeons from Eijerkamp – all were good pigeons. All have left their mark.

Can you tell us about the most important race birds you have had and the ones that established your reputation? Which is your favourite?

I have had many: 'Hermanator', 'Brinkie Boy', 'Tukse Lady', 'Brinkie Girl', 'Red Barcelona' ... there are many. I think 'Brinkie Boy' was my favourite. He was also an excellent breeder.

Did these individuals display any particular traits?

No, they were all normal pigeons.

Have you any idea what made them so great?

In truth I think it was good blood, but many pigeons with good blood do not breed or race well. Good blood is only the start. I really think it is something inside them we can't see. It is this invisible element that makes long-distance pigeon racing so fascinating. The only thing we know is that whatever is present in pigeons with good blood is also likely to be there in pigeons that have proved themselves at flying long distances. It is certainly there in pigeons that have proved their ability to produce top long-distance pigeons when coupled with different mates. There are not many who can do that.

A Life in Pigeons

How do the pigeons fit in with your family life?

My wife Ria is interested but doesn't actively do anything. My sons are also very interested, but at the moment Jan is at University so he doesn't do much. Pigeons are important to me and I can't imagine life without them, but they are not everything. Three or four times a year my family go away on holiday together – they are most important.

Reducing the Odds

Racing pigeons at long distances is always a challenge and full of uncertainties. By its very nature we can never know everything. You have been more successful than most fanciers in the sport, so can you single out the one technique or quality that has helped reduce the uncertainty, shorten the odds and, to some degree, helped produce a successful colony?

The fancier's motivation is very important: if you don't have motivation the loft will be no good. Motivation also goes in cycles. You must keep learning new things. The act of learning motivates.

Making discoveries keeps a fancier interested. If you think you know everything you are already on the way down. If motivation isn't there you cannot even identify good pigeons to keep your loft at the top. Among other things motivation makes one more aware.

Do you have any further ideas and ambitions?

Ten years ago my loft was stronger than it is now, but since my sons were about to go to University I sold half of my pigeons to help with the costs. I am now building up my strength again. I am always trying out new ideas, innovations and methods. All lofts go through their ups and downs. It's just like a football club – you can't have a full squad of the best players all the time. When it does happen your loft is at its maximum strength and you are at the top of competition. Staying at the top is difficult.

Long-distance Racing and its Spiritual Quality

The fact that you are disposed to race long-distance pigeons suggests to me that this type of racing has a spiritual quality about it. Are you intrigued by the pigeons' ability to fly extreme distances?

I've always been interested in the development of the pigeon itself. In sprint and middle-distance racing the fancier is important, but in long-distance racing the pigeon is the key. It's the pigeon that must fly the distance – the pigeon that must make the effort and win the achievement. There is indeed a spiritual quality about racing, but to be honest it gives me great pleasure. When a pigeon makes it back from Barcelona it is very nice. The pigeons make it very pleasing. It is rewarding for the spirit to be the one who has trained and raced a small bird that can fly such a long distance. There is very little in life that gives more satisfaction than this.

CONCLUSION

The Brinkman Contribution to Pigeon History

In summing up Herman Brinkman's attitude toward and experience of pigeon breeding and racing, one becomes aware of what he has decided to leave out rather than what he does. His pigeon operation is uncomplicated. It is basically a simple, no-frills affair: nothing is done at the Brinkman lofts that is not thought necessary for the improvement of the pigeons. The breeding policy is intended to provide sufficient good pigeons, year after year, ready and able to fly the extreme distance. This is easier said than done. In his day-to-day management Herman would rather not do something than do it without reason. He would rather recognize and accept failure than ignore the consequences. The Brinkman philosophy accepts that, when it comes to breeding and racing long-distance pigeons, not everything is even half understood.

An Inexact Science

Breeding, of course, is the basis of most long-distance pigeon racing. To this end there is a constant search for quality pigeons. Herman Brinkman knows better than anyone else that breeding is far from an exact science. He admits his mistakes, but despite failures he is always on the look out for pigeons able to improve the present colony or help produce birds capable of flying the Brinkman distances. In order to stay a part of the loft the youngsters off the imports are expected to pass performance criteria similar to those Herman expects of his own pigeons. This is a tall order, but that is why Herman Brinkman's contribution to the history of pigeon sport has been that of a giant, shrinking the 1,300km (800 miles) distance from Barcelona down to something that can be flown with a measure of consistency. In his way Herman Brinkman has inspired fanciers across Europe. Since 1986, when he first sent a lone pigeon to Barcelona and was 2,163rd from a field of 18,076 birds, he has improved gradually to being 14th International in 2001 from 25,760 pigeons. Breeding excellence is part of his contribution. His birds are valued for their extra strength and tenacity, largely because of the distances they fly.

Extra-High Quality

Only high-quality pigeons are imported. These pigeons are carefully selected and their credentials examined before they are chosen. The choice is based on successful results at a distance similar to that which the Brinkman lofts fly (the Vertelman pigeons are an example), but even with these precautions it is not always possible for every import to be successful. Herman has admitted that, in spite of all his precautions, mistakes can still be made, since breeding can never be exact. Breeding for performance is more of a statistical exercise for the simple reason that there is not enough information from which to make a full assessment. Herman cites the fact that two brothers of the 'Golden Breeder' (the father of 'Brinkie Boy') were imported at the same time, but one produced

- **NL 00 1260004**
'Barca 04'
49 nat St Vincent
78 Int Barcelona 04 24913 b
25 nat St Vincent 03
  - **NL 97 4326712**
'Jompa'
Father Barca 04
    - NL 95 4383308
Full brother 'Golden Girl'
      - NL 90 2269046
Father of Brinkie Boy
      - NL 93 5800634
Mother of 5th nat St Vincent
1994
    - **NL 95 4383345**
Dtr 'Felog'
      - NL 93 4357134
G Father 5, 11,24,47
Nationals
      - NL 90 2269058
Van der Wegen
Mother of 6th nat Bergerac
Vertleman
  - **NL 96 4310672**
Dtr Beul 5th nat
St Vincent
    - NL 95 4383319
'De Beul' 5 x overnight
5th nat St Vincent
      - B 94 2232053
Beullens and son
      - NL 92 4340467
Van der Wegen
    - NL 93 2090879
Eijerkamp
      - NL 90 1910295
G Son Red 07 of 85
W Muller Wilhelminadorp
      - NL90 1911390
Dtr Marseilles Star
W Muller Wilhelminadorp

Pedigree of the latest Champions. 'Barca Boy' – 78th International Barcelona 2004.

nothing of quality while its sibling, bred in exactly the same way, became a cornerstone of the loft.

The Lofts

After the breeding has been done, the next problem to be solved is the housing of the pigeons, the way they live their lives. There is no point in breeding pigeons of potential quality if the loft does not provide the necessary contentment, security, health and happiness. All these are necessary for the pigeons to perform at their best.

Ventilation

Herman Brinkman knows a thing or two about ventilating pigeon lofts. He aims for a flow of continually renewed air without ugly draughts, believing that if the ventilation is right, then the respiratory system of the pigeon itself is also likely to be all right. Ventilation produces good health as well as a pleasant atmosphere. Herman stresses that you can't buy ready-made good ventilation. Every loft is different, due to its location and its construction: a loft that is good in one place may be a failure elsewhere, even though its structure is the same. Continual adjustments have to be made in order to get ventilation exactly right.

An Aviary

The racing lofts also have an aviary in front of each section to further enhance the ventilation and the health of the pigeons. Dry lofts with perfect ventilation are of the utmost importance to Herman Brinkman, but aviaries also serve a necessary function by enabling the birds to take baths without dampness of any kind affecting the main loft. An aviary also allows them a view of the sky.

Dampness

This heading should perhaps more appropriately appear as 'dryness', for it is the dry atmosphere and floor conditions that allow the Brinkman lofts to accumulate droppings and exist without constant cleaning out. This practice not only allows for easier management but is also an example of how Herman Brinkman thinks 'pigeon'. The pigeons are undoubtedly happy to be left as nature would intend them to live. They love the apparently haphazard management (or apparent lack of management), but most of all they love being left alone. The pigeons are happy and comfortable with this style.

The Bond

It is not considered essential for Brinkman pigeons to be managed in a tidy way. Instead the pigeons are encouraged to make up their own minds on the way they wish to live and go about their lives. This promotes a developing bond between them and the place they live that grows stronger with age. That is one of the reasons why Barcelona pigeons are kept until they are four years of age, by which time the pigeon is at full strength, before they are put to the most difficult task.

It goes without saying that a strong bond to their home is essential if we wish to have pigeons exert themselves over 800 miles. A bond to the loft is in itself a kind of motivation. When this bond is further heightened by individual territorial motivation, as it was in the case of 'Hermanator', an exceptional performance may be in the offing, provided the pigeon has the breeding quality and preparation necessary for the job. As Herman always reminds us, however, it is the pigeon that has to do it; we should never forget that.

Ups and Downs

Herman Brinkman has the habit of comparing the sport of pigeon racing with that of other sports. Given his passion for football, he compares the ups and downs of a football team to the ups and downs of a colony of pigeons. This cycle of quality, in pigeons as in football, almost always rests on the star quality of the team as a whole. The ability to produce star pigeons almost completely depends on breeding. Without high-quality stock good pigeons are not produced and the loft inevitably declines.

Motivation

Brinkman also draws our attention to another cycle, the motivation of the fancier himself, which similarly goes in cycles and has its ups and downs. If a fancier is motivated he is more likely to notice the potential star pigeons within his team and take action early in their lives. If on the other hand he is not motivated, or his motivation is low or non-existent, then things tend to get overlooked. In such circumstances good pigeons with a lot of potential may not only fail to be noticed but are often treated wrongly. When a fancier's motivation is high everything is noticed, including the fancier's own mistakes. That is a Brinkman lesson for all of us.

CHAPTER 2

Jelle Outhuyse

Harlingen, The Netherlands

BACKGROUND

Jelle Outhuyse (pronounced 'Yeller Out-Houser') is relatively young to have earned success in the world of long-distance pigeon racing. Usually, those who are successful at this level are mature, well-seasoned men or women who either have a lifetime's experience behind them, or are following in the path of a parent or a close family member. Jelle is neither of these. He is only thirty-nine, has two young daughters and works full-time in a shipyard in Harlingen, his hometown. Yet despite these commitments, a modest loft and not much time, he has already made a mark in international racing. It is for this reason he is interesting. Can he last? Will he improve? Is his success dependent on a particular good breeder that he happens to own at this time?

These questions have yet to be answered, but I think he can last, since this Harlingen man is more than a passing comet that briefly lights up the sky. Jelle Outhuyse is here to stay for the simple reason that his character is that of a long-distance man through and through. He is determined, his only interest is in long-distance pigeons and his stoic temperament is suited to the task. In my opinion he will become a long-distance giant whose pigeons will influence generations to come.

Harlingen, an ancient port in the province of Friesland, is almost as far north as one can go in the Netherlands. Jelle Outhuyse is the longest flyer in this book. Despite this disadvantage – his distance from Barcelona is 1,335km (834 miles) – his pigeons have already flown outstandingly well from Pau, Barcelona, Perpignan and Marseilles. Jelle is a thinking man with the potential to achieve

Jelle Outhuyse – One of the longest-flying fanciers in the Netherlands – His distance from Barcelona is 835 miles. He is only 39 years of age and works full-time in a shipyard. Photo: © Copyright Jelle Outhuyse

Town Hall Harlingen – The majesty of its civic building shows Harlingen and its important past.

A view of Harlingen. This attractive Friesland town of canals and ships has always earned its livelihood from the sea.

'970', the most important stock bird of the Outhuyse loft. This pigeon has already bred the 1st and 3rd St Vincent as well as 13th National Marseilles. His blood is in almost all the pigeons in the Outhuyse loft. Photo: © Copyright Jelle Outhuyse

an even brighter future in the sport. He is much too reserved to postulate on such things, but you can bet he is thinking about it. He is a very determined individual.

THE INTERVIEW

The Start

How old are you and when did you first start with long-distance pigeons?

I am now thirty-nine years of age and I started racing long distances in 1990. No one in my family was ever interested in pigeons of any kind. I was the first.

What stock did you first buy for the long distance and do you still have some of these pigeons in your present colony?

Although I started with programme birds in 1990, my present family of pigeons is still based on Van der Wegen pigeons I bought from Nico de Heus of Hedel in 1992. The main producer of my family is a cock from 1993 that is still breeding. Although he still filled his eggs in 2005 and looks in very good condition, he may be coming to his end. I'm keeping my fingers crossed that he goes on for a few more years. His contribution to the loft cannot be overestimated.

The Cross and its Effects

Have you since brought in fresh imports to cross with your present colony?

Yes, every year I have bought one or two pigeons, including some from the Martha van Geel strain and more of the Van der Wegen pigeons. You must always be on the look out for good pigeons to cross with your own. I look for pigeons bred from birds with results at the long distance. I don't especially concentrate on lofts similar to my own or on pigeons of a similar shape to mine, only on results. It is the genes you buy, not looks. The only thing I do insist on, however, is that the pigeons must not be too big: medium to small birds are better for long distances.

Must they be from an inbred family of performance birds?

I prefer it if that is so, but today there are not so many successful inbred colonies of pigeons based on a related family. So I often encourage inbreeding in my own loft, pairing father to daughter or mother to son in the hope that I can preserve the genes of the good ones. As for performance, racing performance is absolutely essential. As I said before, results are all important, especially when selecting future stock, since this is the only aspect of long-distance racing that is measured. Everything else is opinion or conjecture. It is therefore results and testing by the basket that matter.

How long do you allow before deciding whether the new imports are working with your family and what mistakes have you made?

I give them three years at the most, but if I buy one or more and all the youngsters are lost then immediately they are out – the whole lot of them. All long-distance pigeons in the breeding loft must have the ability to pass on the homing instinct to their young. Some may be better than others and some are more determined than others, but all must have the instinct to home in the first place. As for mistakes, yes indeed, I have made more than I can

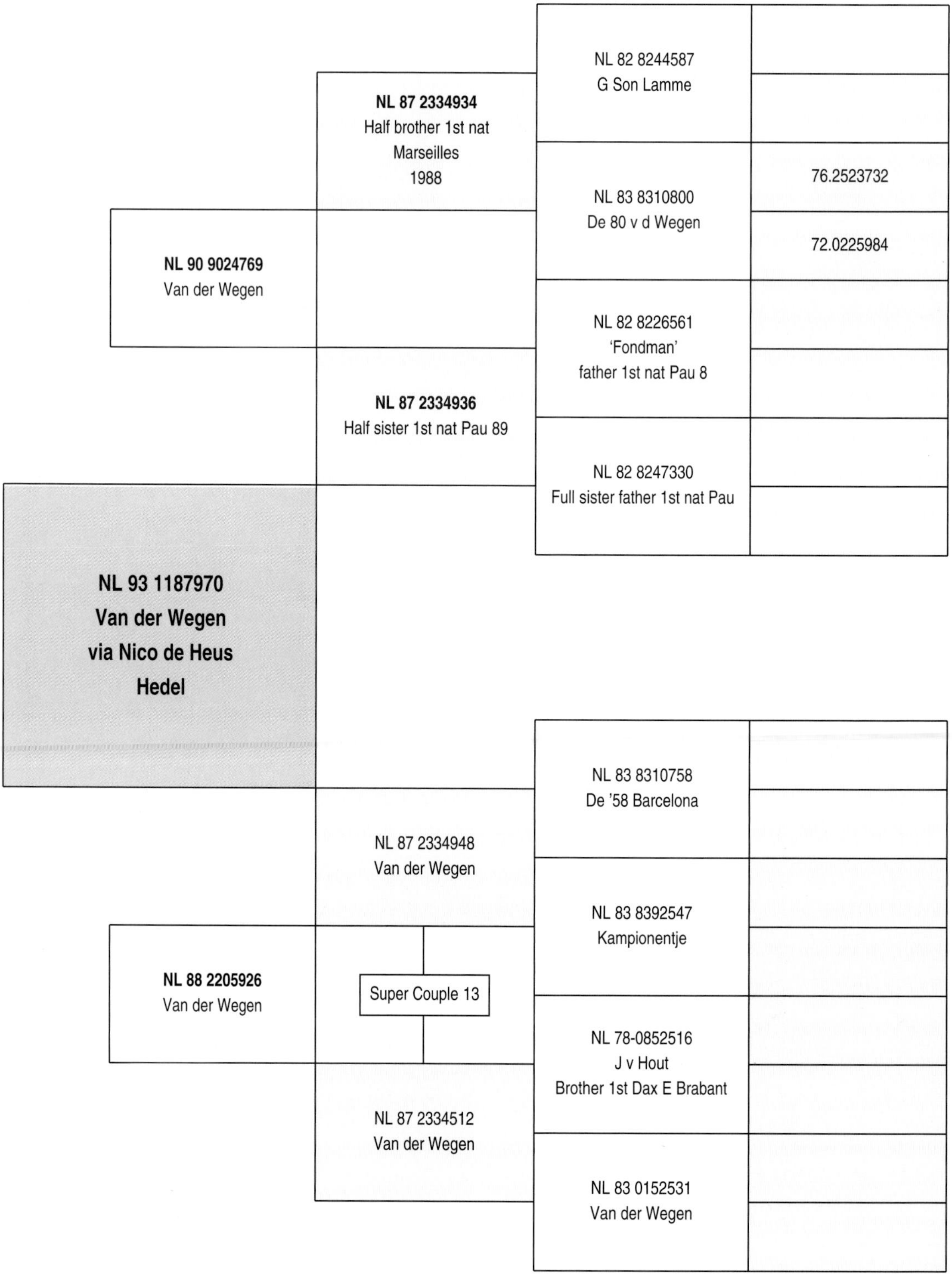

NL 93 1187970
Van der Wegen
via Nico de Heus
Hedel

NL 90 9024769
Van der Wegen

NL 87 2334934
Half brother 1st nat
Marseilles
1988

NL 82 8244587
G Son Lamme

NL 83 8310800
De 80 v d Wegen

76.2523732

72.0225984

NL 87 2334936
Half sister 1st nat Pau 89

NL 82 8226561
'Fondman'
father 1st nat Pau 8

NL 82 8247330
Full sister father 1st nat Pau

NL 88 2205926
Van der Wegen

Super Couple 13

NL 87 2334948
Van der Wegen

NL 83 8310758
De '58 Barcelona

NL 83 8392547
Kampionentje

NL 87 2334512
Van der Wegen

NL 78-0852516
J v Hout
Brother 1st Dax E Brabant

NL 83 0152531
Van der Wegen

Pedigree of '970', the Van der Wegen from Nico de Heus.

count, for what we are trying to do in breeding long-distance pigeons that can fly up to 800 miles is extremely difficult. I don't think I am so gifted that I can be sure of getting the selection exactly correct every time. Introducing pigeons and then breeding off them is not an exact science, but there are some guidelines. The main ones are those I've already mentioned: good pigeons and good results of the type you require. Good pigeons are always consistent pigeons – this applies to breeders as well as to racers.

The Race Team from Year to Year

How do you treat young birds in the year of their birth? Do you race young birds? What do you expect of them?

I train the young birds myself by car. They do not go into organized competition, only on flights that I control. One of the things I do is to train them over the sea. I drive them across the Afsluitdijk, the dyke that connects Friesland with North Holland and divides the IJsselmeer from the Waddenzee. It is more than 32km (20 miles) long. The route from North Holland over the Afsluitdijk to my loft is the most direct route in longer races. Since the majority of birds in National and International races come through North Holland, I train them in this way in the hope that they become accustomed to the sea crossing and it encourages them to fly the most direct route possible.

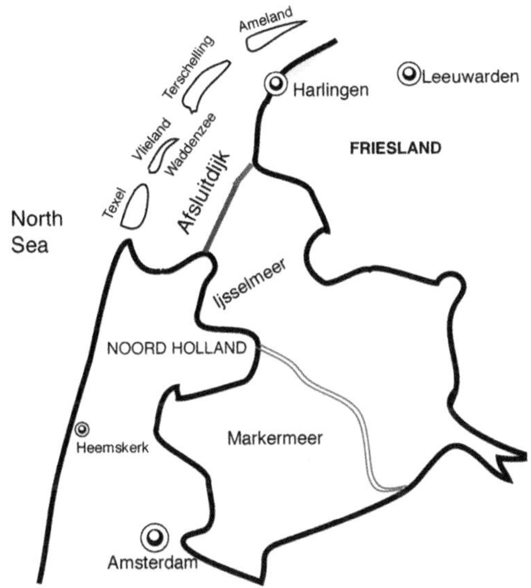

The Afsluitdijk road connects the land of Noord Holland with Friesland. Its construction turned the previously named Zuiderzee into the present IJsselmeer.

The Afsluitdijk – it is over its windswept 20 mile strip of road Jelle Outhuyse trains his young pigeons.

Do you breed late breds and have you had any success with them?

Some of my best pigeons were born late in the year. I rather like late breds. They are bred in the best weather off the best pigeons. If you are prepared to wait for them, late youngsters can be the best in the loft. This year [2005] I bred fifteen. Some went to England but the rest I kept for myself.

How are the late breds treated?

As yearlings these late-bred pigeons have to go to only 600km (370 miles). These are the programme flights. They are not expected to win a prize of any kind. I give them time to develop.

How do you treat yearlings that are bred in the early part of the year and what do you expect of them?

Yearlings that come from the previous year's early-bred youngsters have to go to 900km (560 miles) or perhaps even a distance of 1000km (620 miles). These also are not expected to win a prize. All these flights are day flights in which the pigeons are liberated early in the morning and the birds have to fly all day. The yearlings that survive this treatment are worth keeping.

How do you treat two-year-olds and what work do they have to do?

They must go to a race of at least 900km. When the pigeons are three years old, they go to St Vincent in the Dutch National, a distance of 1000km. They are expected to compete and get

5417 NOS-TT 417 wo 19 jun 22.33:11

duivensport 5/5

zat. 15 juni

Voorlopige uitslag meerdaagse vlucht

St. V I N C E N T

Sector IV:

1	J. Outhuyse	Harlingen	866
2	C. v. der Ploeg	Leeuwarden	856
3	W. Roozendal	Dedemsvaart	850
4	H. Brinkman & zn.	Tuk	846
5	E. Glazenburg	Winschoten	839
6	H. Brinkman & zn.	Tuk	825
7	H. Brinkman & zn.	Tuk	824
8	C. Seinstra	Assen	819
9	A. Hartgers	Hoogeveen	818
10	R. Kooistra	Damwoude	814

e. e. a. onder voorbehoud

Bron: N. P. O.

A picture from Dutch television. In this particular result Jelle Outhuyse was first sector '4' in the NPO National from St Vincent, a flight of more than 1,180km to Harlingen. The low velocities show how hard the race was. Photo: © Copyright Peter van Raamsdonk

among the results. I also observe how they look when they arrive back: are they excessively tired or have they flown this distance comfortably? This is a crucial year for long-distance pigeons. At this stage of their career you can see if you have a real pigeon on your hands, one that has a chance to fly in International races and become a cornerstone of your loft. If pigeons have taken the early years comfortably in their stride they can arrive at the four-year-old stage mature and full of potential. By this stage they have grown accustomed to the loft, the surroundings and everything about their lives. Pigeons that can do this can go on for a few more years and eventually be even more outstanding, but pigeons of this quality are very special. There are not many of them in any loft regardless of distance; at the distance I compete, there are even fewer.

Do Looks Matter?

Is there any physical attribute you particularly look for in a mature pigeon? Are you looking at the wing, the throat, the head, a particular shape of the body or what?

The pigeons must have good soft feather, but perhaps most of all they must have a good expression. They must be alert and clever, not uninterested and sleepy. The throat must not be too big. That is important. Generally my cocks have a little bit of a hen about them. They are not bold, aggressive cocks with big, bold heads, but tend to have a refined look.

Treatment for Disease and Creating Immunity

Do you consider a high degree of immunity to illness is essential for a long-distance loft to perform well?

Absolutely. If pigeons lack good immunity and have to be constantly treated, they cannot be expected to perform long flights year after year. Long-distance pigeons must be naturally strong. Often they may be with other pigeons in a basket for eight or nine days before the longer races. As part of my routine I ensure that everything is open and the pigeons are allowed to go outside in the fresh air. A natural life like this builds up their resistance to disease as well as their bond to the loft and the environment.

Do you clean out your lofts on a daily basis and, if not, what is the reason for this?

No, I don't clean out the lofts every day. The droppings are allowed to accumulate beneath grills on the floor. The pigeons are happier with this than if I were constantly scraping, cleaning and disturbing them.

For what conditions do you vaccinate annually?

I inject for paratyphus and paramyxo every year.

If illness, such as a respiratory condition, were to arise spontaneously, would you immediately suppress the individual or its offspring without attempting to treat the pigeon, or would you allow it to persist and wait for the pigeons to get over it?

Fresh air is the best thing. Sometimes when a pigeon is ill I take it out and put it in a box away from the others. I will then assess it and treat it on its own, but never with the rest of the colony. But provided you have a dry, well-ventilated loft you

Inside Outhuyse loft – dry droppings on the floor encourage contentment and good health.

The Outhuyse racing loft. A tidy, but modest, back garden loft but one that contains outstanding long-distance pigeons of international class. Photo: © Copyright Jelle Outhuyse

do not usually have a problem. The rule here is 'prevention is better than cure'.

Does this change as the pigeon gets older – for instance, are you much more severe on the young bird team than on older birds?

No, they are treated the same every year of their lives. Even when pigeons are entered for the really long races like Barcelona I don't treat them with anything. They just get good food and plenty of it. The rest is left to the pigeon.

How often do you treat for canker or coccidiosis?

I treat for canker early in the year when the pigeons are mated, but the rest of the time I don't. Nor do I treat for coccidiosis.

Is any routine medical treatment an essential part of your preparation for the race season or for a particular race?

No, I don't treat for anything at all.

Advice for the Novice

What advice would you give a novice attempting to build a team of long-distance pigeons, and what stage should he have reached after three years?

First he must get good pigeons that have all been bred from a line that has already done the distance required and been consistent and successful doing it. He must build a good loft with plenty of ventilation. He must breed a lot of young ones and test them. Gradually, if he is a good fancier, he will eventually thin the birds down to the best. It is these and their parents he must concentrate on. He should breed more off these pigeons and the ones that bred them.

If he is a good fancier and is well motivated in himself, he should be sending birds to, and doing well in, races in distances up to Ruffec or Bergerac – not the international or longer flights, these will come later. But he must also take this three-year period to evaluate himself. If and when he gets good pigeons from such places as Ruffec or Bergerac and he has youngsters coming along from them he can then start on the International races with some confidence. Perhaps it will take him six years or more before he can enter an international race. It might take even longer, perhaps eight years. Of course, and this is more than a possibility, he may fail completely. If that is the case, he has to pick himself off the ground and start all over again by trying to find out how he went wrong the first time. Long-distance pigeon racing is the most difficult of all the disciplines. Regardless of the blood, only a few out of all the pigeons that are bred will do it successfully. The reward lies in seeing one come home. At that moment the struggle and work involved will be forgotten.

Before the Race

Do you fly widowhood, on the nest, both systems or something else?

Everything is played on a natural system, including the yearlings. The pigeons have a nest for the whole of the season.

How much exercise do the pigeons take every day?

Because I have to leave early to go to the shipyard in the morning, my only option is to exercise the pigeons in the evening for an hour between seven and eight o'clock. Everything goes out of the loft: cocks, hens, yearlings – the whole lot. I put the flag up for an hour and they must exercise around the loft flying the whole time. The pigeons get used to the regime and accept it; exercise becomes normal routine for them.

Are some hens raced and what system do you use?

Hens are also raced on a normal natural system. I like to test both sexes.

Can you give me some idea of how you would treat a three-, or four-year-old widowhood pigeon being prepared for the big races of the year?

They are paired on or about 25 March so they are not too advanced in the moult in August, when the long races are held. They are first given some short races to loosen them up and then three or four weeks before Barcelona they have a race from 800 or 900km. Twice a week I give the pigeons garlic juice on their food, squeezing the cloves with a garlic squeezer I get from the supermarket.

What happens in the final week before a big race?

They train around the loft every day for one hour. I give them as much food as they can eat and allow them some small seeds as an extra. The pigeons are then sent to the big race sitting on small youngsters of perhaps three or four days old.

After the Race

When a tired pigeon returns from a long race is there any special treatment you give him before he rejoins the flock for normal training?

I allow plenty of rest but give only clean water. At that time the cock sits in his own place – it is very important that a cock has his own place, his own territory. When a cock is away for a long race I shut the box to preserve his territory until he gets back.

The Moult and Winter Treatment

Are the pigeons separated for the winter and, if so, when?

They are separated for a month before they are coupled for the following year.

Are they given any special food or treatment, such as baths, to promote the moulting of the feathers?

They get plenty of baths. A good set of new feathers is essential for good performance the following year.

Does winter separation improve or detract from a good moult?

I think it is good they are together, but also good that they are separated before pairing. This helps if you want to switch pairings for the coming year. Everything in my loft is done to promote the pigeons' contentment. The only thing they are forced to do is to exercise around the loft, but even this, when it is done regularly and with caution, is not a problem. As the pigeons get fitter they exercise better and, strangely enough, become happier.

Pairing up the Birds

When do you pair the race birds?

I couple both race birds and stock birds on the same date, about 25 March.

Do you do anything special beforehand?

No, nothing special.

What physical characteristics do you look for when pairing up the birds? Do you compensate for size or colour of the eye, etc?

I don't look for anything special like size or such things, but I do have one faddish preference: I don't like pigeons with a lot of white on them. I think that's my only fad.

The Loft

What do you consider important for the construction and ventilation of the racing loft?

The loft must be well ventilated and, above all else, dry. It must also have an aviary where the pigeons can go out all day to look at the sky and the surroundings and have a bath. You can't tell whether a loft is good or not until you see the pigeons in it. A lot depends on the location of the loft and what surrounds the loft, such as trees or buildings. Getting the loft absolutely right needs constant adjustment. I have recently altered the loft by making it so that the stale air comes out from above the pigeons, and I hope this will be an improvement.

Numbers

How many birds do you have in your race team and stock loft, and how many youngsters do you breed each year?

I have eighty pigeons in the race team, thirty breeders in the stock loft and every year I breed almost sixty young pigeons.

Would you like to have more pigeons?

I think I should have more – not too many, but a few more. If I was very wealthy, what I would really like would be more time. Time is something you must spend with the pigeons, and at the moment I do not have enough time to do as I would like.

Martha van Geel elf penner (eleven flighted), the other breeding influence in the Outhuyse loft.

- **NL 98 1866054** Double Eleven Flighted Martha v Geel Top stock bird
  - NL94 9464818 **"Robijn Dolle"** M v Geel
    - NL 88 2041532 **"Kaalopje"** M v Geel
      - NL 83 0706065 "Dolle 83" M v Geel
        - NL 67 2052951 "Dolle" M v Geel
        - NL 79 7982474 "Dtr Dolle" M v Geel
      - NL 83 0705002 "Intelt Lange" 17 o/night 17 prizes
        - NL 82 1036100 G Son"Lange" 100 v Geel
        - NL 82 8266092 Sister "Puk" M v Geel
    - NL 93 26131213 **"Batenburgje"** Batenburg
      - NL 85 1273760 "Bonte Kweker" Batenburg
        - NL81 1533120 "De Witbuik" Batenburg
        - NL 84 1597133
      - NL 86 03 16076 "Braakhuis" Braakhuis
        - NL 83 1788934 Braakhuis
        - NL83 1788150 Braakhuis
  - NL 93 9347330 **"Mischa"** 50% M v Geel
    - Ukraine 87 0000014 **"Mischa"**
    - NL90 2850240 **Dtr "Green Eye"** M v Geel
      - NL 86 2102296 "Zivajo" Ason M Poot M v Geel
        - NL 83 8315951 "Manke Poot"
        - NL 81 8152434 Dtr Barcelona 83' M v Geel
      - NL 87 2282190 "Groenoogje" M v Geel
        - NL 81 8152434 "Vlekje" M v Geel
        - NL 79 1445799 "Dtr Dolle" M v Geel

Pedigree of '054', the Martha van Geel stock hen.

Do you consider a certain number of breeding pigeons an essential minimum for maintaining the quality of your colony?

I think if you are to maintain an output of good birds from within your existing colony you probably need more than I have at the moment, but quality is the most important thing. If you buy in pigeons, you must ensure that the quality is better than your own. Over time, as your results improve, you get to the point where it becomes increasingly difficult to import pigeons that are good enough.

What do you consider the minimum number of birds necessary for the programme of races you take part in?

I would say I need all I have at the moment, with the proviso that quality must, of course, come first. If you do not have the quality you must reduce the number of races you take part in. It's hopeless sending second-rate pigeons to International races and hoping to succeed. At my distance the finest quality pigeons are essential just to stand still. Nevertheless, it is a challenge to race at International level. I enjoy this challenge. It inspires me.

The Main Birds

Which individual stock birds were essential to the development of your colony?

'054', the Martha van Geel hen, and '970', the good Van der Wegen cock of Nico de Heus. I'm looking for something to replace these. I recently exchanged some pigeons with Herman Brinkman and have some good pigeons from Jan Roelofs of Alkmaar. My first pigeon from Ruffec this year was from the Roelofs pigeons. I also have a grandson of the old Van der Wegen stock cock of Nico de Heus. This cock is already breeding good pigeons – my Barcelona of 2004 that was 219th International was from him.

Can you tell us about the most important birds you have had and the ones that have established your reputation? Which is your favourite?

The good breeders, of course: '970' and '054'. This pair of pigeons is in the blood of most of my family. They are my most important pair. My 'Barcelona' and the 'Marseilles' are both good ones and my first National win from Bergerac was also a good pigeon.

Have you any idea what made them so great?

They are ordinary pigeons, they show nothing special. To get good pigeons you must have good muscles, but many ordinary pigeons have good physique but are not good. I think you must have a little bit of luck or breed something into them you can't see.

133rd nat Barcelona and 219th International Barcelona of 2004 835 miles International and 216th Barcelona 2006. From '054', the Martha van Geel stock hen. Photo: © Copyright Jelle Outhuyse

A Life in Pigeons

How do the pigeons fit in with your family life?

Of course the pigeons have to come second to the family, but my young daughters are not yet old enough to become interested.

Can you imagine a life without pigeons?

No, I can't – long-distance pigeons are a central part of my life. Breeding and creating a family of long-distance pigeons is my interest. I want to be successful doing it.

Reducing the Odds

Racing pigeons at long distances is always a challenge and full of uncertainties. By its very nature we can never know everything. You have been more successful than most fanciers in the sport, so can you single out the one technique or quality that has helped reduce the uncertainty, shorten the odds and, to some degree, helped produce a successful colony?

I am always trying something different, something extra. I never sit and think I have done enough already. I am continually thinking in terms of breeding better pigeons. Breeding is the key to almost everything. If the pigeons are good it is easy, but if the pigeons are not so good then everyone struggles, regardless of how they are handling their pigeons.

- **Nl 00 1147976**
219 Int Barcelona 04
25 nat St Vincent 03
350 nat Perpignan 05
216 Int Barcelona 06
  - NL 96 1372639
Son Ruffec
2nd Nat Ruffec
    - NL 95 1031575
      - NL 89 2164336
J S Outhuyse
        - NL 86 1926501
J S Outhuyse
        - NL 88 2693665
J S Outhuyse
      - NL 94 2163467
Sister 1st St Vincent
J S Outhuyse
        - NL 93 1187970
vd Weaen De Heus
        - NL92.1986392
Mother 1st St Vincent
    - NL95 1031527
De Ruffec (2 nat)
J S Outhuyse
2nd nat Ruffec 1996
      - NL 89 2164336
J S Outhuyse
        - NL86 1926501
J S Outhuyse
        - NL 88 2693665
JS Outhuyse
      - NL94 2295957
Mother 2nd Nat Ruffec A.
Ruitenberg Zwolle
also 8th and 10th Ruffec
        - NL 91.2460240
Jac vd Wesen
        - NL 91.9169541
Jac vd Wegen
  - NL98 1866054
Double 11 flighted
Martha Van Geel
    - NL 94 9464818
Robijn Dolle
M v Geel
      - NL 88 2041532
'Kaal kopje'
M v Geel
        - NL 83.0706065
'Dolle' 83 M v Geel
        - NL 83.0705002
Inteelt lange M v Geel
      - NL 93 2613123
"Batenburtje"
Batenburg
        - NL 85 1273760 Bonte
Kweeker Batenburg
        - NL 86 0316076
"Braakhuis"
    - NL 93 9347330
"Mischa"
M v Geel
      - UK 87 – 0000014
Mischa From Ukraine
      - NL 90 2850240
Dtr 'Groenoogje'
Green Eye v Geel
        - NL 86 2102296
"Zivajo" son M. Poot
M v Geel
        - NL 87 2282190
"Green eye"
M v Geel

Pedigree 133rd nat and 219th 2004 and 216th International Barcelona 2006.

Do you have any further ideas and ambitions?

Yes, I'm always trying different things. I have some new pigeons from Jan Roelofs of Alkmaar and a few I exchanged with Herman Brinkman of Tuk. These are both very good long-distance men, the best in their class. The Roelofs pigeons have started well. I enjoyed visiting him – like me he doesn't clean the lofts too often. The conditions he keeps his birds in are very similar to my own, but his pigeons are smaller and do not have such a strong back as mine, though perhaps this may not matter. Already they have begun to show themselves: this year my first and third pigeons from Ruffec were bred from the Roelofs stock, so I am hopeful they will prove to be a sound investment and of the right quality.

Long-distance Racing and its Spiritual Quality

The fact that you are disposed to race long-distance pigeons suggests to me that this type of racing has a spiritual quality about it. Are you intrigued by the pigeons' ability to fly extreme distances?

Long-distance pigeons are the only ones I'm interested in. I should say I am fascinated by nature when it is able to produce anything outstanding and rare. Top long-distance pigeons are rare.

Does this extreme of the sport have a more spiritual feel about it? Are you in some way guided by this feeling and does it manifest itself in the way you manage your pigeons?

Out of more than sixty fanciers in Harlingen I am the only one who tries to race the long distances. I do not value pigeons when they have a flight from 160km (100 miles) and the whole line-up arrives together – it means nothing to me. One is no different than the others. These pigeons in my opinion are not proving anything. Perhaps there is a spiritual quality in hard work and effort. I also like to run in half marathon races. That's also a part of my character and I think the two are connected.

The whole thing about pigeons is definitely not about money. I try to improve the pigeons by getting them to achieve more difficult things year by year. I also attempt to achieve greater reliability at difficult distances. Only a few manage it, but that is my aim and that is what interests me. I can definitely say I am not in it for the money, otherwise I would sell my best pigeons. I would sell my 'Marseilles' and my 'Barcelona' and the old Van der Wegen. I have already been offered a lot of money for the Van der Wegen, the father of the loft, but I do not even consider such things. Some things are greater than money.

'The Marseilles'. The outstanding performance of 2005 for the Harlingen loft was being 13th from Marseilles out of the whole of the Netherlands flying a considerably greater distance than all the others. Photo: © Copyright Jelle Outhuyse

CONCLUSION

Jelle Outhuyse Compared

Consciously, or unconsciously, those who write about pigeons and pigeon fanciers attempt to make some assessment from a historical point of view. This unconscious practice happens more in long-distance racing than any other. Writers tend to compare one fancier with another, one up-and-coming young man with a similar period in the lifetime of another. This is because champion breeders and fanciers make a deeper impression on the sport at long distances than any other. Great feats of endurance have always imprinted themselves on our collective memories. In the sport of pigeon racing long-distance feats tend to be more prominent than any other.

Extending the Possibilities

There is a very good chance that J. S. Outhuyse of Harlingen may emerge as a powerful influence in the future, either because of the distance his birds have to fly (he is 835 miles from Barcelona) or because of the consistency his birds achieve. Or perhaps both reasons may count. People are always attracted to birds that fly extra-long distances owing to the stamina required to complete the task. Pigeons are steadily extending their range: the criteria for recognizing 'extra-long distance' are themselves increasing. What was once considered difficult is now almost normal. Today, fanciers are extending boundaries beyond what was previously thought possible.

Jelle Outhuyse is one of these fanciers. He is at

NL 011074272
13th Nat Marseilles 05
J S Outhuyse

NL 93 1187970
Nico de Heus
V d Wegen
Number One Stock bird
J S Outhuyse

NL 90 9024769
V d Wegen

NL 87 2334934
A and L vd Wegen
Half brother 1st nat
Marseilles

NL 82 8244587

NL 83 8310800
De 800 Duivin

NL 87 2334936
A and L vd Wegen
Half sister 1st nat Pau

NL 82 8226561
Fondman I

NL 82.8247330

NL 88 2205926
V de Wegen

NL 87 2334948
A and L vd Wegen

NL 83 8310758
De 58 Barcelona

NL 83.8392547
Kampioentie

NL 87 2334512
V d Wegen

NL 78 0852516
J v Hout

NL 83 0152531

NL 97 9766834
G Dtr 1st nat Perpignan
Comb Kleef de Jong

NL 88 2945045
Son Perpignan
Comb Kleef de Jong

NL 84 1710333
Son Goudplevier

NL 70 2150005
Goudplevier

81 1029912 half sister
Mustang Pol Bostiin

NL81 8112076
1st nat Perpignan

75 2003365
Arend

80 0534451
Rode Kweekster

NL 95 1834279
Van der Wegen

NL 92 9271809
Son Stefan

78 7876460
Stefan

80 8015460
Sister 16

NL 92 927197
Sister Tarbes

81 0003090
Benjamin

85 8548496
Intelt Lamme

Pedigree of 'The Marseilles'.

Pigeon	Parents	Grandparents	Great-grandparents	Great-great-grandparents
NL 01 1074215 **Barcelona Witpen** **273 Nat Barcelona 05**	**NL 00 1147977** **Brother 133 Nat** **Barcelona**	NL 96 1372639 Son 2nd Ruffec father 133 nat Barcelona	NL95 1031575 J S Outhuyse	NL 89 2164336
				NL 94 2163467 1st St Vincent
			95 1031527 De Ruffec 2nd nat Ruffec 1996	NL 89 2164336
				NL 94 2295957 Mother 2, 8, 10 Ruffec
		NL 98 1866054 Double 11 flighted Martha Van Geel	NL 94 9464818 "Robijn Dolle" M v Geel	NL 88 2041532 M v Geel
				93 2613123 Batenberg
			NL 93 9347330 "Mischa" M v Geel	Ukraine 87 0000014 "Mischa"
				NL 90 2850240 Dtr Green Eye
	NL 96 1372651 **Half sis 1st St Vincent** **vd Wegen**	NL93 1187970 vd Wegen Nico de Heus Father of 1st St Vincent 13th Marseilles	NL 90 9024769 v d Wegen	NL 87 2334934 A and L vd Wegen
				NL 87 2334936 A and L vd Wegen
			NL 88 2205926 Nico de Heus	NL 87 2334948 A and L vd Wegen
				NL 87 2334512
		NL 94 2295957 Mother 2 , 8, 10 Ruffec A Ruitenberg Zwolle vd Wegen	NL 91 2460240 Jac v d Wegen	NL 87 8791895 De Blauwe 95
				NL 79 7984710 "t Tikske" Jac vd Wegen
			NL 91 9169541 Jac v d Wegen	NL 87 8791869 De Jonge Parel Jac vd Wegen
				NL 89 8918683 Het Lichtje Jac vd Wegen

Pedigree 273rd nat Barc 05 – The two top stock pigeons of the Outhuyse loft are represented here – Both the Martha van Geel hen and the Nico de Heus-Van der Wegen stock birds are represented in the pedigree of this pigeon.

273rd nat Barcelona over 835 miles. Photo: © Copyright Jelle Outhuyse

present the only fancier in the town of Harlingen, and one of the most northerly in the whole of the Netherlands, who is a regular in International results. His success will undoubtedly attract more to follow in his path.

Circumstances

Another thing pigeon writers do, this time more consciously, is assess the circumstances behind each fancier or each colony of pigeons. We all want to know how many pigeons are kept, how many are sent to the races and how many are in the race team. We also like to know how many breeders are kept or how much help the fancier gets in the day-to-day running of the loft. It is not unknown in the pigeon world for a fancier to keep pigeons in two, or even three, active locations with professional help in all three. It comes as a mild surprise, then, to find that Jelle Outhuyse benefits from none of these things. What you see is what you get: a modest back-garden loft managed in a modest way.

What's more, Jelle Outhuyse is still only thirty-nine years of age and he has been racing at international level for only two years. He also works full-time in a shipyard in Harlingen and has a family with two young daughters under six years old. If this is not enough, there are limits on how much exercise his pigeons are able to have. Because he has to leave for work so early he cannot exercise his birds in the morning, only in the evening.

The background to this loft's competitive approach over these enormous distances beggars belief. Here we have the only such loft in the whole of the Harlingen area, managed by a relatively young man with a demanding and busy domestic life. Yet from a relatively modest loft he has still achieved remarkable results that compare with many competitors who are far better endowed with time and are flying a much shorter distance.

International Life

International competitive life for Jelle Outhuyse is not just about popping round the corner to the local club to race his pigeons: he has to travel 75km (45 miles) each time he wants to mark and check his birds for races. The complete task of racing and managing his pigeons under these circumstances is daunting. How does he do it and could a loft in better circumstances and with more time perform better? Many may think it could: if they were able to exercise the birds twice a day and fly a lesser distance they believe they would improve on Jelle Outhuyse's performances. But we should not jump too soon. Jelle Outhuyse has strengths that defy simple measurement.

Dedication is Difficult to Measure

Obviously, he manages his time well. He concentrates on competing and flying only old birds. His natural system is simple. Both sexes are used and tested. Since his first success at long distance by winning the North Section of the Bergerac National ignited his interest in long-distance racing, his progress has been phenomenal. It is difficult to measure this degree of dedication and the simplicity of his method. Perhaps highly motivated widowhood cocks might fly as well at this distance. It may well be that exercising twice a day detracts rather than helps the performances. It is possible that too much time spent with pigeons would lead to the over-management of the loft rather than his present practice of under-managing and leaving the birds very much alone. All these things have to be taken into account. Jelle Outhuyse himself might be unaware of the one crucial factor that brings success. Whatever is it, we hope he does not change his ways.

A Bit of Luck

Jelle acknowledges his luck in acquiring '970', the super Nico de Heus-Van der Wegen foundation stock bird whose blood runs through most of the loft, but the hard work continually put into testing and evaluating must also have helped. He has been determined to maintain the high quality of his loft. Testing in races lies at the heart of this policy. Regardless of reputation, the offspring of all his pigeons are tested every year and those that make it through these tests prevent the loft going backwards, while those that excel keep the loft moving forwards. It will be time to change when the loft ceases to produce star pigeons.

The real secret lies in such practices, since without continual but realistic testing even outstanding stock birds would probably never have been discovered. It is easy to identify good racers by virtue of their performance, but outstanding stock birds also have to be discovered. This is more difficult but it is an ongoing process in the Outhuyse loft. It is thought essential for the future.

High Demands

Here we have a loft that sets high standards and is prepared to wait for them to be met. Jelle Outhuyse is a patient man who is more than aware of the traps into which famous lofts of the past have fallen. One of these is, of course, that of overselling. He could have sold his principal stock birds time and time again, but he has not done so. He hopes to avoid the mistakes others have made. If his wisdom and determination is taken into account he probably will. We will all watch this young man's progress with great interest, for it is men like this, pushing the boundaries of what is possible, who are more likely to influence the future than those who never try or, more likely, those who try and give up.

Some of the Main Birds

The old 'Father of the Loft' is the Nico de Heus-Van de Wegen NL 93.1187970. In the Outhuyse loft at present there are twenty-five children directly off this good pigeon, among them the following:

2163409	1st nat St Vincent 1996
94.2163467	67th nat Bergerac and 8 other prizes
00.1147968	3rd nat St Vincent 2005 and total of 8 prizes
01.1074282 Cock	7 prizes
95.1031581	21st nat St Vincent 98 (now at stock)

01.1074272 Hen
Brive 2003 606th nat from 2,903 birds
Bergerac 2003 110th nat from 2,898 birds
Ruffec 2004 113th nat from 5,075 birds
St Vincent 2005 117th nat from 1,537 birds
Marseilles 2005 13th nat from 3,679 birds

CHAPTER 3

Mevr Deweerdt and Sons

Kortemark, Belgium

BACKGROUND

The Deweerdt lofts are today managed by Bernard and Freddy Deweerdt, the two sons of Emiel Deweerdt, who passed away in 1990. The racing title is now in the name of their mother, Mevr Lies Deweerdt, a dignified but agile lady of eighty-two. The loft title is therefore 'Mevr Deweerdt and sons'. They have made Kortemark, a small town in the Belgian province of West Flanders, famous in the world of pigeons.

Of the two sons Bernard is fifty-one and Freddy is fifty-seven. It was Bernard who answered my questions. Those who are lucky enough to know Bernard Deweerdt will recognize his style, a mixture of jokes, serious comments and quite profound insights into not only pigeons but also the world. Bernard is one of the few fanciers who can stand back from pigeons and pigeon racing, take a detached view of what exactly we are doing and interpret it for the rest of us. The ability to detached oneself is a rare accomplishment.

Over the years the Deweerdt pigeons have won almost everything, including 1st International Barcelona Hens and 1st International Bordeaux. They have been at or near to the top of international racing for more than thirty years as European Champions and winners of various national and provincial titles. Possibly the surest test of their family of pigeons, and of the quality of the loft as a whole, came during the International Barcelona race in 1987, a notoriously difficult event in which, out of 21,545 competitors, only one pigeon was recorded as flying faster than 800 metres per minute.

The modern Deweerdt family L to R Bernard, Emmy (Bernard's daughter) and Tim (the son), and Fred.

The Deweerdt lofts were 193rd, 568th and 615th, but it was their overall performances that shone. They entered seventeen pigeons in that race and timed ten of them in the international result including seven hens, which tend to do well in hard races. Whereas many lofts failed with both hens and cocks, or had only a small proportion of their team in the result, his lofts' achievement, even at an early stage of their participation in long-distance pigeon racing, proved to Emiel Deweerdt that he had the basis of a good breed. The strain is now even stronger. Race conditions like this force pigeons that would normally fly in flocks to be broken up and to fly as individual pigeons. Each pigeon has to work on its own. Races flown in such conditions, although not welcome because of the heavy losses, examine the hardness of the strain.

THE INTERVIEW

My brother and I both work in local government, not in the same place but in similar jobs. My father was also in local government. He died in 1990 at the age of sixty-nine, but our mother, who is now eighty-two, still takes an interest in the pigeons and is always asking about them. She has a picture of 'Spiritus', one of our most famous pigeons, on her living-room wall. We still fly under her name. My son Tim, who is twenty-three, has his own section in the racing loft above the house. He looks after them on his own just as I did when I was a boy, but because he is away at university a lot his time with the pigeons is somewhat limited. Fred's son Filip, who is thirty, has a loft of his own in his own name. He has had considerable success. His '735' of 1993 is a real champion, being in the top 2 per cent in international races three times. Both our sons race pigeons bred down from our stock.

Did your father keep pigeons?

Yes, of course. He started the family of pigeons sixty years ago, first with sprint pigeons in the 1940s, middle-distance pigeons in the 1950s and then later with long-distance pigeons. My brother and I carried on from where our father left off.

When did you first start with long-distance pigeons and what stock did you buy?

In 1971 we started long distance, but as we are old-fashioned people it took us four years to get a team to compete in all the International races – Barcelona, Perpignan, Marseilles, Pau and Dax. So it was not until 1975 that we were fully up and running for long-distance events. The big change came in 1983, when we designed and constructed the house I now live in, which has a racing loft in the attic included in its design. This has been a boon to us, since it has allowed us to practice the system we use to this day. The extra space provided by the loft in the attic allows us to be patient with the development of the birds. It also allows us to really develop the pigeons at a pace that tests our birds. When we started long distance we continued with the original stock we had for middle distances, refining them for the longer races. The bases of these pigeons were the Van der Espt of Ostend and Marcel Desmet of Waregem.

My father knew Charles Van der Espt. He was in hospital in Ostend after the war and from the hospital window he could see the Van der Espt pigeons flying every day. After he got better he visited Van der Espt and it turned out that he and my father had something in common, because Van der Espt had also been in hospital after the First World War for similar reasons. Anyway, my father ended up with some of the best of the Van der Espt pigeons. The rest is history.

The Cross and its Effects

Since then have you brought in fresh imports to cross with your present colony?

After our official start we introduced the pigeons of André Vermote, also of Ostend, through the line

The attic loft. The loft and house, built in 1983, provided much-needed extra space for the pigeons. Since then the loft has expanded along with its commitment to international racing.

of 'Atleet'. A sister of 'Atleet' bred our famous 'Spiritus' of 1974, which was 1st National Cahors and 'Ace' pigeon of Belgium.

Nothing much has changed since then and our pigeons are still basically of the same blood. We have had a few crosses from individual pigeons that have stayed with us, such as the 'Rocky' of Vaneenoo of Wingene. There were some from Paul Lemahieu that were basically our blood. A hen from Emiel Denys that was a granddaughter of the famous 'Bliksem' was particularly good. There were also some from Roger Florizone of Nieuwpoort. These few imports cover more than thirty years of breeding, so I think it is possible to say the pigeons we now own are our own strain.

What influences you when you bring a cross into the loft?

We are still trying to find a good cross. We mostly get them from West Flanders. We've tried them from eastern Belgium but they have always

3302048.74
SPIRITUS
Foundation bird of the Deweerdt lofts
1st NatCahors
Best bird of Belgian Nationals 77 and 78

3302042.73
ADAMO
Also sire of Merlijn 2 nat Montauban – Donna 4 nat La Souterraine

3302035.72 Wannes full brother to Argenton 11 x nat 11 x prize 1st club Argenton

3332043.66
Jef
Very good long distance racer

3446629.65
full sister Keppe

3402130.71

3164970.61
Prince
son of Prince vd Espt which is last son of Prince H Desmet

3302003.70
Dtr Koekoek and 125.67
Marcel Desmet Waregem

3152519.73
Full sister Atleet A
Vermote Ostende
2 Nat Ace Pigeon 71
Mother of Spiritus and Harry
1st nat La Souterraine

3164490.67
Diepe Zwarte

3198093.64
Old Blauwen
Father 1st prize nat Cahors 71

Spreeuwte

3164482.67
Tintin Hen
C Denys Gistel

3301864.61
TINTIN
Won from Angouleme, Barcelona and Marseilles

BULTE
Brothers Deny's
Gistel

Pedigree 'Spiritus'.

'Spiritus', a Belgian National winner and an 'Ace' pigeon that was itself the result of a cross. This pigeon, more than any other, can claim to have infused into the Deweerdt family a new level of achievement and reliability right across the board. Bernard says of 'Spiritus', 'We should have bred more off him, but at that time we did not have the space or the attitude we have now.' Photo: © Copyright Jan Van Wortengham

been a failure. Perhaps it is our fault, I don't know. Perhaps it is because we are more familiar with the lofts of West Flanders and are likely to get better pigeons from the area we know and have flown against. I don't know the real reason, but it is generally a fact that West Flanders pigeons are the ones that have stuck with us.

Have you ever tried crosses from the Netherlands?

We have, but none stayed with us. I'm not talking about masses of pigeons. On average every year there have been only one or two imports altogether.

Is it essential that the birds you consider importing into your own family descend from an inbred family of birds, and how long do you give them to succeed or fail?

Yes, I would say if possible we go for inbred pigeons or pigeons from a related family of birds. We have tried importing pigeons, sons and daughters of champions who were themselves superb pigeons but not inbred or related to a family. I have to say they were not a success. Nowadays we don't consider a cross unless it comes from a family of pigeons. There are fanciers who have a super pigeon from time to time, but apart from that nothing. Importing pigeons from this type of pigeon has always been a failure.

We try to keep the offspring for five years. When you only import a few pigeons each year the offspring must be given a good test. The offspring must be quite mature pigeons before we throw them out. It is interesting, though, to keep on trying with new pigeons just to see if their offspring can succeed under our methods and our selection. Perhaps new pigeons first have to adjust to our rather unusual methods. This is another reason we give them a good test over a long time.

Have you made any mistakes importing pigeons?

We've made more mistakes than we've had successes. That's life, the game we're in is a chancy business. All we are doing is attempting to cut down the odds by keeping to the pigeons of our basic family – after all, it's these we know and these that have responded to our 'no-frills' management. There are no certainties in pigeon racing, only fewer mistakes. Occasionally we hit the jackpot, but more often than not we fail.

The Race Team from Year to Year

How do you treat young birds in the year of their birth? Do you race young birds? What do you expect of them?

There is a difference between those that are born early and those that are born later. Those that are born early are trained and may go to a few races and some may eventually go to the longer Young Bird National races depending on their condition at that time of the year. Not many go to longer races, perhaps fifteen or so. Those that are born later are trained. They have to go through the system of training from a short distance whatever the conditions. I take them to work and liberate them there, for example; this is just 20km (12 miles) away. I call this period of their lives, rather euphemistically, 'The Torture Chamber'. They are expected to survive this period without help of any kind. No medicine, no special food, nothing but themselves and how they are bred. They are put either in the aviary lofts at the bottom of the garden or in a separate section in the attic loft and trained from there. We continue to train them even in the winter with every condition thrown at them. Those trained in such a way often go on to make the best pigeons. In my opinion they are even better than those early pigeons that are trained and raced in the longer races. Even if early pigeons do well in these races, they do not always turn out to be the best pigeons. I prefer the ones that haven't been raced but are locally trained to the ones that are raced.

Do you breed late breds? Have you had any success with them and, if successful, what is the reason?

We've had a lot of success with birds bred later

Bird	Parents	Grandparents	Great-grandparents	Great-great-grandparents
94.3341846 **MAGNUS** 19th Int Dax '97-7194 b 36th Int Perpignan '97 – 12,367 b 33rd Int Dax '99 329th Int Perpignan '99 128th Int Dax 2000	93.3357732 Masahiko 373 int Perpignan 256th Cahors 386th Montauban	89.3316151 EMIEL 1st Int Bordeaux	83.3324036 BARTO 118,145,260,290 nat Cahors	75.3300141 Bartje
				80.3402024
			84.3200297 sister Kristoff 1st prov 2nd nat Perigueux	77.3402159 FILIP
				78.3402200
		90.3326257 Sister PAUL H Sister Tony	82.3294280 MARCO H Brother Danka 7 x Barcelona	73.3302033 MARCUS
				79.3355540 Sn SPIRITUS Dtr Adamo
			86.3158245 P Lemahieu Sister 1 prov Limoges	79.4533434
				81.3457720
	93.3357847 H Sister Matsushima	90.3326001 HARPO 178th Brive 50th Cahors	87.3321249 TONY 42 nat Limoges 7th nat Dax	81.3462638 PILI
				86.3158245
			83.3426509 dtr Taunus g dtr SPIRITUS	77.3402047 G Son Prince Van der Espt
				78.3402085 Dtr SPIRITUS Son Adamo
		92.3363501 g dam Magnus	91.3313100 half bro Athus sire Bartali	85.3329089 VARAZUR
				90.3240706 g dtr KOUROS
			91....1499 sister Resso Dofix Emmylou	83.3324181 KOUROS
				87.3321082 EMMY

Pedigree 'Magnus', a modern multiple winner at the Deweerdt loft.

in the year – 'Iban', 'Ted', 'Magnus' – a high proportion of the very best pigeons in our team were bred late in the year. Yes, now I remember, 'Zinka' was also one. I would say a higher percentage of late-hatched young pigeons turn out to be good later in life. I don't know why this is but they are generally better.

How do you treat yearlings and what do you expect of them?

We send them to the yearling programme (Châteauroux and Limoges) and some, but not so many, to the long-distance yearling races. The late breds are not raced, only trained. That's also the reason we don't use the Automatic Timing System. We were planning to race the old birds with Automatic Timing and the late breds sent along as trainers with a rubber on, but you are not allowed to send a mixed team. It is all or nothing. That's why we do not have it.

Are the yearlings expected to win prizes?

When a yearling is a nice pigeon of the best origin it doesn't matter if he or she is doing well or not. In such cases we allow them to develop further. If one that's not such a nice pigeon and is not directly off the best birds isn't doing well, we will probably send it on to the longer races as a yearling. All this, of course, is much easier when you have a closely related family of birds. To some degree you can pick and choose on the basis of what went before with pigeons bred in a similar way.

How do you treat two-year-old pigeons and what work is expected from them?

The majority of the two-year-olds go to a maximum of 600 or 700km (370–430 miles). That's the same as the yearlings. This year [2005], for example, our late breds from 2003 are now in their second season but have only been to Limoges (600km). We are a bit old-fashioned in how we treat them. We take our time, but more to the point we give the pigeons time.

What is this 'old-fashioned'? Is it that by waiting for them they develop a greater connection with the loft or something?

A yearling is not a mature pigeon, nor is it mentally mature. We never show the hen on basketing day, for instance. Some yearlings go the whole season before they understand the system. The time we give them allows them to develop both physically and mentally in their own time at their own pace. The yearlings have very little stress in their lives. You can only take out of the pigeon what is in the pigeon. Our system is designed to put physical ability and confidence into the pigeon during the whole of its life. This is also why the two-year-old pigeons are also treated easily. When finally they are asked the big questions in the big races, they are more likely to respond if they have been treated easily in their early life and their reserves and natural inclinations have not been abused.

How about the three- and four-year-old pigeons? How are they treated?

Here we have a slight problem. All the pigeons are mixed together, yearlings, two-year-olds and older birds. Sometimes when we are building up particular pigeons for long races they do not race for three or even four weeks. Because of this the yearlings and often the two-year-olds also have to stay at home because they are in the same section. This is not ideal for the yearlings and the two-year-olds for they really should race every week.

We try to avoid problems of this kind but often it is difficult. The three- and four-year-old pigeons go to the longest races and often race until they are six or seven years of age. The future of the loft rests on their performance, so we give them priority over the rest.

Do Looks Matter?

Is there any physical attribute you particularly look for in a mature pigeon? Are you looking at the wing, the throat, the head, a particular shape of the body or what?

When the pigeons do well it doesn't matter what they look like, but usually those that do well are nicely balanced and have a good wing. What I do like is good feather quality. I really like good feather. I like silky feather. I don't like pigeons with very dry feather. We did have a few good ones with dry feather, but usually the following generation, the ones bred from such pigeons, are not so good. I remember in particular one pigeon that had some middle-distance blood in him. He was very good but his brothers and sisters were not. The feather quality of his wings was really bad. He was not a good reproducer. We still have two sons, I think, but they have to perform well this year or that will be the end of this particular line.

Some of your pigeons are deep and bony in the hand. Is this a good sign?

I must admit I don't particularly like this shape, but I have to accept it because so many of our best pigeons are shaped this way and have turned out to

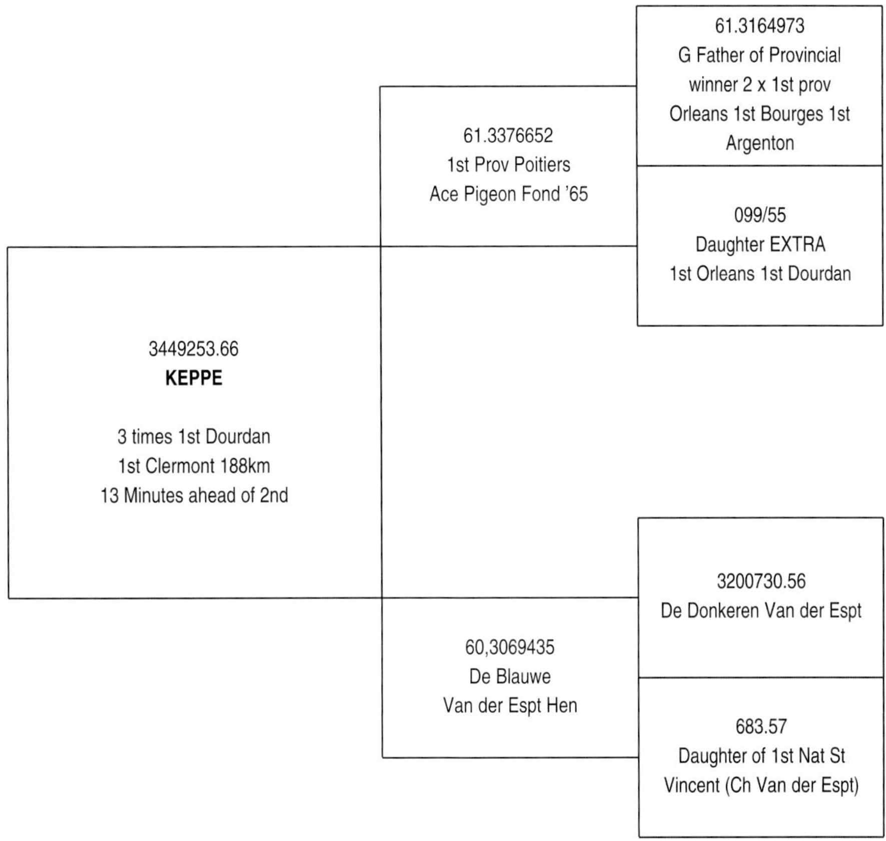

Pedigree 'Keppe', a foundation pigeon that goes directly back to the original founding Van der Espt birds. The fact that Emiel Deweerdt was in a hospital bed overlooking the Charles Van der Espt lofts was one of those lucky chances in life (not seen as being lucky at the time) whose effect was to last for another 50 years.

be really good. Some are rather deep especially when young and underdeveloped. As they grow and mature it is not so obvious. A couple of our good pigeons with this bony shape have been 'Spiritus' and 'Magnus'. 'Iban' was a bit deep. 'Magnus' had a cousin that was beautiful and had a really classic shape. I liked this pigeon and expected him to do really well, but I was wrong. He turned out to be a complete duffer, while 'Magnus', his close relation but not such a good-looking pigeon, turned out to be a champion. I think this deep shape comes from the old original Van der Espt line. 'Keppe', bred from direct Van der Espt pigeons, was this shape. It probably goes back to the old original pigeons of Vandervelde of Ostend. These pigeons played a huge influence in the Van der Espt family.

Treatment for Disease and Cultivating Immunity

Do you consider a high degree of immunity to illness is essential for a long-distance loft to perform well?

There is very little in the pigeon world that's more important. I hope that transport will not become too fast. I like slow transport. I don't know anything about doping, but I think the slower the transport the harder it is to dope, creating better conditions for cultivating pigeons and pigeon families of true quality.

Those pigeons that possess a high degree of natural immunity will emerge as the fathers and mothers of dynasties of future long-distance pigeons. Those that do not, will not. The shorter the time between basketing and liberation the easier it becomes to treat the pigeons.

- **3321147.87**
KORNEEL
1990
1539 Int Marseilles 15,648 b 1990
288 Int Perpignan 10,444 b 1990
34 Int Barcelona 27,167b 1991
1030 Int Perpignan 13,573 b 1991
112th Int Barcelona 26,807b 1994
  - 3339510.81
Mirko
A full brother of Mirko is the sire of Tamar 568th Barcelona smash of 1987
    - 3302048.74
Spiritus
Foundation bird of the Deweerdt lofts
      - 3302042.73
Adamo
Also sire of Merlijn 2 nat Montauban – Donna 4 nat La Sout
        - 3302035.72 Wannes 11 x nat prize 1 club Argenton
        - 3402130.71
      - 3152519.73
Sister Atleet a Vermote Ostende
2 Nat Ace 71
        - 3164490.67 Diepe Zwarte
        - 3164482.67 Tintin Hen C Denys Gistel
    - **73000695.74**
Anja
1"Dourdan
1st Int Barcelona Hens '80
      - 3067574.67
Rosten
A Leenaert Heule
Desmet Stichelbaut
      - 3302049.72
Sandra
nest sister to Alfa
1st Angouleme 74
  - 3158213.86
    - 3275731.84
Full brother to 1 prov Limoges for P Lemahieu Diksmuide
      - 4533434.79
      - 3457720.81
    - 3423339.84
Full sister Barto
Sire of Emiel
      - 3294076.82
Kristof
2 nat Perigeux 4245 b
        - 73402159.77 Filip
        - 78.3402200
      - 3402024.80
half sister of Claude Rinus
Mia etc...

Pedigree 'Korneel' the Deweerdt pigeon that was 112th from Barcelona at 7 years of age.

'Korneel' was a pigeon that flew many International races in its long racing career. Korneel was finally 112th Barcelona International from over 26,000 pigeons in 1994 when he was 7 years of age. Longevity in both pigeons and humans is a sure sign of vitality. Photo: © Copyright Jan Van Wortengham

Cycling trainers don't stop here on the way to the Tour de France, then?

No, no, not here. They give us a miss.

Do you clean out your lofts on a daily basis and, if not, what is the reason for this? Do you vaccinate annually?

In the racing season the lofts are cleaned daily, though sometimes it is not possible. Between basketing for the final race and the new season of the following year, however, there is no cleaning. A lot of the ways we do things here are down to convenience because we have little time. This makes us decide what is really crucial for the well-being and future of the pigeons. What is important, and what is not so important, we have learnt over the years. We now vaccinate for paramyxo and pox, each given individually since I was told by the vet and by another fancier that the combined vaccination is not effective against pox. Some fanciers I know very well used the combined vaccination and they still caught pox. I also vaccinate for paratyphoid. That too is given on its own. The vet always comes along to vaccinate – we do not do it ourselves.

If illness, such as a respiratory condition, were to arise spontaneously, would you immediately suppress the individual or its offspring without attempting to treat the pigeon, or would you allow it to persist and wait for the pigeons to get over it?

It happens so very seldom, but when it does we treat the individual. During the racing season, when the pigeons can be under a certain amount of stress, we treat them, but in the off-season we don't treat for anything. Not a single pigeon is ever treated during the close season.

What we are concerned about are the really serious illnesses like paramyxo and paratyphus. These diseases cause physical damage. Even when a pigeon gets over the condition it is left damaged. If a pigeon raced over middle distances is damaged you can say its career is over, but when you race long distances the pigeon gets lost. You can't take any risks with conditions such as this. Most of the champion pigeons have very good health. Health and vitality go hand in hand. Health breeds confidence. Confidence is important to a pigeon. There are always exceptions, of course, but here I am talking about what happens most of the time.

How often do you treat for canker or coccidiosis?

We treat them for canker when we race seriously. Many late breds are treated for the first time when they are two years old. As for coccidiosis, samples are taken to the vet before the season starts. If the count is high we treat them, but never in the winter, when coccidiosis disappears. Coccidiosis is likely to attack when a pigeon is racing and is under a certain amount of stress, but when a healthy pigeon is just resting, or exercising normally, coccidiosis gets cured.

You once told me you expected the birds to fly with a bit of trichomoniasis. Is that still your opinion?

In the past we used to treat pigeons for trichomoniasis prior to breeding while they were sitting and also prior to racing. Now, because so many fanciers' lofts suffer from a resistance to certain strains of trichomoniasis, not a single bird is

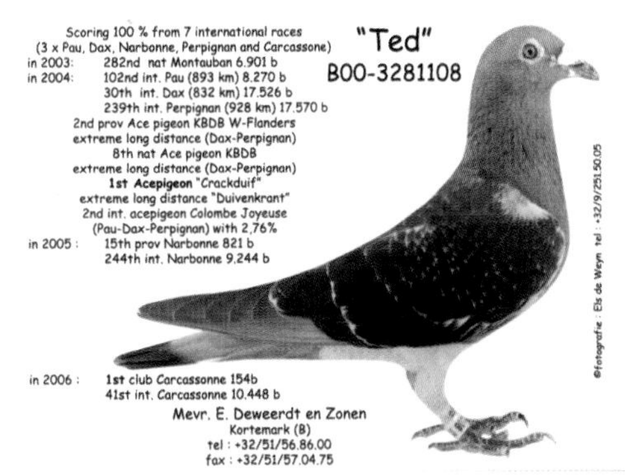

'Ted' – 2nd International 'Ace' pigeon Colmombe Joyeuse 2004. Photo: © Copyright Els de Weyn

3281108,00 **TED** **Dark Cheq** **102 Int Pau 8270 b** **30 Int Dax 17526 b** **239 Int Perpignan 17570** **2nd Int Ace Pigeon Colombe Joyeuse** **8th Ace Pigeon KBDB Dax, Perpignan** **41th Int Carcassonne 2006 10448 birds**	98.3266496 ED	95.3289671 KEDIR 34 Int Dax 78 Int Dax 143 Int Perpignan	93.3307264 KEDIR Snr 317 Int Marseilles 15.586 b
			91.3369489
			91.3313219
			92.3363501 g dam Magnus
			91.3313100
			91. ...1499
		96.3321955	94.3299394 Wimbledon 19 nat Brive 5736b
			89.3313328 Bles
			89.3316304
			95.3336931
			92.3317133 Kasper 1 prov Tarbes
			94.3299383
	98.3266091 LOLA	96.3321951 br Texas h btr Athus	88.3316250 Gerard 1st Chateauroux 2nd Dourdon
			84.3331121 Limogoc
			84.3243491
			90.3240706
			89.3185432 P Lemahieu
			87.3321142
		96.3321486 h Sister Magnus	93.3357732 Masahiko 373 int Perpignan 12367 b
			89.3316151 EMIEL
			90.3326257
			95.3289497 Sister to Seikan
			90.3326229 AGASSI
			90.3326056

Pedigree of 'Ted'.

treated during the winter from after the last race has been flown until after a couple of races the following year. If the pigeons come back from the early races having picked up a bit of trichomoniasis it's very good. We like to build up as much resistance in our pigeons as possible without being foolhardy. We don't start searching for a bottle as soon as things appear to be going wrong.

Advice for the Novice

What advice would you give a novice attempting to build a team of long-distance pigeons before he started?

My advice would be to build a good loft with good ventilation. But you have to learn by experience whether the loft is good or not. It all depends on the environment, the direction of the entrance and many of the surroundings, such as buildings situated near the loft.

I know it might seem old-fashioned, but I would suggest trying to build your own family. We did it: we started with two or three families of pigeons and then started to build a new family of our own. Every year you should import two or three new pigeons and be patient with them. But that is old-fashioned as well. Above all you must have some time during the racing season. Of course, that can be a problem as well, so I would advise people new to the sport to race in partnership. If you have a regular professional life there are times when you are not available and cannot take time off. At such times your partner can take over, while you can cover for him when he is not available. It can be hard work when you do it all on your own. Pigeon racing, although it has huge rewards, can also destroy.

What would you advise a novice to avoid and at what stage should he be after three years?

Avoid giving too much medication and, yes, overcrowding. When you are racing long distances and the loft is overcrowded the problem will be solved automatically, but above all our novice must be patient. After three years a novice reaches a vital stage when you have to select without pity. This is a crucial time. Only the best must be kept. You have to be patient, but at the right time you have to make fundamental decisions.

If you have pigeons that come home looking tired and losing weight you can ignore this once, but if it happens twice you should get rid of them. Also, if you have birds that have difficulty flying – some call it 'one-wing syndrome', in which one wing is slightly lower than the other – then they also are finished, so get rid of them. You have to be a bit careful and decide whether it is because of an injury or because of 'one-wing' lameness. I don't give a second chance. It appears that some people are having serious problems with it, or so I hear.

The novice should love the idea of building a family of pigeons and gradually improving across a broad front. This takes the form of getting more pigeons to fly certain distances, getting more pigeons into the results, breeding a better standard of pigeon. If this idea is at the back of his mind he will gradually begin to make more good decisions than bad ones and the overall strength of the colony will improve. If the novice is patient it is to be hoped that one or two champions will begin to emerge. But perhaps that is an old-fashioned idea as well, because the majority of today's fanciers are not patient; everyone is in too much of a hurry for success these days.

Before the Race

Do you fly widowhood, on the nest, both systems or something else? Are yearlings also on widowhood?

We fly both systems. Some hens are flown but not many. As for the yearlings, they are flown on widowhood, but as I said before we do not show the hens, so quite often the yearlings have to go a whole season before they learn the system.

How much exercise do the widowhood cocks take every day?

They exercise in the evening. In the past it used to be for about one hour, but this is no longer possible since after an hour we cannot get them in.

'Magnus' a pigeon that has been 3 times in the first 50 in International races – 19th Int Dax – 19th Int Perpignan 97 and 33rd International Dax 99. He went on to score 128th Int Dax in 2000, but ruled himself out of the final Perpignan race that year after catching a mild dose of pigeon pox. The Deweerdt loft now vaccinates against this disease.
Photo: © Copyright Els de Weyn

PICABO
01.3250485 Dark Cheq
1st prov Barcelona 04
28* nat Barcelona 04
91 Int Barcelona 04
306 Int Perpignan 03
52 Int Perpignan Hens 03

- 95.3289653 Son of Eleni
  - 90.3326053 Half Brother Emmy and Korneel
    - 83.3324181 Korous 1st Club 4th Int Perpignan
      - 80.3402021 Stany
        - Brother sire Adamo
        - Daughter sire Adamo
      - 82.3429379
        - Filip g son Keppe
        - Daughter Spiritus
    - 86.3158213 G Dtr Kristof 2 x nat Perigueux
      - 84.3275731 P Lemahieu
        - Son Adamo
      - 84.3423339 G Son Keppe
  - 91.3313241 Eleni 2 nat 3 Int Barcelona hens 22 int Barcelona 26,807 b
    - 90.3380780 Athus Imbred to Korous
      - 87.3321143 Gunter
        - DtrElza g dtr bthr sire of Adamo
      - 90.3240706
    - 88.3316078 Amporo 2nd nat La Souterainne
      - 82.3294291 Tamar
        - Daughter Kouros
        - Son Spiritus X Anja
      - 83.3426530
        - Filip
        - Daughter bthr Spiritus x Elza
- 00.3253199
  - 98.3266053 Zwarte Zeno
    - 94.3299094 Zeno 102nd nat Barcelona 12,731 3 x Barcelona
      - 90.3326244 Zem
        - g son Tamar
        - g dtr Spiritus
      - 90.3326200
        - Gunter
        - g dtr Adamo
    - 93.3307293 Nest Sister Matsushima
      - 90.3326001 Harpo
        - g son Filip
        - dtr Spiritus
      - 91.3313340
        - Athus
        - Amparo
  - 98.3266367 Sister Raldo
    - 89.3316150 Aldo 5th Poitiers nestbrother Emiel
      - 83.3324036 Barto
        - Son Kempe
      - 84.3200297
        - Flip
        - g dtr Adamo
    - 92.3317158 4 x Barcelona half sister Zaina
      - 91.3313199
        - g dtr Tamar
        - g dtr Filip
      - 89.3316084
        - Kouros
        - Emmy g dtr Spiritus

Picabo, a pigeon of this century has in her a pedigree of pigeons going back to the very foundation of the Deweerdt family in the century before. This pedigree is a good example of Deweerdt breeding methods. Highlighted in Blue are pigeons that repeat themselves in later generations.

Picabo: A modern provincial winner of the Deweerdt loft – This time 91st International Barcelona. Many fanciers liken a provincial winner to a UK Federation winner. This is far from the truth – The nearest comparison to a similar UK result would be to win the section in the National Flying Club with double the birdage. West Flanders, the Belgian province where the Deweerdt lofts compete, is usually one of the largest provinces in Belgium in terms of the numbers competing. In recent years, though, the proportion of Dutch pigeons from Eastern provinces bordering Germany and along the Valley of the River Maas has increased. For this reason Western provinces of Belgium and the Netherlands no longer enjoy the same advantage they once did. Photo: © Copyright Els de Weyn

We exercise them in the morning only when the main races are coming. In April and at the beginning of May it is still cold in the mornings, so we do not exercise them then in those months. When we raced middle distances we used to race the whole team every week, and then it was possible to train them for just an hour because the pigeons were not fed so much and were a bit hungry. Because we feed more for long distances it is no longer possible to do this. Sometimes some pigeons are not raced for three weeks. These pigeons are not hungry and they fly when some of the others that have been raced come in to feed. Often they are out for an hour and a half. I don't want them to be out longer, but sometimes I haven't finished the cleaning, so they have to stay out longer.

Are some hens raced and under what system do they race?

They race to the nest. Sometimes they are sent to a race on eggs, and later on a young pigeon of about a week old. We try to exercise them at home. For this we have to come home at midday. Again this is not ideal, but we do it. They fly for perhaps 20 minutes. Sometimes I take them to work and liberate them there; this is only 20km so again it is not ideal. Compared with the cocks they do not get enough exercise, but still they sometimes put up good performances. Joan, for example, was 10th International from Barcelona in 2005 and 109th Perpignan in 2003, so I think it is the blood that counts more than the exercise. If the good long-distance genes are there, hens seem to overcome fitness disadvantages when flying in Marathon events. This would not happen in middle-distance races. Here the birds do not need to be of such good blood provided they are fit. At long distances, breeding matters more. Breeding and good blood based on performance is essential.

Is there any particular herb or supplement, for example garlic or onion, you use either in the water or on the food?

I don't give anything like that. I'm not saying that they're bad, but as a rule I don't have the time to prepare such things. Others may do it, but generally they have more time or fewer pigeons than we have.

That brings up an interesting question concerning how much time a fancier has for the sport and where should you go to get your pigeons. In every system there are pluses and minuses. A man with fewer pigeons and more time has fewer bad pigeons. That is a plus. When you go to a man who has more pigeons but less time it is the quality of the pigeons that is making the performance, not the method. That also is a plus and from that point of view it is better to go to the man who has the bigger team and less time.

Is there perhaps a kind of a happy medium that's manageable on the one hand, but has a big enough genetic pool on the other to produce one or two very good pigeons every year?

You have to know the man. If he is a good pigeon man who is not exaggerating you can be successful with birds from a small team, but on the other hand buying from a small-team man who may be using all kinds of products and tricks that you cannot use … well, you probably won't be happy with those pigeons. A man with a bigger team can work on natural immunity. So can a man with a small team, but it is more difficult, so many small-team men don't. If a man who is breeding, say, only twenty to thirty young birds in the loft experiences some illness, well, firstly it costs less money to treat them. Secondly, if ten die out of twenty that is a disaster, but if ten die out of a total of 150 in a big loft then that is a blessing.

So you don't use garlic, tea, honey or any other herbs?

No, we don't. I once won a bottle of 'garlic extract', or something like that, and it sat on a shelf down the loft for perhaps three or four years. A journalist came to see the pigeons and noticed this bottle, so he thought we were using it. The only things we use are grit, Vitamineral and, when they have babies in the nest, Pickstone clay.

I remember Dad always used to say tea was for humans.

In the run-up to the big race, a week before Barcelona, for example, do you give them peanuts or small seeds as some fanciers do?

No, we don't use any of these things. Perhaps there is an opening for some improvement here? Our system is to see to the pigeons in the morning and the evening. We have to basket pigeons and do many things for them. If on top of that we had to cook special potions and do all these other things ... Our hobby is to watch the pigeons coming home after the races. If we had to do all these things while we were waiting, well, it wouldn't be much fun any more. When we have to give them a treatment I hate it – it's extra work. I avoid all these things as much as I can.

After the Race

When a tired pigeon returns from a long race is there any special treatment you give him before he rejoins the flock for normal training?

No, we don't. I won't say that's bad, it probably isn't. One of the things we do use when they come back – we put some glucose in the water. My father used it. But many of these things are more of a tradition, more a necessity for the fancier than for the pigeon. It's like sportsmen who are ... what's the word in English? ... 'superstitious'. They have a gold chain around their neck or they put their boots on in a certain order; they don't like not to do it in case they have a bad race or a bad game, but when they have a bad race or a bad game it doesn't get the blame. Pigeon products is a very good business – that's where the money is.

How long is the hen allowed to sit with the cock on his return?

This is also very irregular, but the hen is always there when he comes back. If he is tired she sometimes stays overnight, but there is no set pattern. We do what we feel at the time, depending on how we see things. It also depends on how many birds are sent from a section. If only one is sent from a section then he won't have his hen for very long because we don't want to upset the other pigeons, but if the whole section is sent then they have more time with their hen. When they come home from Barcelona we tend to take them out of the loft and put them in an empty nest box in another empty section. We have a few nest boxes at the back, away from the main sections, that we use for this purpose. We lock them together and perhaps feed them in the box for the rest of the day. Usually the next day, when the others are out for exercise, we put them in their original box with the hen and then take the hen away when the others come in after exercise.

Are the pigeons allowed to rear a young one after racing before they are separated?

Yes, they are allowed to rear some youngsters. That is why this is the main breeding season. Separation is not immediate after racing. They are allowed to sit again and again, often until December. If I wanted to ring the last late breds of last year [2005] I could have rung them with rings from 2006. This also happened in 2004; the last youngsters of that year had 2005 rings on them. We get the rings on 31 December. The last late bred off 'Ted', for example, was an early late bred of 2006 but Ted is one of our best birds so we must have more youngsters from him. His loft was only separated when the early breeders were beginning to mate the following year.

We have now mated some pigeons, perhaps three or four sections. When I see a particular section has not made it through the moult well they won't be mated in December, and perhaps not until March. We don't keep the lights on when they are mated early; they have to cope in the dark. As for food, they only have breeding mixture, which is mainly 'Natural', but we do use some from Versele-Laga.

The Moult and Winter Treatment

Are they given any special food or treatment, such as baths, to promote the moulting of the feathers?

In the winter we give them moulting food containing small seeds. As for baths, I always want to do it but again time is a problem, so I never do it. I would say that most of the time the pigeons don't have a bath, but as usual this is very irregular. During racing maybe we give a bath once or twice. It is all very irregular.

Pairing up the Birds

What physical characteristics do you look for when pairing up the birds? Do you compensate for size or colour of the eye, etc?

I don't especially look for the eye, but when I notice a particular pigeon has a very light eye I mate it with one with a dark one.

Because you have a family of pigeons, can you sometimes see characteristics particular to your family that indicate you might have bred a good pigeon?

Sometimes, yes. But it is not always physical, it is often behaviour. Sometimes when I see certain behaviour in the loft I notice it and keep the pigeon in mind. 'Iban' and 'Ted' were two of the favourites I noticed – they became champions. 'Magnus', on the other hand, was not one of my favourites; I missed him. His cousin from the same section, on the other hand, was a favourite but he was a duffer. I like to see an individual attitude in a pigeon, one that does not dive in for the food immediately at feeding time but looks around, waits and then selects where he has to stand.

The Loft

Turning to the environment of the loft, the use of the aviary, etc, what did you have in mind when you constructed the loft?

Pigeons like to sit high. That is why we have pigeons in the attic, but it has its drawbacks in the spring when the wind is strong and because we live near the sea; if the pigeons are out too long they loose condition instead of gaining it. People with garden lofts that are often protected by nearby buildings and trees have a better time of it.

Are there improvements you would still like to make to your race loft and, if so, what are they?

We made a big investment a couple of weeks ago. We divided one section because the pigeons were too difficult to catch. The pigeons are quiet and very gentle most of the time, but as soon as they see the nestbowl they run away – they know this is a sign of basketing. You can't get them into the nest box any more. The bigger the loft the more problems you have. There are two types of pigeon. Both are really smart: the first type know the hen is coming and go into their box; the second type think 'He's going to catch me' and refuse to go into the nest box. That's why we made the section smaller, so they're easier to catch.

Numbers

How many birds do you have in your race team?

We have about a hundred nest boxes, but it is never completely full. The yearlings are mixed in with the old birds. It is better to have yearlings in their own section, but then you have the problem of transferring them from one loft to another. Our system is to allow the pigeon after it is mated to have the same box for its whole life.

How many breeders do you have?

We have thirty nest boxes for the hens, but they are not completely full.

How many young birds do you breed?

On average more than two hundred. Perhaps three hundred. But young birds are tested quite hard. Even late breds are tested. If they survive this testing then they have a comfortable life for two or three years. Testing for suitability has to take place early in life.

Would you like to have more pigeons?

No, I wouldn't have more even if I won the lottery and had all the time in the world to look after them.

Do you consider a certain number of breeding pigeons an essential minimum for maintaining the quality of your colony?

Ah, yes! The gene pool must be big enough to withstand the testing we give them and also big enough to produce champion pigeons from time to time. If champions do not appear for some time then you know you are doing something wrong. If that happens you are in deep trouble, but if champion pigeons keep coming from within your family then it is still healthy from the genetic point of view.

The golden rule is you should never sell a pigeon you cannot do without. We do not sell our champions or our top breeders. We could, of course, always sell the bad pigeons, but we would want to get rid of pigeons like that from our loft in any case, so in the long run it does not do any good to sell bad birds. Our policy is we only sell what we ourselves would keep.

'Emiel', 1st International Bordeaux 1992 – 100% prizewinner from 5 Nationals. Photo: © Copyright Els de Weyn

61.3376652
1st Prov Poitiers
Ace Pigeon Fond '65

66. 3449253
'Keppe'
3 x 1st Dourdan
1st Clermont

60.3069435
De Blauwe
Van der Espt Hen

75.3300141
Bartje
6 prov Orleans
7 and 23 prov Poitiers

67.3402125
G Dtr 1st Int Barcelona
M Desmet Waregem

3324036.83
Barto
118 nat Cahors
145 nat Cahors

3302042.73 Adamo
Also sire of 2nd nat
Montauban

78.3483403
Brother 'Spiritus'
1st nat Cahors

3152519.73
Full sister Atleet A Vermote

80.3402024

71.3302068
Sister Rika
1st nat Brive

3316151.89
EMIEL
1st Int Bordeaux 1992 34565 b
100% prizewinner from 5 nationals

72.3302048
'Mannix'
6th nat Tulle

77.3402159 FILIP
10 nat Cahors
18 nat Brive

66. 3449253 'Keppe'
3 x 1st Dourdan

75.3445175
Dtr 'Keppe'

84.3200297
sister Kristoff
1st prov 2nd nat Perigueux

3302042.73 Adamo
Also sire of Merlijn 2 nat

75.3445222
'Tiki' brother 'Spiritus'
1st nat Cahors

3152519.73
Full sister Atleet A Vermote

78.3402200
Sister 'Tara'
3rd prov Chateauroux

'Elza'
5 x Barcelona
43rd Int etc..

Pedigree of 'Emiel'.

KOUROS 83.3324181 Dark Cheq	80.3402021 Stanny	Giba 73.3302007 Dark Cheq	Jef 72.3332046	J Verschuere
				J Verschuere
			65.3446629 Sister Keppe	Rik 61.3376652
				60.3069435 Bue van der Espt
		Rina 79.3355549 Light Cheq	Rinus 76.3301043	Jo 72.3302068
				3302068.71 Sister Rika
			Sister Spiritus 78.3402206	Adamo 73.3302042
				73.3152519 Sister Atleet A. Vermote
	82.3429379	Filip 3402159.77 Zwarte Zeno	Mannix 72.3302046	Max 69.3302033
				71.3402147
			75.3445175 Dark Cheq	Keppe 3449253.66
				67.3402125 Marcel Desmet
		3462611.81	Spiritus 74.3302048 1 nat Cahors Ace pigeon 77-78	73.3302042.73 Adamo
				73.3152519 Sister Atleet
			Anja 74.3000695 1st Int Barcelona 80 Hens	Rosten 67.3067574
				Sandra 72.3302949

'Kouros', a pigeon that was sold but left an enormous influence.

Every year the same question arises: what will be the quality of the breeding? We try to keep the quality high and mate them with this intention, but every year we don't exactly know if high quality is coming. All we know is that there are good genes in the history of our family and in all probability something good should come out, but we are not sure where. I think historically the hit rate of champion pigeons produced in our lofts is high and, more pertinently, it has remained high for a number of years, not just for one or two years. 'Time at the top' is still one of the greatest tests of a good loft. Of course, not every year is the same but our average over the years is good.

The Main Birds

Which individual stock birds were essential to the development of your colony?

'Spiritus', of course. We should have bred more from 'Spiritus'. In those days we didn't have the space and the attitude to breed as many as we do now. We raced all his babies – that is something we shouldn't have done. He was, of course, mated with different hens, but not on a bull system, so it took a long time.

I don't know how many we have bred this year from the main cocks in the loft, but we have bred quite a lot from 'Iban', 'Ted' and 'Emiel'. 'Emiel' is, of course, one of our main cocks. He was mated with three hens at the same time, although not fully 'bull system', so nothing too strenuous; the first two were put under other pairs and the last pair he reared by himself. We used a similar method with 'Magnus', 'Kedir' and others.

'Kouros' was one of our top cocks, but we sold him when he was seven years of age. He was one of our best, so again it was an exception to our rule. We got some babies back – that was in the deal – but it is rare for us to sell a pigeon of this quality that is representative of the best we have.

Iban: The Deweerdt loft also contains workhorses of quality. No modern international loft can survive at the top without pigeons such as this being regularly produced. Photo: © Copyright Els de Weyn

Ivani. Photo: © Copyright Els de Weyn

So there are 'Spiritus', 'Magnus', 'Emiel', 'Ted', 'Kedir', 'Kouros', 'Masahiko': we're not living and dying just because of one pigeon. It's a long and generous list. The style of our loft is that it doesn't depend on a single magic mating to succeed. It looks for gradual improvement on a broad front. If one part of the front is not producing, then another probably will.

There were others, such as 'Sylvester' and his half sister 'Roxanne', a very good hen. We have a pigeon that was 4th International Dax in 1992, so we started breeding from him then. One of the best is 'Iveni', a grandson of 'Magnus', and he is breeding very good pigeons.

As for racers, it depends on what standard you are making your judgement. There is really only one standard on which to judge and that is the standard at European level: 'Ted' was second 'Ace' pigeon on the European list, based on three races. On two races he was number 8 in Belgium. So 'Ted' was a very important pigeon.

All the best pigeons are related. Sometimes there are many generations in between, but they are related.

'Spiritus' was always a favourite of my father's. Although he was in my loft when I was a boy he was not a particular favourite of mine. My favourites were 'Emiel' and 'Ted', but not so much 'Magnus'. I liked 'Kedir' very much from the beginning, but 'Kouros' was a very wild pigeon. He was frightened by a German fancier and never forgot about it. Some of the others recovered, but not Kouros. Since then I don't take visitors to the racing loft any more. We built the house in 1983 and moved the yearlings there the following year.

I have never seen anything like the time 'Kouros' was frightened, before or since. There were nine pigeons in this particular section. The German fancier opened a sliding door to the loft. He was wearing one of those typical hunters' hats with a feather in it, like they wear in Germany. I wanted to tell him not to open the door but the harm was already done. These nine pigeons took off together and all hit the window with a smash. I don't know if it was the hat, the feather or what, but that's what happened.

A Life in Pigeons

How do the pigeons fit in with your family life?

My wife used to help with the pigeons, but she doesn't do it now – she is allergic to pigeon dust.

Are other members of your family interested in the pigeons?

Yes, as I mentioned, both my son Tim and Fred's son Filip are interested. My son is now at University, so his life is taken up with his studies, but he has his own section.

Can you imagine a life without pigeons?

It would be very difficult. I have been around pigeons all of my life. I am a pigeon person through and through. It would be very, very difficult to imagine a life without pigeons, but still pigeons are not the whole of my life. I do have other things.

Reducing the Odds

Racing pigeons at long distances is always a challenge and full of uncertainties. By its very nature we can never know everything. You have been more successful than most fanciers in the sport, so can you single out the one technique or quality that has helped reduce the uncertainty, shorten the odds and, to some degree, helped produce a successful colony?

I simply don't know what makes the difference. Is it luck? I simply don't know, but because I have been associated with pigeons all my life it has probably become a culture to me. It's like a cook who can prepare a menu without thinking. He's simply doing it. On the other hand, there may be a man who's not a bad cook but always has to look at the recipe.

Do you have any further ideas and ambitions?

I will be happy to stay on the same level while enjoying racing the pigeons. I am certainly not going to push harder than the breeding of the pigeons allows. The Deweerdt loft is mainly about breeding, keeping the colony intact and the standard as high as we can get it.

Long-distance Racing and its Spiritual Quality

Does the keeping of pigeons have a spiritual quality about it? These small birds try so hard and perhaps suffer some pain in getting home. Is there something that captivates you about the whole process?

I am certainly captivated by the whole thing. I am still amazed when a pigeon gets back from a race over many hundreds of miles. But I think the most important race is the one you are preparing for this week. Next week it is the same, that's important, too. One of the nice things about racing pigeons is you are always thinking about tomorrow – racing and breeding and planning for the future. 'Pigeon racing' is a lot about looking forward.

Obviously you have respect for nature?

Very much. Yes, very much. I like to race pigeons and breed pigeons, but I can't talk too much about it. We have known each other for quite a while now. I think we talk a lot, but I can't stand pigeon men who can only talk about pigeons. I like to talk about different issues. Often when we go to a pigeon presentation you don't have a choice where or with whom you sit, and there are always some people who only talk about pigeons. It's the same when I have to attend a professional lunch and some can only talk about work. If you have a problem, it's normal. You try to solve it. It's a part of your life, but talking about nothing but work bores me.

Some jobs may give a satisfaction similar to that we get from the pigeons, but not many. Everyone needs a challenge in life. If you have a medical education, the challenge might be to find new ways of treating illness. Yet many people, if they were being honest and sat back to consider if what they were doing was important and making people better, would have to admit it was not. For me pigeons is that challenge. Even in this field there is always research going on, always questions that have to be answered and problems to be solved.

When I compare today with what we were doing twenty years ago very little has changed. We have stopped racing young birds – that was one major change. After cortisone was introduced you couldn't do well racing young pigeons any more, so we stopped altogether.

Would you say the pigeons keep you sane?

Yes, [laughter] I think I could say that. I find the possibilities of meeting people from different countries, with different professional lifestyles and different backgrounds, are always interesting. I

David Glover, ex editor of the British Homing World, in deep discussion with Fred Deweerdt.

don't think I could do my daily job if I didn't have pigeons.

When I listen to my colleagues – some of them, certainly not all of them – at a meeting I am amazed by their limited view of life. Of course, we are government officials and much is to do with legislation. You have to do things this way because that's what the law says; then ten years later there is another government and you go back to how you did it in the first place. Some colleagues can make a big thing of this: it's the law and the law changes. I find this aspect of life amazing. Many of them are so awkward in their dealings with our clients, the citizens. Some think they are so important. Of course, some of them have other fascinating hobbies, which I think is a good thing in life. However, I also think that if I were professionally involved in pigeons I would not gain the satisfaction I do as an amateur. That is why the Deweerdt lofts always preserve their independence and have always done so. We are not contracted with anyone. We like to remain unattached and make our own decisions in our own time at our own pace for our own reasons.

Avian Virus

Does the Avian Virus worry you?

The 'Avian Virus' is worrying some pigeon men to death. For some this is more than a worry, it's a necessity, for they have to race. As for me, I don't like it but I can put up with it. I can easily wait another year. I would hate it but I can wait. I could probably wait for eight or nine years if necessary. Of course, we would have to reduce our stock, but we would if we had to do it.

I think this sport is such a wonderful hobby. It has given me a lot. It has widened my view of life and kept me sane in a mad world. I can hardly think of any other pastime that would have provided me with as much. I love it. I love the pigeons. I look forward to every time we manage to produce and train a new champion. Champion pigeons don't know they are champions, though. They know they have to mate and rear their young, but they are certainly unaware of the reward they give their owners. I like that about pigeons.

CONCLUSION

Building a Strain

The Deweerdt section of this book may appear to be laden down with pedigrees. We apologize for this, but it is unavoidable. The Deweerdt lofts are primarily a family of pigeons based on the concept of founding, maintaining and building a strain of related pigeons. The best way of showing this is through the pedigrees of the founding and famous pigeons. Those who are inclined to study pedigrees will come to some understanding of how this strain has been put together and how they themselves might imitate the procedure with their own pigeons. If, after thirty years, they have achieved a similarly related family of pigeons, with similar

Bernard telephoning the arrival times. Every Belgian pigeon timed in International races has to be verified by telephone within one hour.

Zaina: Another workhorse that would be welcome in most lofts. She has scored from both Barcelona and Perpignan and is sister to a Geoff Cooper's BICC National winner "Wriggler" here in the UK. Photo: © Copyright Els de Weyn

Liesbet: 1st prize National Barcelona 1981 from 6,729 pigeons. Photo: © Copyright Els de Weyn

performances to the Deweerdt's, they will have achieved a remarkable thing.

Breeding performance pigeons is notoriously difficult and inexact. More is unknown than known. This should not intimidate would-be future strain-makers from trying. The Deweerdt lofts are probably among the most successful lofts that have had the patience to do it. They continue to build their family of pigeons today. It has taken two generations to get to where they are, but if they should make a wrong move or the wrong choices the strain could easily disintegrate beyond repair. This could happen more quickly than it took to build it up. I have used the pedigree of 'Picabo', a recent champion, to show the integration of related pigeons of the strain on both sides of her pedigree. Her lineage is typical of the Deweerdt breeding method. We hope this helps readers see the process of thirty years of related breeding in the hands of master breeders. Up to now the Deweerdts have avoided making big mistakes. The fact that the Deweerdt lofts are themselves still strong and competitive is itself proof of this. They can also claim that their birds win regularly in the lofts of others.

Anja: 1st prize Barcelona International hens 1980 and 15th in the whole International from 13,637 birds. Photo: © Copyright Els de Weyn

Going Back in Time

Interviewing Bernard Deweerdt is also a bit like going back in time. Bernard refers to the Deweerdt lofts as being 'old-fashioned'. Does 'old-fashioned' mean a time when more emphasis was spent on breeding and developing the pigeon as a sporting bird? A time when the pigeon had to race and perform entirely on the talents carefully bred into it? Perhaps more importantly, does 'old-fashioned' mean the time when building a family of pigeons within one's own loft was the object of most of the pigeon fraternity? I think it does, but it is important to stress it does not mean going back to some mythical 'Golden Age'. The Deweerdt loft is very much a loft of our time and utterly realistic in the world of modern pigeon racing. Nevertheless their philosophy does include the principle of doing things for the long term. This has been their principle from the day the strain was founded and it still guides them today.

The Deweerdt lofts are primarily concerned with qualities developed by breeding, as opposed to those improved by technique. On the face of it their technique looks crude and slightly unmanaged. It is certainly a no-frills approach. This appears on the surface to be counter-productive to good results, that is until one looks more deeply into the world of breeding and racing pigeons.

No-Frills Management

On this level their 'no-frills' management can be interpreted as allowing the pigeon to show its true qualities unaided. In short, because their no-frills management gives a better and more accurate picture of their breeding, it must eventually show itself in more consistent results. This better picture is one that over time must also produce a better pigeon in the lofts of others. Certainly the Deweerdt loft is not standing still. Their hit rate of good pigeons is high and, as a side product, they have produced a family at or near the very top of international results for nearly forty years. This has been achieved using relatively few crosses. Few modern lofts can make such a claim, using the best of technique and depending almost entirely on a successful cross to keep their performances near the top of international competition.

Medicines Do Have their Benefits

Despite their no-frills approach, Bernard Deweerdt is not so set in his ways as to ignore improvement and change. Medical help does have its benefits, which the Deweerdt lofts have not ignored. They are certainly keen to protect their birds from what Bernard feels are the most dangerous of conditions that can damage. In common with most lofts they treat for trichomoniasis, although sparingly, and regularly vaccinate for the paramyox virus, paratyphus and pigeon pox. They have moved forward cautiously with science, while at the same time keeping to their core belief in 'improvement through breeding' and the creation of an untarnished family of pigeons.

Amateur Status

This enlightened approach is typical of the Deweerdt lofts. It is not only intelligent and far-sighted but also holds true to their amateur status. The sense of being an amateur delights Bernard Deweerdt. They are not dependent on time. The Deweerdt lofts can pick and choose the path they take and do it entirely in their own time. Bernard touched on this topic when I interviewed him. Through the pigeons he maintains he achieves a sense of purpose. He goes further: 'Without the pigeons I could not do my job.' The Deweerdt brothers are not under any pressure; they enjoy their birds while still holding to what they believe. It's a very civilized view of life.

The Tortoise and the Hare

Generally in this kind of loft good results occur more at long and Marathon distances than lesser distances. The conflict between everything scientific and the 'old-fashioned', as Bernard Deweerdt calls it, may well prove to be a re-enactment of the tortoise and the hare. The old-fashioned, patient tortoise, in it for the long term, may well have a place against the modern, impatient hare. Certainly the tortoise is not under pressure. It is the hare that is expected to win. The tortoise can win if we think in terms of establishing a family of improved pigeons through the process of related breeding over the long term. It will most certainly win if we once again begin to think in terms of history and the creation of a strain and having purpose in our lives.

Of course in the days before science had taken such a hold in animal affairs, there were good fanciers and not so good ones, there were big lofts and small, but the one difference between then and now was that the good lofts tried to create a certain standard of improved pigeon they could call a strain. Today this is more difficult and the effects are not so obvious because many lofts have good pigeons. Many pigeons today have reached a high plateau of race ability that has been produced by technique. As technique improves the room for improvement through breeding alone is less clearly marked and less obvious in the short term.

A Sense of History

In those days the keeper of a good loft held at the back of his mind the idea that he could, if he were good enough, produce a strain that might secure its creator a place in the annals of pigeon history. Most fanciers of those days had a sense of history.

Joan: A super hen that was 10th International Barcelona in 2005 the last year she raced. She was unfortunately lost in the final International race from Perpignan the same year. This is the price one has to be pay when racing at the extreme long distances. Great pigeons can and do fail to return. It is this element of danger and the possibility of failure that makes Long Distance pigeon racing. A safety net does not exist. Photo: © Copyright Els de Weyn

Emiel Deweerdt, the father of Bernard and Fred. Emiel, whose influence still exists in his two sons. It was Emiel who founded the Derweerdt strain and forged its precepts. His two sons carry on in much the same way, rejecting much of what can be called 'modern' in favour of a steady build up of better and better quality pigeons across a broad front. Photo: © Copyright Foto Sinaeve

They wanted to be remembered in the next generation. They worked for it and towards it. They wanted to improve the breed and be noticed for doing so.

This is not so much the case today. Good results do not automatically indicate intrinsically good pigeons that will do well in the lofts of others. Good results can often be isolated within a particular loft and not be transferable. Bernard Deweerdt, in his advice to our imaginary novice, clearly calls for creating a family as they have done. He urges our novice to attempt longevity by aiming to be at the top of competition for twenty or thirty years with the same basic family of pigeons. Today, however, a family of related pigeons and the creation of a strain is a rarity compared to fifty years ago.

Carry on the Same

The Deweerdt lofts have, in their wisdom, gone down the long-term breeding path to success. Unfortunately, the long-term will always be old-fashioned. The Deweerdts are now maintaining three generations of pigeons in their family. They appear not to be in a hurry. When asked about his ambitions, Bernard calmly opts for carrying on at the same level as they are now, 'without drastically changing [our] methods'.

Theirs is certainly the tortoise approach to life. Although it is steady and prone to ideas of the past, it is not idealistic in the sense of being unworldly. They know what they are up against. They know what is happening and are prepared to vaccinate in a modern way to protect themselves, but most of all they are also prepared to go a long way towards protecting what they have built. Their family of pigeons, with its inbuilt resistance to most disease and an ability to produce champion pigeons on a regular basis from within the breed and within the loft, is not about to be thrown away. Like the tortoise, they are in long-distance pigeon racing for slow, patient improvement over years, if necessary. Their pigeons, often bony and not always conventionally good-looking, may well win against the modern hare. The Deweerdt point of view may also require an approach to the pastime of pigeons as one that also feeds the inner self.

CHAPTER 4

Geoff and Catherine Cooper

Peasedown St John, Bath, England

BACKGROUND

Geoff Cooper has been keeping pigeons and been in contact with animals, birds and nature all his life. He was first influenced to keep pigeons by his uncle when a small boy, but as he grew older he gradually learnt the trade of 'racing pigeons' himself. He made mistakes, of course, but learnt the trade well enough to establish a reputation in his own right. Those on the UK pigeon scene now associate the names 'Geoff and Catherine Cooper' with sound ideas and quality pigeons. Geoff understands the basic reasons why things should be done and why things should be left alone. He has developed in this way because he has the mind of a detective, ferreting out the mysteries of nature. His wife Catherine is similar. They are unconventional in the sense that they do not always do things because current thinking dictates it. I think it true to say they are original. They are innovators without thinking of themselves as innovators. Without reason both would flounder; reason and reasoning keep them sparkling and alive in the world of pigeons.

THE INTERVIEW

The Start

How old were you when you first started playing with pigeons and did your father have them?

I was still at school – I think I was eleven at the time. My father didn't have pigeons but my uncle did. He was the local bookmaker and was a little tight by nature: I had to work for a long time, cleaning and scraping and occasionally timing the pigeons, until in the end he gave me a pigeon. I worked hard for that one pigeon.

Another local person also gave me one, so that is how I started. At that time we lived in an old farmhouse about 300 yards from here. The house has now gone, but of course a lot has happened between then and now, even though I have not moved very far.

Were these original pigeons good ones – sprint, middle-distance or what?

Geoff with the Oliver Dix trophy for the National Flying Club member with the best average from Nantes and Pau. Geoff won it in 1998.

No, they were nothing. I built my own loft at the time from any odd bits of wood I could lay my hands on, but I struggled to win a race. I think I was sixteen before I won anything, then I won three races on the trot. During the lean years, when I was learning my trade, I used to send to the long races but the pigeons never came home. This taught me one thing, you definitely need good pigeons. If you are to do any good in this sport, quality pigeons are the essential ingredient for success. They are indeed vastly more important than any other consideration that might appear absolutely essential at the time. Without quality pigeons there is nothing to work on.

The First Long-distance Stock

When did you first succeed with long-distance pigeons?

I had an old black hen; she was a stray without an identification ring. It was she who bred me my first 800km (500-mile) winner. She bred me a hen that won the Thurso race two years in succession. I then went and saw Reg Venner of Street in Somerset. He was the best in the area at the time. I bought three pigeons from him. These three pigeons, together with the black hen, made up two pairs. I then began to breed some good ones.

Did you join the National Flying Club at this time or were you still flying on the North?

I was still on the North, but I think it was in the mid-1960s that I joined the National Flying Club. I was moderately successful, but mainly at the long-distance end of the sport. By this time I had left school and was working for my living. I suppose my main success came in 1976 when I was second open Palamos with the British Barcelona Club. Palamos is their longest race and a true test of good long-distance pigeons.

The year 1976 was the hottest summer on record. This Palamos pigeon came home on one of the hottest days of that year. There were only six

FLIGHT of FANCY

A BUTCHER'S 24-year-old hobby got the chop yesterday when 39 of his racing pigeons came under the hammer.

Twice a year auctions of racing pigeons are held at the Miners Arms, Farrington Gurney, and yesterday was the one Mr Geoff Cooper, 37, of Pleasant View, Huddox Hill, Peasedown, had not been waiting for.

Mr Cooper, who runs a butcher shop in Peasedown, has bought a similar business in High Littleton, which his son David, will soon take over.

He had about 61 birds and took 39 to the auction.

This is the first time he has sold any birds, and he said, "My wife Iris and I had a tear in our eyes when we left home this morning with the birds I was to sell.

"It has taken me a lifetime to build my loft. I am very sad to have to sell them, it is purely for business reasons, but I still have about 24 left and when things are sorted out at High Littleton, I shall start again."

The auction was conducted by Mr Ken Otton of

Mr Cooper says goodbye to one of his pigeons at yesterday's auction.

Street, a member of Glastonbury and Farrington Gurney Flying Club.

About 150 fanciers from Wales, London, Sussex, Leicester and local members of flying clubs attended the auction, which took about two hours to sell 57 birds.

Prices ranged from £5 to £170 — for a red chequered cock bird belonging to Mr Cooper, who raised a total of £1,861 at the auction.

Mr Otton later said he had sold birds at other auctions at prices around £200, but added, "There is not so much money about today."

Black Hen 1st Thurso – The first 500-mile winner for Geoff Cooper. Photo: © Copyright The Bath Chronicle

Spanish Maiden 1st Section 6th Open British Barcelona Palamos 1980. Photo: © Copyright Anthony Bolton

Spanish Princess 1st Section 2nd Open British Barcelona Palamos 1976. Photo: © Copyright Anthony Bolton

birds on the second day. Palamos was more than 1,100km (700 miles) from my loft. The birds were up at 7.00am on Friday and I clocked at 7.25 on the Saturday evening. This hen I called 'Spanish Princess' was the only one in my section on the day ('Fear Bros' of Clandown were second section the next morning). She came out of a pair of Venner pigeons. She in turn, when paired to a Truman Dicken cock, produced a hen I called 'Spanish Maiden', which was 1st section 6th open Palamos, and in turn this hen produced a young cock that was 1st section 2nd open BBC young bird Rennes race, and that produced a pigeon that won the Saintes race. That pigeon produced 'Silver', which was 2nd and 3rd section Pau in the National Flying Club. These pigeons are still in my blood today and some of them are in the blood of Brian Shepherd's famous 'Legend', the Dax International winner of 2003. All these pigeons came down from the original Venner pigeons.

The Belgian Experience

You had these Venner pigeons at this time. Did you think of bringing a cross into them?

No. My thinking at the time was that English pigeons were the best and Englishmen were the best fanciers. Then in 1981 I went to Belgium with Roy Clark, who showed people around Belgian lofts. This trip opened my eyes. I realized that we were not the best and were not even at the cutting edge of pigeon sport. I bought two pairs of pigeons on that trip from André Vermote of Ostend. I wanted to buy pigeons from Emiel Deweerdt of Kortemark, but they were too expensive so I ordered some for the following year. I wanted them out of the best he had. I went to both fanciers because they were using each other's pigeons and the cross was very successful.

Were you in the butchery business at this time? Did you have your own shop?

Yes, I had a shop here in Peasedown.

Did you go back to Belgium the following year to collect the pigeons from Deweerdt?

No, I had a pair sent over – a nice little hen out of 'Filip', though at that time I thought it wasn't big enough, and a big bony cock, the most ugly pigeon I have ever seen. I thought, 'What have I paid all this money for?', and was certain I had made a disastrous mistake. I wasn't impressed at all and the thought 'I've done a bad thing here' kept on racing through my mind.

That year I moved to High Littleton, just six miles from here. I moved the old loft and just left it propped up. In fact it was just thrown together. I bred three pairs from those pigeons. The cock bird then hung himself on one of the pieces of wire I had used to hold the loft together. I thought at the time it was probably a good thing, because this

'21' brother to 'Nicholls' is famous for breeding good hens that further strengthen the hen side of the family. He is the sire of 'Miss Somerset', 'Miss Pau', timed Pau International 2005 and Miss Dax 93rd Int Dax 2005. Photo: © Copyright Anthony Bolton

Nicholls – 3rd NFC Pau and 4th Central Southern Classic Pau. Photo: © Copyright Anthony Bolton

ugly cock would do me no good at all. It was a case of 'good riddance to bad rubbish' – or so I thought at the time.

All this was really sad thinking because the three pairs I bred at High Littleton off the original Deweerdt pair were absolutely brilliant. There was 'Bernard', which won the Nantes Combine and went through to Pau. There was 'Stumpy', who went all the way through to Pau. Then there was what we called the 'Old Deweerdt cock', which was a brilliant producer. A Pau National winner for Harding Bros of Bristol was down from Bernard and Stumpy.

A lot of my best pigeons go back to those original pigeons. The mainstay of my loft today goes back to those crossed with present-day Deweerdt pigeons.

A Big Mistake

Have you bought other pigeons since and have you tried any more?

I've tried many pigeons since. I tried a few more Vermote pigeons because they were round and of a good shape. At the time I was concentrating on crossing the Deweerdt pigeons into the Vermotes, that was a mistake. What I should have done was

Geoff Cooper outside his loft.

cross the Vermote crosses back into the Deweerdts. I realized this after many failures.

Did you go back to the Deweerdt loft to buy more pigeons after you realized your mistake?

Yes. In 1984 I purchased a daughter of 'Liesbet', the Deweerdt National Barcelona winner of 1981. I had to save up for a year. 'Liesbet' was a nice, compact, good-shaped pigeon. The one I bought was another big, bony, ugly pigeon, but with a similar head to 'Liesbet'. When I went to collect her, Emiel Deweerdt said to me, 'We have got something special for you, Geoff.' She certainly looked good on the perch, but when I came to handle her she was another of those big ugly pigeons. I never let the Deweerdts know how disappointed I was – I was still of the opinion that you needed to have good-looking pigeons.

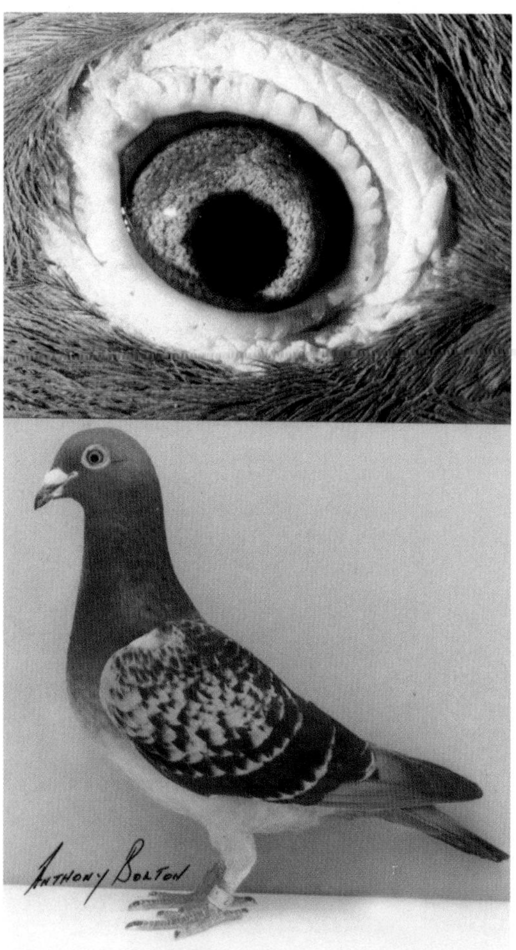

Gold Dust – daughter of 'Bulldog' and the 'Ashmans' hen. Photo: © Copyright Anthony Bolton

The opinion that you always have to have good lookers is a hard thing to shake off. This kind of thinking persists despite the evidence against it. This daughter of 'Liesbet' and the two original Deweerdt pigeons proved to be absolute gold-mines. They bred good pigeon after good pigeon. What really sealed it for me, and started to change my thinking, was Bob Ashman of Hagley. I borrowed a Deweerdt pigeon from him that I called the 'Ashman's Hen'. She won six firsts including 1st Saintes and 1st section Pau National, the only bird on the day over 600 miles. I thought she was the best hen in England at the time. I borrowed her to go with 'Bulldog', my NFC section winner, on the basis that we would split the youngsters. When he brought her down I looked at her and yet again this was another long, deep, 'no back' ugly hen.

When people handled her, almost without exception they called her the ugliest pigeon they had ever handled. When people started making remarks like that it brought it home to me. They were wrong; they were definitely wrong. How could pigeons be the wrong shape and at the same time be so good? They had got to be the right shape, otherwise they would not fly so well!

Over the years, starting as a child and right up to the time I started to fly well, I used to read the 'Old Hand' books, among others: pigeons had to handle like this or handle like that. Without exception all these books used to stress the need for balance. A lot of the Deweerdt pigeons did not have this balance. Some were big and ugly with bits sticking out all over the place. The only good thing I would say is that they all have long wings and all have silky

An international gathering:-Back Row l to r Bernard Deweerdt, Mark Gilbert and John Haynes; Front Row l to r Annie Deweerdt, Geoff Cooper and Catherine Cooper.

feather. Apart from that only a few can be described as beautiful, but beauty is, of course, in the eye of the beholder. It's a hard lesson to learn, but once learned it will hold any fancier in good stead for the rest of his life.

Buying Genes

What influences you when you import stock into your loft? The Deweerdt lofts are near the sea, while you are some way inland, so does location matter?

No, I don't think location matters. To be honest, getting back to Bob Ashman, I don't think Bob liked the Deweerdt pigeons. I may be doing him a disservice, but I don't think he liked them, even though he raced brilliantly with them in the Midlands. I'm almost 100km (60 miles) from the sea, I do pretty well. Mark Gilbert races near to London, he does well. We are all in different locations – it's just a matter of having good pigeons. That's all that matters, good pigeons with the right genes.

What do you look for when you go back to Deweerdt to buy more pigeons? Do you always buy off performance pigeons?

When I go to buy I don't care what they look like, providing they are off the best pigeons and providing they are healthy and have good feather. Apart from that I don't care at all. You buy a bundle of genes. That's all you are buying: it does not matter whether they are big, small, long or short. It's just the genes you are buying.

'Morning Glory', bred and raced by Paul Kendall of Wantage, was twice 2nd NFC Pau. The mother of 'Morning Glory' was bred at the Cooper lofts and the father was half Cooper. Photo: © Copyright Bryan Siggers

So when you get the imports or other pigeons in your loft, all you have bought is good genes in an endeavour to make your loft as strong as possible?

Yes, totally. That's all I want.

Cleaning Out

Your management and Bernard's management appear to be totally different, or are they?

If you had asked me that a few years ago I would have agreed with you. Emiel Derweerdt's management and mine were totally different in so many ways. Bernard's and mine are similar in a lot of ways. Emiel used to clean out every day – everything had to be straight and tidy. Bernard, on the other hand, is different. Some would say he is a lazy fancier, but I disagree. I came to this opinion after reading a book by Wendel Levi called *The Pigeon*, in which he tells of the management of pigeons for meat production. He kept tens of thousands of pigeons, so it was commercially essential for him to find the best way to health. To this end he tried different ways of keeping pigeons healthy. He tried mechanical scraping and cleaning them out every day. He tried wire-bottomed fly pens. Finally he tried deep litter composed of dry droppings. He found he had a far superior health rate on deep litter made from dry droppings than the wire grids. Now that surprised me, so ever since I have kept pigeons on dry droppings. I have found that even with youngsters I can keep pigeons healthier on dry droppings that are allowed to accumulate than on a scraped floor.

In the past I have tried scraping the loft every day, burning off the floor and nest boxes religiously to destroy bacteria and creating a lot of work for myself, but even this method is not as good as keeping pigeons on dry droppings.

Testing New Imports

How long do you give the new imports to see if they are working in with your family?

It takes a long time with long-distance pigeons. You have to give them five years. It is possible that there can be failures, of course, but I can honestly say that up to now I have not had a failure from the Deweerdt pigeons. I have bought the best, of course. Perhaps that is the reason I have been so lucky.

Have you tried pigeons from elsewhere?

Yes, I have tried many. I have had lots of failures, but with the Deweerdt pigeons I have never had one. I don't say I will never get one, but up to now it has not happened.

Have you tried Dutch pigeons, for instance?

I have one pigeon of Dutch origin in the stock loft now. It is of 'Invincible Spirit' origin. It is too early to say if this line will stay, but up to now it is proving satisfactory. I have learned a lot over the last few years about breeding and the more I learn the less I am inclined to commit an opinion too early. If you intend to establish a colony of pigeons you must have a successful base of related pigeons that have a proven record of breeding and racing. This base must outnumber all others in the loft. It is they who must be of the greater number. Into these successful related pigeons you add others from time to time. What you never do is add pigeons from the good base into others, that just dilutes the basic blood. You always add into the successful family of related pigeons, never from the related pigeons into a different family.

In the case of the 'Invincible Spirit' blood, this blood is added to the numerically dominant Deweerdt blood. I hope it will be successful, but it will take five years or more to tell. In my loft the Deweerdt blood must always be dominant. It took me years to realize this. I notice many fanciers who still do not understand this basic principle. They cross and cross in an undisciplined fashion. Occasionally they come up with a very good pigeon, and sometimes a champion, but it is never sustained in future generations. Unless such lofts have enormous resources and can continually import champion pigeons every year, they tend to fail after a few years. Lofts such as this get to a position where champion pigeons are just not produced any more. Breeding is a tedious business. Offspring have to be continually tested. I have had a few other Dutch pigeons in the loft, for example, but none have ever stayed. They have all failed.

Pigeons that Stayed

The only pigeon that has stayed and continued to influence is a sprinter from Serge Van Elsacker of Schilde in Antwerp province. I sold most of the Van Elsacker pigeons and then later found this one to be quite good. This pigeon of Van Elsacker produced 'Daybreak' crossed with the Deweerdts. 'Daybreak' was a National Flying Club merit award winner. 'Daybreak' also has close connections to other good pigeons, being the grandfather of Mark Gilbert's International Dax winner. So this blood is now running through some very good pigeons. To sum up, excepting the Deweerdts, of course, and a tiny proportion of the original Vermote pigeons, the Van Elsacker pigeon is the only one that has definitely left its mark.

The Race Team from Year to Year

How do you treat young birds in the year of their birth? Do you race young birds? What do you expect of them?

It is all according to when they are bred. The early cocks have to race to 140km (89 miles) – the furthest point inland – or occasionally perhaps 190km (120 miles) to Guernsey. Providing they come home fresh and not too tired they are allowed to stay. The hens are different. I don't race old hens. The young hens have to go to every Channel race I can send them to: I need the ones that can really survive and cope with the hard races while at the same time showing no signs of distress. They are the future of the loft. They are the ones I keep.

Do you breed late breds and have you had any success with them?

I only breed a few late breds off the best pigeons. Some have made good pigeons.

As young birds, when they are twelve weeks old they are trained three or four times from about 30 to 50km (20–30 miles). As yearlings they go to a

Wriggler – the best late hatched pigeon in the Cooper lofts. Already he has flown in the prizes both in the NFC Dax and the International Dax.
Photo: © Copyright Mrs Catherine J. Cooper

Belge 85 3329089
Varazur
Deweerdt
76th Int Pau 541 lb 88th Int Perp
l16l4h

Belge 91.3313351
Deweerdt
Son of Varazur

Down from Stumpy
and Filip

Belge 94 3299293
Bernie
Sire of Jumpy and Wriggler
Brother to Zaina 97 370th Int Barc
24908b 130* Int Perp 12367b

Down from Stumpy
and Filip

Belge 89.3316084
Deweerdt
Sister to Emmylou, Doffix,
Resso

Belge 87 3321082
Emmy
Co-Winner 1st nat
champion KBDB

GB03N 01302

Wriggler
Full brother Jumpy
1st BICC Falasise 2464b 05
5th NFC 1248th Int Dax

Dark Cheq
3rd section G 79th Open
NFC Pau
Sire of 1st NFC Pau

Thurso
1st West of England NRC Thurso
1st West of England NRC Thurso
1st West of England NRC Coupar
Angus-Brother Ashgrove King

GB 00 N 00527
Miss Thurso
Dtr Thurso 2 X 1st WENRC
Thurso etc
Bthr to Ashgrove King 1st NFC
Pau-Dam of Jumpy and Wriggler

G Dtr
EMIEL

Pedigree Wriggler.

race of perhaps 320km (200 miles) and as two-year-old pigeons they are as good as any. At that stage they can go to an 800km (500 miles) race once in a season. The 'Wriggler', for instance, was a two-year-old late bred when he was 5th National Dax and 1st BICC Falaise.

Early bred two-year-old pigeons go to a 500-mile race once in the season, but as they mature to three-year-olds they can go to 500 miles or even to 650 miles. Their programme may include two 500-mile races and a 650-mile race. It is quite natural for a mature three-year-old pigeon that has scored from Dax in the international to go back to Perpignan, also an International race, three or four weeks later. Here we are talking about mature pigeons, pigeons that are at the height of their power and pigeons that have survived a selection process that has been on going since their birth.

Do Looks Matter?

Is there any physical attribute you particularly look for in a mature pigeon? Are you looking at the wing, the throat, the head, a particular shape of the body or what?

I've only got two fads – long wings and silky feather. I will compromise a bit on the wing, but the pigeons have to have silky feather.

Treating for Disease and Cultivating Immunity

Do you consider a high degree of immunity essential for a long-distance loft?

Immunity is essential for long-distance racing. I don't treat late breds for anything at all. Young birds that have a National race may be treated if things go wrong during their preparation, but this is an exception. Normally I don't treat young birds at all except, of course, for their annual vaccination. As for old birds, I have raced some years and not treated them at all and have been very successful. Some years you are not so successful, but to keep things on an even keel I now treat annually. Before racing starts I treat for canker. During racing and before the big races I treat for canker and respiratory disease. For canker I use the normal commercial brands that are readily available. I like to vary the brand so that as wide a spectrum of effective ingredients are active against as wide a spectrum of canker strains as possible. I only ever treat for canker twice in a year and for respiratory once. Of course, when you get to the 500-mile races the pigeons have to be spot on, so a few weeks prior to that time I use Doxycycline or some such medicine as a treatment for respiratory coccidiosis.

If illness, such as a respiratory condition, were to arise spontaneously, would you immediately suppress the individual or its offspring without attempting to treat the pigeon, or would you allow it to persist and wait for the pigeons to get over it?

If it were a really good pigeon I would do everything in my power to cure it. If it were a young bird then it's different. Every year since I've been at this address, about twelve years, I get 'Young Bird sickness'. At first it used to frighten me to death. I used to take pigeons out to try to let them get over it. After they recovered I would put them back in the loft, then another would go ill. Now I don't bother over much. The first thing you see is vomit on the floor – green diarrhoea and all the usual symptoms of Young Bird sickness. When that happens I don't feed the birds until they have eaten all the vomit and the regurgitated food that is on the floor. The next day there are perhaps five or six being sick. After five days every young bird has Young Bird sickness. The perches are awash with green diarrhoea. The loft looks a right mess. Within fourteen days they are all over it.

During this process I haven't used medicine, antibiotics or anything. I used to try all sorts of things: glucose, lemon, all the usual potions and medicines in fashion at the time. Now I just leave them to get over it and after fourteen days they are all right again. This year I had one die. Last year I had one die. Gradually the strong ones are becoming immune to the effects of this illness. I have had young birds that have suffered and perhaps sit in the corner for a week or ten days huddled up, but they get over it and come back to being normal again. I have had some come back from the brink of sickness and have gone on to make my best pigeons. If they die during this period I take them out, if they don't I leave them. I would not treat a young bird for canker. If it dies, so be it, but I very rarely have a young bird with canker.

Coccidiosis

I have only ever treated a section for coccidiosis once in my whole life – three days after treatment the count was zero, then a week after that it was back to where it started. I thought it was a waste of time. If you have a high coccidiosis count it tells the health of the pigeons. Look with a microscope and you will immediately tell the health of the pigeon by the coccidiosis count (the number of oocytes in a given sample). If you put what is causing the ill-health right, then the count will go down. Treating for coccidiosis is the wrong way of

Even in such a famous loft, the occasional watery droppings still occur. It is not that such things happen it is understanding what is happening in such cases and how to deal with it. In this particular case it happened just before the pigeons were treated for canker.

going about health. Coccidiosis won't kill a pigeon and treating for coccidiosis won't solve the problem that is causing the high count. If the count is high normally it is canker – not always though, but canker is the most likely cause more often than not.

Advice for the Novice

What advice would you give a novice attempting to build a team of long-distance pigeons?

In any form of pigeon racing, first of all make up your mind what you want to do and the distance you wish to attempt. When you know what kind of racing you want to do, you then go to a man who has been winning at this distance for some time – not someone who has just started winning or who won well years ago. What you want is a current champion who is winning now and has been doing so for a number of years. When you have selected the man, you buy from him. A lot of people say you buy from two or three lofts and make your own family. I say no. Invest in one man. He has a successful family that is currently winning and has been doing so for a number of years. That is good enough. After you have established a good team of pigeons that are flying and winning at the distance you require, you can then try your first cross, but do it very carefully.

Obviously the novice must have a good place to house the pigeons. Ventilation is very important. Dryness is also very important. So long as the loft is dry and the ventilation's good, it doesn't matter if it's an old tumbledown shed. Overcrowding is, of course, a great sin. The novice must avoid the temptation to house too many, or otherwise he will undo all the effort he has put into the original selection.

Cutting Out Trial and Error

At what stage should the novice be after three years?

Well, the way to success is to follow the methods of the fancier from whom you acquired the original birds. Forget what everyone else is telling you. If your original man is winning and doing well, his methods have got to be right and his birds have got to be right. After you have had them a few years and begun to learn a bit yourself you can perhaps tinker a little, but don't tinker too much.

That is the short way to success. The long way is the way I did it. I made a lot of mistakes, trying different methods and gradually sorting out what works and what does not. The short way is to copy someone else. The long way is to learn by yourself. Mark Gilbert, for instance, came to my loft with about three other fanciers. He bought a couple of pigeons, but he said to me right from the start, 'I haven't come especially to buy your pigeons, but to make friends and to learn how you do it.' There is a lot in that approach. If you go to a man to learn, by so doing you are cutting out twenty or thirty years of trial and error. Most people, of course, can't believe what they are told most of the time. They just don't believe it. They come with preconceived ideas, determined to fit what they already know into what they see and hear. If something runs counter to their ideas they generally reject it. That is why I don't advise novices to go to two separate lofts. They generally mix the ideas of both and end up with the worst of each.

Before the Race

Do you fly widowhood, on the nest, both systems or something else?

I basically use the widowhood method with my pigeons. Very occasionally I will try a hen or two on the nest, but I generally fly widowhood cocks.

Are the yearlings also on widowhood?

Yes, the yearlings are raced on widowhood, just the same as the older pigeons.

How much exercise do the widowhood cocks take every day?

Once it's warm the cocks fly an hour twice a day. They are locked out of the loft to induce them to do this. In the early part of the year, when there are likely to be cold east winds, the pigeons are exercised only once a day in the evening, but as the cold

Flying freely – All the race team are encouraged to fly freely for an hour, morning and evening. In the early part of the year, when it is cold, they fly only in the evening, but as the year progresses they enjoy flying morning and evening for at least an hour apparently without effort. It is then that the pigeons are fit.

weather disappears they are expected to fly twice each day for an hour.

Sometimes I flag them a bit, but pigeons that are fit should fly well on their own without inducement. If the pigeons won't fly there is usually something amiss. I then try to find out what it is. In April we exercise once a day but, as the year progresses, if the feed is all right and the loft is all right then you should have no trouble getting them to fly twice a day for an hour each time. I must inject a slight word of warning here: even in May it can sometimes be quite cold.

I do very little training: the old cocks get two tosses about 20 miles, as do the yearlings. The cocks are then raced every week until we get over the

Outside the lofts. Nothing special to look at but the walls and roof are insulated to enable an even temperature with little variation between night and day.

water, then they go every fortnight. When we get to the longer national races they go every three weeks. The hen is always there when they get home.

The Nest Cycle of Mature Pigeons

Can you give me some idea of how you would treat mature three- or four-year-old widowhood pigeons that are being prepared for the important races of the year?

Take a race like the Dax International, for example. Dax comes quite late in the year. We pair the first week in December and rear a pair of youngsters. When the youngsters are twenty-four days old, the hen and the youngsters are then taken away. The cocks are then on widowhood. Sometimes we re-pair the pigeons in the third week of March, sometimes we don't. If we do, we only allow the pigeons to sit for four or five days maximum, then they are separated again. That way we expect the cocks to have a good wing for the first or second week in July, when the Dax race is likely to be flown.

Early in the year the pigeons only go out once a week. They have to be reasonably fit or sparrow hawks will take them. I have got to keep them reasonably fit but I also want to avoid winter form, so they are not at their peak. When April comes around we start trying to get them out every day, gradually improving their fitness. In the third week in April the races begin. I'm not particularly interested in these early races, but they still go every week. When it comes to races over the Channel they race every other week. This is the routine up to about 650km (400 miles). For Dax and the main 800km (500 mile) races I only allow them to race every three weeks. By the time these races come

The chimney in the ceiling through which the stale air goes out.

The grill where incoming air comes over the heads of the pigeons to ventilate the loft.

around the pigeons should be really fit. Feeding is simple. We use a normal widowhood mixture: we don't break down or anything like that, but in the last three or four days before a big race we put as much fat into the feed as we can.

Herbs, Seed and Vitamins

Is there any particular herb or supplement, for example garlic or onion, you use either in the water or on the food?

The only thing I ever use is pressed garlic cloves. These are put in a liquidizer and put in the water.

Do you do this once a week, twice a week, once a day or what?

I have used it once a week, every day or not at all, and to be honest the performances have not altered a lot. The one thing I would say is that garlic keeps the skin clean. Garlic is the only thing I use. I don't use vitamins, but the pigeons always have minerals. They also have a pickstone and fresh grit in front of them all the time. There is nothing else I use.

Do you use seeds or anything like that?

There is always a lot of seed in the mixture. When I mixed my own there was always 15 per cent in the mixture. Now I use Versele-Laga mixture. The mixture I used to make myself was as good, in my opinion, but I couldn't always guarantee the quality of the corn, so, even though Versele-Laga is a bit more expensive, I set this disadvantage against the assurance that I can always guarantee the quality of the corn. The maize in my own mix was sometimes of dubious quality and you would not know until it was too late.

What about peanuts? Do you use them?

I used to use them but I don't now because again you cannot always guarantee the quality. If you get bad peanuts you ruin everything, so I don't buy them any more except as a treat. To encourage trapping I use hemp. This is as good as anything, but in our loft there is always food available at all times, so we just put a pinch of hemp in each box as a tit bit.

After The Race

When a tired pigeon returns from a long race is there any special treatment you give him before he rejoins the flock for normal training?

The same mixture is available, together with clean water. Each cock has his hen for three or four hours and after really long races perhaps overnight. I don't use either glucose or electrolytes, as I have found they don't benefit the pigeons.

The Moult and Winter Treatment

Are the pigeons separated for the winter and, if so, when?

In the first week of August they are re-paired after the season and rear a round of youngsters. They then sit a round of pot eggs, after which they are separated. You could let them rear all winter and then separate – it would probably be as successful, but I don't do it.

After the pigeons are separated and during the moult the pigeons are fed on Versele-Laga moulting mixture. At breeding time they are fed on breeding mixture from the same firm and for racing, as I have already told you, they are fed on widowhood mixture. In my view Versele-Laga corn is as good as any. It is more expensive and to be honest it hurts the pocket, but it's good corn. The pigeons are given plenty of baths at this time. When I used my own corn I always had 15 per cent barley in the mixture. People used to say, 'What do you want barley in the mixture for?' For them barley and re-growing the feathers are not compatible. My answer is that I never like pigeons fat at any time of the year. Barley achieves this for me because the pigeons, if given the choice, always eat barley last, so barley works as a control for the amount of food necessary. I used to let the pigeons get fat in the winter, but that was a mistake. I simply hate pigeons getting fat. I never keep pigeons short of food because they always have barley in the hopper. If you keep pigeons short of food to prevent them getting fat they eat more and gorge themselves at every opportunity. Barley, and the use of barley as a staple in their diet, prevents this.

Does winter separation improve or detract from a good moult?

I don't think it is better in that pigeons that are separated necessarily achieve better quality feather, but separation makes them moult quicker, so separation is not absolutely essential.

Pairing Up the Birds

Do the race birds rear one or two youngsters?

I used to let the race birds rear only one youngster – the idea was that I was conserving their energy and hopefully each pair would put more into the one youngster than they would into two – but now I let them rear two. Healthy pigeons have more than enough energy and vitality to rear two youngsters. Healthy youngsters reared in this way can go on to prove themselves in important races. If the vitality of the flock rests on giving a helping hand to nature I would sooner not have this kind of vitality. The real and long-term advice is to select and breed vitality into them in the first place.

The stock birds are paired up at the same time as the racers. They can and do easily rear six rounds of youngsters themselves without stress of any kind. They are not given anything special to get them into good condition. Your pigeons should always be in good condition.

A perfect breeding loft – Breeding pairs in good condition can quite easily rear six rounds of youngsters every year.

What physical characteristics do you look for when pairing up the birds? Do you compensate for size?

Yes, I won't put two big ones together or two small ones together. Medium can go together, big can go to small and big can go to medium, but never big to big or small to small.

Do you take the eyes into account?

I spent seven years studying eyes. I read every book available on the subject. I recorded every eye in the loft. I had three cardboard boxes full of all the eyes of my pigeons and details of how eyes should look. After two years I thought I had it cracked. After three years I found out what a load of rubbish all this eye sign stuff is. You can tell the health and vitality of a pigeon by the eye, but no one can tell a future champion by looking in its eye. You can't tell the genetic make-up of a pigeon by looking at the eye. You can't tell how good a pigeon is going to race by looking at the eye. Those who think they can are fooling themselves.

The Loft

Turning to the construction of the loft, what idea did you have in mind when you made yours?

At the front of my mind was the need to ensure good ventilation while at the same time achieving an even temperature. The racing loft, which is exposed to wind and weather, is situated at the top of the garden. The roof and walls are both insulated. The floor wasn't, but I think it should have been. The glazing on the front is polypropylene, which has a double wall in its manufacture. Air comes in at the top of the loft, drops to the floor and goes out through a chimney in the roof. This is designed so that there is a slow change of air at all times without causing draughts. Some people have air coming in the bottom and out at the top, but all this causes is draughts and you know yourself that when you're sitting in a house with draughts you are uncomfortable. The pigeons are the same.

GB 01 N 15518
'Farm Boy'
7th Euro Diamond 'Ace' Pigeon
190th NFC Saintes 03
56th NFC Saintes
132nd NFC Pau
475 Int Dax 19420b 04
12th Int Dax 17526b 05

B 99.3286915
Emiel II
Sire of 'Farm Boy' 12 int Dax etc...

B 89.3316151
Deweerdt
EMIEL
1st Bordeaux 1992 9493b

83.3324036
Barto
118 and 145 nat Cahors

84.3200297
sister **Kristoff** dtr **Filip**
1st prov 2nd nat Perigueux

B 97 3311016
Deweerdt
Dtr Bartalli
78 Int Bare 256 Int Perp

92.3317121
Deweerdt
Bartgali

94 3299375
Deweerdt
Sister Ch Magnus

99. .3286983
Deweerdt
Miss Kedir
Dtr Kedir

B 95 3289671
Kedir
34 Int Dax – 78 Int Dax
143 Int Perp 16025b

B 93 3307264
Kedir Snr
317 Int Marseilles 15586b

B 92 3363501
Deweerdt
'501'

B 98 3306043
Deweerdt
Dtr Jochen

B 96 3273851
Deweerdt
Jochen
61st nat Perigueux 5739b

B 97 3311132
Deweerdt
Dtr Ch Magnus

Farm Boy, 12th International Dax 2004 and 475th International Dax 2003. He was also 7th Euro Diamond. He is now in the stock loft breeding absolutely top pigeons. Photo: © Copyright Mrs Catherine J. Cooper

How did you manage the environment of the loft and the use of the aviary?

I have an aviary for the hens but not for the racers. As far as I am concerned the loft and the environment in and around the loft is working, so I intend to leave well alone until such times as I have definite proof that things could be improved.

The Early Life of Young Birds

You have told me that when you have youngsters you allow them to have open hole and be free to exercise as they wish. Is that still your policy?

I now have two rounds of youngsters. The older ones had open hole from February, when they were beginning to fly, until early in April. Those pigeons that were early bred were then flying an hour and a half to two hours. The younger ones were flying five minutes. If I began to train those that were flying only five minutes I would lose three-quarters of them, whereas I would lose hardly any of the ones that were twelve weeks of age and were flying up to two hours. Last week the later bred pigeons were beginning to fly an hour or an hour and twenty minutes. After another week of that I shall give the lot four or five tosses of up to 80km (50 miles) and then they will be fit for racing. At the moment the older ones are exercised once a day, while the younger ones are allowed out the whole day.

While the youngsters are out race birds are flying overhead on their way home. Every day birds in training are coming up and down. My youngsters are out the whole time and I lose hardly any. Even on Saturdays, when racing is taking place, the pigeons are allowed out to learn about the sky and what is passing over. They learn to be aware of the hawk and to cope with it. They learn to get back after they have been carried off with a team of racers going through to the Midlands. They learn everything at this crucial stage of their lives. If they get lost off the loft, then they are fools and I don't want them. The benefit of having them out all day, as opposed to just having them out for certain periods, is that they learn so much. They flop on and off the loft getting acquainted with the area. They become accustomed to what may frighten them. The more they are out the fewer the losses and the better the pigeons. There are peregrines and sparrow hawks around here. People tell me I'll lose pigeons to them. I do lose pigeons to both sparrow hawks and peregrines, but the rest learn how to get out of the way and subsequently they make better old pigeons because of it. Some friends of mine, Harding Bros of Bath, used to keep their pigeons in and only let them out at certain times. By the second or third race they had nothing left. They used to see my pigeons out on Saturday mornings when the race birds were going through and couldn't understand the risk I was taking. 'We can't keep a pigeon', they said, and I replied, '*Easy* – let them out and go away … Don't bother with them, don't try and protect them.' Before they were frightened and didn't trust the pigeons to learn for themselves. They now do it and lose far fewer. Less management is better for the early experience of young birds.

Numbers

How many birds do you have in your race team?

I have room for seventy-six cocks but I don't like to keep more than sixty cocks maximum. I think this year I have fifty-nine, including yearlings. The ventilation is good for the numbers I have. I have two stone sections with sixteen boxes in each. If I kept the maximum of sixteen pigeons in these sections I would win nothing, so I always have some empty nest boxes.

How many breeders do you have?

I have sixteen pairs at the moment, but normally I like to keep between twelve and fifteen pairs.

How many young birds do you breed?

I like to breed as many as I can accommodate. I can house between 110 and 125 young pigeons.

I like to work the early ones hard in an attempt to lose the fools. I honestly believe 25 per cent of the pigeons anyone breeds are fools and absolutely no good at all. 50 per cent of pigeons bred are average; this makes them good enough to win at club level, but ambitious fanciers want pigeons that are better than that. That leaves just the top 25 per cent. These are the ones that are needed and are going to take your loft forward. If I breed a hundred youngsters only about twelve or thirteen are going to be really good cocks, so the more you breed and the quicker you get rid of the others the better your chances.

Would you like to have more pigeons?

I don't think I could manage more than sixty cocks maximum, not on my own.

Do you consider a certain number of breeding pigeons an essential minimum for maintaining the quality of your colony?

You have got to have six really good breeding pairs to stay at the top. This is very difficult. I would like to think I could aim at twelve good breeding pairs, but this is so difficult as to be near impossible. At the moment I know I have seven good pairs out of those I have at stock.

Of course, you are importing pigeons from time to time and they have to be tested?

John – An outstanding pigeon in Cooper history, was twice 6th NFC Nantes 1986 and 1987. He was also 12th NFC Pau. Photo: © Copyright Anthony Bolton

I used to try importing pigeons from anywhere and everywhere – 99 per cent ended up in failure. Now I just wait for the Deweerdt loft to have a new champion. When they breed a really good new pigeon I want something out of it.

The Main Birds

Can you say which individual stock birds were essential to the development of your present family of pigeons?

I would say the original three from Deweerdt that I had at the start, plus a daughter of 'Liesbet' and 'Ashman's Hen', which was a Deweerdt out of direct Deweerdt pigeons. I have super children off the imports of Deweerdt winning pigeons.

Obviously you are trying to keep the quality as high as you can make it.

Yes, the crosses I now make are my old Deweerdt family crossed with the modern Deweerdt pigeons from current champions. That works and it seems to give hybrid vigour as well.

I know this might appear a silly exercise, but hypothetically which six pigeons (three hens and three cocks) from the whole history of your loft would you choose if you were able to restart a family?

The 'Twenty-Pound Hen' and its mate were the best pair of National breeding pigeons I ever had. In a way I want them but the line ended there: their offspring did not produce anything. To produce a family it would have to be the original pair of Deweerdts and the daughter of 'Liesbet'. '350' was a super breeder that I bred myself. I would definitely have '21', which is a grandson of the original pair and in the stock loft at the moment. My imaginary stock loft should also have 'Farm Boy' and I would include a sister to '21' and 'Nicholls' as well. The Classic hen is three-quarters Derweerdt and a quarter Vermote and 'Ashman's Hen'. All these were super breeders that have left a mark in the loft as it is now.

In a similar way, which half a dozen would you have to race?

'John' was brilliant. He was 12th NFC Pau and I would definitely have him. 'August' (5th NFC Nantes), one of the original ones, was also brilliant. 'Nicholls' (3rd NFC Pau) would also be there and so would 'Farm Boy' (12th Int Dax) and 'Bulldog' (5th NFC Nantes and a Pau section winner). 'Bulldog' should also be in the stock loft – I forgot how tremendously influential he was. 'Wriggler' is a current champion. He is the best late-bred two-year-old I have ever had.

Garden party in the Cooper Garden at Peasedown St John to commemorate the UK's first International win. Brian Sheppard the International winner is in the centre of the second row. The second, Crowley and Green are behind him looking down.

Have you got to the stage where you can make any suggestions as to what to look for in a pigeon? Do you have any ideas on what makes it a future prospect?

I like pigeons that walk around your feet – not pigeons that are tame or pigeons that allow you to handle them, but busy pigeons that aren't nervous of you. I can tell more from the character of a pigeon than I can by putting it in my hands.

Are you good at picking good pigeons from within your young bird team?

If I were to study them, yes – but I don't study them overmuch. Nowadays I just race them and keep what is left. I let the basket do the selecting. Even though I don't put much time into it I do notice the odd pigeon that has something different about it. Reg Venner said to me, 'Always watch the pigeons that are always around your feet.'

I think this is true.

A Life in Pigeons

How do the pigeons fit in with your family life?

We, the whole family, revolve around the pigeons. My wife Catherine is really interested, but she does not manage the pigeons. She believes that one person is enough for the pigeons to relate to. She has made that decision and I go along with it. The family, of course, has everything they need for their well-being, but to be really successful a lot has got to give. Catherine and I are interested in the sport as a whole. I serve on various committees and do various jobs for various clubs. She writes articles for pigeon magazines and also for magazines from different cultures such as China and Taiwan. We are both interested in International racing as the basis for the future of the sport. My wife ran, organized and staged two garden parties to celebrate the UK winning the only two International races this country has ever won. She is as fully committed to pigeon racing as I am. I have to admit I am obsessive about pigeons. Catherine is almost as obsessive as I and possibly a little more ambitious, but we are definitely a team enterprise.

Reducing the Odds

Racing pigeons at long distances is always a challenge and full of uncertainties. By its very nature we can never know everything. You have been more successful than most fanciers in the sport, so can you single out the one technique or quality that has helped reduce the uncertainty, shorten the odds and, to some degree, helped produce a successful colony?

'Pigeon racing' is easy. It is 'pigeon fanciers' that make it difficult. If there is an easy way of doing something and a difficult way, then choose the easy way. But the part of the sport that is most difficult is breeding and producing good pigeons. Establishing a good stock loft is difficult because difficult choices have to be made. Most fanciers have not cracked the breeding part of pigeon

'Flipper' – Flipper was 8 years of age when he was 86th International Perpignan from 12,551 birds. He was the oldest pigeon in the first 100 places. Age is always a sign of vitality when it is coupled with a winning performance. Photo: © Copyright Anthony Bolton

racing. They tend to think that technique is the only thing they have to learn. They are wrong. It is breeding, especially for long distances, that is the most difficult. But it is the one thing everyone should study if they are to keep at the highest level in the sport for as long as possible.

Do you have any further ideas and ambitions?

Yes, I want to win an International race. I may not succeed but I will definitely be having a good try. That is the overriding ambition I have yet to achieve.

Would you say there is a spiritual quality to pigeon racing in the sense that how these little birds, which you have bred yourself, home from great distances seems to confirm that nature can achieve great things right here at your back door?

It is indeed magical. There is nothing more magical, especially when, at the end of the day, you see in the evening twilight a pigeon come home from a long race. I think I have some special kind of respect for nature. As a young boy I had owls, kestrels and all sorts of living things. I even had a pet grass snake, which I used to carry up my shirt to school. As I grew older people always told me that I could do things with animals that others couldn't. I think this is a part of my personality and comes from the respect I have for other species. I think all living things have a life that is worthy of respect.

CONCLUSION

Breeding and managing a small bird so that it can fly 1,050km (650 miles) in just over a day is not the most philistine activity known to man. Pigeon racing can be enlightened stuff. You could say it is intellectual in its own kind of way. Even though most of the world's great 'long-distance' pigeon fanciers are continually asking questions but find only partial answers, they still persist. In this sense they are research scientists in a field where race results are the outcome of experiments. When it comes to identifying the homing mechanism, conventional science has so far failed to find more than incomplete answers. You could say scientists have had no greater practical success than pigeon fanciers, although they come to the problem from different directions.

This should not surprise us, but it does. In this modern age we are mesmerized by the role of reductionist science in research. Science seeks to identify individual components in order to deduce mechanisms. Science may be wrong. Homing ability could well be a combination of components or the joint karma of the flock. The worst of pigeon racing may be artless and non-scientific, but so is the worst of science. Fanciers such as Geoff Cooper can make a valid contribution in seeking solutions that can be reached only through statistical measurement over time in an extended series of long races. He is prepared to go it alone, if necessary, based on what he has found. You could call his approach intellectual.

Early Learning

There is little doubt that some of Geoff Cooper's answers overturn many of the fashionable mumbo-jumbo ideas held by some fanciers, such as 'eye sign' and the theory that long-distance pigeons have to be a certain shape. Perhaps the most important, but the least obvious, is how he treats his young birds when they are starting to fly. They are allowed to learn their surroundings by themselves in their own time. This is called 'open hole'. Geoff is convinced this practice results in fewer losses in his young bird team. I suspect the effects may well be more far-reaching than that: this revolutionary method of teaching pigeons, by giving them their freedom at an age when learning has its greatest effect, may well set the pigeons up for their whole lives. A pigeon that is capable of winning top prizes from long races as an adult may owe some of its ability to the lessons it learnt when it was young.

Without a comparative test, in which some youngsters are allowed freedom and others not, this assumption cannot be tested definitively. Those who disagree with the freedom method may do so on the basis that pigeons need to be taught control at an early age in order to race well, but it may be that even greater racing ability is achieved by allowing the pigeon freedom to learn by experience in a hostile environment.

Certainly there is enough evidence that imprinting the pigeon to the loft by allowing it freedom to make mistakes is a good thing for later life. This may indeed be the early stage of instinct building or at least instinct strengthening. Remember how a cock bird appears to spin with joy when it returns after a long flight: it looks as though the pigeon feels happy to be once again connected with the loft. This is not a very scientific observation, but most fanciers, including Geoff Cooper, know it to be true. Our instinct tells us that strengthening the basic instinct has, in the long run, a firmer hold throughout the life of a pigeon than any amount of forced control.

Breeding

And now for Geoff's next trick – probably the most important he has. Geoff has realized that looks do not matter, but relationships do. Once again it has an anti-reductionist slant about it. A family of related pigeons that are of proven good quality (though not all champions) is itself important as a unit. Because breeding for performance is by its nature precarious and uncertain, this unit (the related family) itself becomes an important player. When a related family of known quality gets to a certain size it takes on a life of its own in the way it reproduces. It is then almost certain that champions will regularly begin to emerge from within this 'unit', providing, of course, that continual testing goes on at the same time.

It should therefore be stressed that any large-scale dilution of the genes of such a family is a massive turn in the wrong direction. Any new blood used for a cross should be added to the related family and not the other way around. This maintains the quality of the basic family and the whole of the loft of pigeons, while at the same time invigorating the family from time to time with new blood.

Geoff found this out when he tried introducing the 'Deweerdt' blood into the physically better-looking 'Vermote' blood. What a mistake this was: although initial results were positive, breeding ended after the first generation. It takes a noble man to acknowledge his mistake, but Geoff did so and has benefited from it. He opened up a whole new prospect. By using a base of good related blood (the Deweerdts), Geoff found that he could go on getting good pigeons every year, although he did not exactly know from which pair they were to come. This system put an end to those sterile periods where the crosses simply didn't work. Geoff claims that he has never had a bad 'Deweerdt' import. Every one has bred some useful pigeons of at least 'National Standard'. This is a mind-blowing revelation for the breeding of pigeons, setting everyone who takes notice of such things on a path of improved certainty. When it comes to breeding small birds that can home at speed from 650 miles, improvement of any kind is a giant step.

CHAPTER 5

Robert Ben

Calais, France

THE INTERVIEW

How old were you when you first began playing with pigeons?

I was 14 years of age when I first started with pigeons. I was born here in Calais just after the end of the Second World War; I am now 57. I am the second eldest of ten children. My father had pigeons, but he would only allow me to go in the loft on rare occasions. Eventually I, too, had pigeons. At that time I just had them as pets for fun and didn't enter competitions, but eventually I started entering short races of about 100km (60miles). My brother René, who lives here in Calais, also has pigeons, so you could say we are a pigeon family.

'Super Ben' is certainly the best long-distance pigeon to have ever flown into France and possibly the whole of Europe. His five times in the top 50 places in International races has yet to be bettered in modern times. The best Long Distance pigeons are marked not by how many first prizes they have won but by how consistent they are over many races. Photo: © Copyright Peter van Raamsdonk

When did you first begin to tackle long distances?

I started thinking about the 'long distance' in 1989 and introduced pigeons from the Netherlands fancier Peter van den Eijnden. In 1991 I bought more pigeons from the Netherlands, this time from Mevr Sprenkels, but in 1993 I suffered an enormous setback when all my birds were stolen except for twenty pigeons. I still don't know to this day who did it, but it had had a profound effect on me. Of the twenty pigeons left behind by the thieves, fifteen went on to make really good breeders.

The Effects of the Theft

How did the theft of your pigeons affect you?

The experience of having your loft invaded and birds stolen can act in two ways. It can either demoralize you or it can create a new and greater resolve. With me it worked the second way: my 'long-distance' motivation was set at a higher level as a result of the theft. Some of the pigeons I had left were the original Van der Eijnden birds. These were close related to his famous '55', which is a son of an even more famous hen, the '131' of Jan de Weert of Steenbergen. The birds from Mevr Sprenkels pigeons were also of good pedigree. They were Jan Aarden pigeons from the best of the famous 'Dolle' line of Martha van Geel. These few pigeons were to form a large part of my future family.

Have you ever considered what kind of attitude you must have to be successful with pigeons and pigeon racing? Must you have a scientific mind, be aggressive or have some other characteristic?

I think you must be a multi-layered person able to be different things at different times. When pigeons are young they do not necessarily do their best, so you must then be patient. Later, as the pigeons mature and you require them to perform, you must be a little bit strict. The whole thing is

"Super Ben"
F98 -361048
3rd Internal Perpignan 03 17,338p
5th Internal Barcelona 04 24,900p
20 Internal Barcelona 03 20,204p
21 Internal Perpignan 04 18,192p
44 Internal Barcelona 01 25,760p

- NL96-2261688 'Donkere 68 Direct Chris vd Velden Zuid Beyerland
  - NL94 2709178'Brother Fits' 11 Nat NPO Montauban 98 34 Nat Dax '96
    - NL81 210329 'De St Vincenter' Overwegend Aarden 10 X prize. 28 Nat Dax
      - NL801413132 Chr vd Heuvel
      - NL77 2633227 Ch vd Heuvel
    - NL92 1176627 'Dtr Wittbuik' B Batenburg and son Klaaswall
      - NL81 1533120 'De Witbuik'
      - NL91 2128945 'Dtr Ruffec'
  - NL94-2709106 64 Nat Tarbes '96 111th Nat NPO Montauban '96
    - NL93 2867789 'Son Pau Doffer' A. Kooy Heinenoord
      - NL88 1866275 6 Int Pau 91 Father 2nd Nat Bergerac
      - NL90 2574744 6 Nat St Vincent 92
    - NL91 2232237 'Dtr Perpignan', AP Overwater Strijen
      - NL90 2489419 Sort vd Eiinden
      - NL88 1814196 'De Perpignan 7 Nat Pau 91 – 21 Nat Perpienan 90
- F 97 370196
  - NL91 2393715 Direct Mevr Sprenkels Lepelstraat
    - NL90 2696404 'Bonte 404'
      - 82 8213866 Blue Bonte 7 Nat St Vincent Line Dolle and Barcelona 17
      - NL88 2024948 Dtr 'Kras Dolle' Super Breeder and mother of 'Good Barcelona' 914.87 (6 x Barcelona incl 25 nat '95 5737 pigeons
    - NL90 2696368 'Blauw 368'
      - NL83 8370429 Cheq 429
      - NL86 8611199 Blue 199
  - NL89 1737311 Direct Peter vd Eijnden Deurne
    - NL87 2505124 Cheq 124
      - NL83 967148 'Cheq 48' of Bang G Son of the famous '55'
      - NL82 371326 'Cheq 26' G Dtr Old Doffertje VD Wegen
    - NL86 8653725 Dtr 25 of '86
      - NL84 8438547 Donkere 47 G Son of the famous '55'
      - NL85 1770768 G dtr "Spin Aarden 1"

Pedigree of 'Super Ben'.

very complex, while at the same time being very simple at a basic level. No one attitude can work the whole way through. When the pigeons are three years old, if they don't do well they must be removed from the loft. At that time you must be decisive and think clearly. You must also watch the breeding performance of the stock birds.

Since you were left with only twenty birds after the theft, have you bought in more pigeons to build up your stock?

Yes. Every year I try to go to the Netherlands to buy pigeons. I travel by train and visit the lofts I have found from a study of international results. In 1996 I bought in pigeons from Lei Kurvers of Hulsberg in the Netherlands. I also bought in pigeons from Theo Ernst of Halsteren and Gerard Van Tuyl of Hellow. And I have a pigeon from the Dingemanse Bros from Arnemuiden. This pigeon came from a friend who gave a 'Bon' to the club – these 'Bons' are gift pigeons presented by club members to other members.

I always prefer pigeons from the Netherlands because they have to fly a greater distance. When I am considering buying pigeons I look for consistent Netherlands lofts that are up and coming. I study the results for three years or more in an attempt to find consistent lofts. Then I try to buy off their best birds. Van Tuyl, for example, has since won the International Barcelona and Lei Kurvers has won the International Perpignan in 2004, so it seems my selection process through the study of International results is above average. I am not correct all of the time, of course, but I am some of the time.

When you go looking for pigeons in the Netherlands, how do you decide to have this one or that one, or indeed pigeons from this loft or that?

I don't take notice of the person or the looks of the pigeon, but only the results. Results count above everything but these must be against the best competition. I closely analyse the International results over the winter months when I have little else to do. I try to find the Dutch fanciers who are both regular and improving. They must have good results for three years. This is the minimum time over which you can assess a loft. I do not take account of reputation or supposed fame. I base my selection purely on results. Generally I try to visit second-division lofts that are doing well with limited resources. It is better to have pigeons off the top birds from a second-division loft than off second-best birds from a first-division loft. Investing good money in pigeons without studying results is a lazy man's way of buying pigeons. I don't particularly bother if the lofts are cleaned out every day or only cleaned out once a year. I don't bother if the lofts are near the sea, like mine, or are in the country far inland. I must stress my investigations are based on 'Results, Results, Results', and nothing but the results of the loft as a whole.

Do you prefer cocks or hens, or is there no difference?

If I had enough money I would buy ten cocks and ten hens from the lofts of my choice. I don't have the resources, so I have to content myself with less. Sometimes I can afford to buy five hens and five cocks from one loft, but that is an exception.

Have you made any mistakes?

When I import pigeons I usually couple them with birds from my own loft, so very few are complete failures. That is not to say they all breed champions. They do not. They all have to undergo an assessment to see just how good their breeding performance is and whether they will eventually make a contribution to the loft overall and towards my objective.

The Race Team from Year to Year

How do you treat young birds in their first year?

I usually treat the young birds quite hard. This is necessary because I don't have a car and don't drive, so I have to rely on either a few friends or my daughters to give them their education. This means I do not do the same thing every year. Some years they get hardly any training at all. Some years they get quite a lot. I really think it is necessary to give young pigeons experience, if at all possible, because if they are not trained as young birds the next season is more difficult for them. Late-bred

Late-bred youngsters enjoying the sunshine.

young pigeons are a special case. At this moment I have eleven late young birds and so far they have had only two flights of about 13km (8 miles) each. I will have to be very patient with them next year. I wish I had more time to give to the young birds.

What happens to your yearlings?

Most of the yearling cocks are single. They do not have a mate and are not paired. They have to race to the perch only. I do this because I do not have enough space to give all my pigeons a nest box. Occasionally if I have some box space I do allow a young cock to be paired and to have his own nest box. At the moment I have ten yearlings that are paired and twelve that are single. Single yearlings exercise with the normal widowhood pigeons twice a day. They usually have to race up to 600km (375 miles) at the yearling stage. If you care to make a comparison between single yearlings and yearlings that are paired and have a box, the yearlings with a box are better when the race is hard, but when it is a normal race of medium velocity the single yearlings can often beat the paired ones. Later in life I don't think there is any difference between them.

Do Looks Matter?

When you are studying pigeons to decide their value, are you looking at the head or the wings, down the throat, in their eyes or what?

I don't look at anything. I solely buy pigeons that have been bred to fly long distances. I don't keep anything else. If they can't do this and fail to fly long distances in good times they are removed. Everything is judged by results and not by looks.

Do you intentionally try to cultivate a high immunity to sickness in your pigeons?

An inquisitive champion.

My pigeons are hardly ever treated – certainly not as young birds. I vaccinate them every year against paramyxo, but not against paratyphus. Once when I used to vaccinate against paratyphus one of my best birds died, so now I am afraid to do it. Since 1996 I have not had a single instance of an old pigeon becoming sick, although I do treat them once a year for canker. This year I did it for the second time two weeks before Perpignan. Sometimes a young pigeon can fall ill, but with old pigeons it never happens.

I do worry about my pigeons catching something when they are in the basket for six days or more and are drinking from the same water as all the other pigeons. I don't do anything about it other than keeping treatments to the very minimum to ensure they are armed with the maximum immunity against common conditions.

Advice for the Novice

What advice would you give a novice attempting to build a team of long-distance pigeons before he started?

Firstly, he should never keep stray pigeons when they drop into the loft. Almost all young fanciers and a few old fanciers are tempted to do this in the fond hope they have gained something for free. Here we have many English pigeons that are afraid to cross the sea or are not fit enough. These pigeons often come into our lofts. Do not be tempted.

Our imaginary novice must first buy pigeons from a local man who has been successful at International level. After that he must begin to work.

Should he make friends with a local fancier to learn how to condition and prepare long-distance pigeons?

No, he must learn on his own. He must learn from his own mistakes by careful observation. If he copies someone he will not begin to understand basic reasons, only to imitate the method of the fancier. It is better to learn on your own as I have done, that way you appreciate things much better and the lessons really sink in. I have learnt only one thing from a fellow fancier: if you have a pigeon that is sick at the beginning of the season, forget it for the whole year and don't race it at all. That is the only piece of good advice I ever learned from someone else. The rest I have learnt myself.

How many years will it be before he can send in an International race?

In my case I started with long-distance pigeons in 1990 and I finally raced in an International event in 1996. I would say it would take our novice

General view of the 'Ben' garden and the lofts. The lofts are not palatial only the results.

at least five or six years from the first breeding, if everything goes smoothly and according to plan.

The Daily Routine

When the pigeons are racing do they exercise regularly morning and evening, and how do you manage this?

The widowhood cocks exercise for one hour in the morning and one hour in the evening, but this is not exactly the whole story. I like to see the pigeons fly for ten minutes, then drop onto the loft, then strike up again and fly for another quarter of an hour, perhaps, before they come down again. I like to see activity in the birds rather than continuous flying in a robotic kind of way. I like to see the pigeons interested in life and their surroundings. Perhaps they will chase a small bird or fight among themselves, then suddenly scatter and explode into the sky. This is the kind of activity I like to see. This year for some reason I don't think the pigeons exercised so well. I don't run pigeons by the watch. Actually I don't own a watch – I do things more by feeling. It is not possible to perform really well with pigeons if you regiment them by time alone. That is only a part of the story. It is difficult to explain the other part, but achieving happiness and a zest for life comes into it for both the owner and the pigeons. When the two are combined, providing you have good pigeons, magic happens and good results follow.

How do you prepare the mature pigeons that are expected to do well in the really big races, such as Barcelona and Perpignan?

The strategy for the important races and the important pigeons, pigeons that have probably scored in previous years is nothing special. I like to show the hens before the race. I usually give them ten to fifteen minutes with the hen immediately before the pigeon goes to the race, but I must stress the hen is on one side of a barrier and the cock is on the other side for most of the time. At the end of this time, for just a few vital minutes, they are allowed together but of course the cock must not tread the hen. He is only allowed to get into the nest bowl and call her. I don't give herbs such as garlic or herbs for purifying the blood. I don't like the smell of garlic.

Do you give any special food to build them up before a long race?

I do not give anything special but I do use clay blocks. I think it is good for them to pick at a clay block, since it relaxes them and perhaps stops them going to the fields and picking at something really bad that would make them ill, or at the very least put them off form. Clean grit every day is also very important at this time.

... and a pinch of hemp?

A little pinch of hemp in each nest box at the end of the day is the only kind of seed I use. Again, though, this is not just for the food value but also as a titbit to reinforce their territory. They love it and will always eat it, even after they have been fed. A really fit bird whose digestive system is working at its most super-efficient does not always eat as much as it should. A titbit of hemp helps the appetite. I do not feed peanuts.

If I weren't so lazy I think I would give some brewers' yeast powder on their food the evening before they go into the basket for the race, but generally I don't do it.

Is anything special given to the birds after they return to get them back into good condition?

They are fed a commercial mixture of depurative food a few days after they have returned, but apart from that nothing special, only clean water. Good pigeons generally recover very quickly. It is only bad pigeons that need a lot of help. A cock that returns from a very long race early in the morning is allowed to sit with his hen for the whole day, or perhaps through the night if it is late when he arrives. This is good for morale, but a lot depends on the severity of the race and the pigeon's condition. Of course, while they are away at the race they may be absent for a week or more. Their nest box must be closed at this time so that the pigeons left behind are not tempted to take control of the vacant box. Tired birds should not be

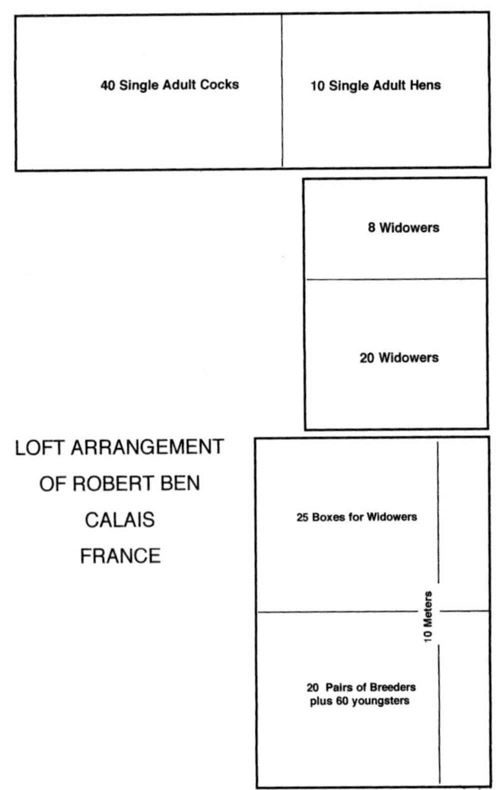

Plan of the Ben lofts and how each category of pigeon, breeders – widowhood racers and single racers, and youngsters are accommodated.

obliged to fight for their box when they return. They should have as much peace as possible to enable them to recover quickly.

After the racing has finished, are the hens and cocks separated for the winter?

Up to now I have been obliged to keep them together for the whole winter because I do not have too much space, but next year it will become possible to separate them. I now have the facility to keep pigeons in the garden at my daughter's house and I intend to keep some hens there.

Do you feed anything special to help with the moult and do you give them plenty of baths?

I feed them nothing special apart from a commercial moulting mixture. As for baths, again I do it infrequently. Pigeons are perverse birds: if I put a bath out and it is sunny they don't get into the bath, but if it is raining then I find they go in. Occasionally I have medicated the bathwater to help get rid of feather lice or such things. The pigeons taste the water and they don't like it, so now I have to spray under their wings and around their bodies before each race to achieve a similar end.

Pairing Up

When do you pair the race birds together each year?

Up to now, again because I am limited for space, the race birds are together the whole year, including all winter. Each time the hen lays eggs I have replaced the eggs with pot eggs so they are not actually rearing young birds, but after eight days, of course, they lay again. This year I intend to do things differently. After the International Perpignan race, the last International race of the season, I will let them rear one young bird each, then I will separate them for the winter. The race birds keep the same mate throughout their entire life.

The breeding pigeons are different. They are separated to allow their mates to be changed from year to year. Not all are changed: some special pairs, if they are breeding very well and are producing good pigeons, are allowed to stay together.

Usually the first young pigeons of the year from the stock pigeons are born in February. If I were to compete for 'championships' that include races for young birds as a part of the championship, I would have young birds born in January.

When you are pairing the pigeons do you compensate for qualities? For instance, do you pair a big one to a small one, a dark eye to a light eye, a red to a blue or anything like that?

I try to couple similar sizes to each other. I don't take all the other things into account. I think the eye is an English fad to which I do not subscribe. I'm led to believe the best English fanciers don't believe it either.

The Loft

Do you take much notice of the ventilation and temperature in the loft and the way it is built?

I think I do, because at the beginning of the season my new loft has much better form than the old one. Often five pigeons will come to the new loft before I have seen one from the old loft. I have seen this happen this year and last year. This does not mean I am going to knock down the old loft and replace it with a new one. I think both have their uses. Even if I had enough money I would not change. There have been more than enough good pigeons from the old loft to make me want to keep it. Perhaps it's a matter of temperature, as you

Inside the lofts – the birds are healthy.

hinted at in your question, but the season is long and the temperature varies throughout the year, so I think I will keep both lofts and not change too much while the going is good. I think it would be a big risk to change too much. Environment also plays a part in the happiness of pigeons. Pigeons get used to things – they don't like change, they like to feel secure – so I will keep the old loft.

Do you think you are a good selector of pigeons? Can you go to a strange loft and immediately select the champion pigeons without being told?

I'm not able to select the champions. Of course, I can select a nice-looking pigeon just the same as anyone one else, but I don't know if it is a champion racer or not. I even make mistakes with my own pigeons, so I have no chance selecting good pigeons in another loft. I'm afraid I must always look at results. If a pigeon has good results then it is beautiful. Potential ability, as judged by those who think they can select pigeons, is hardly ever tested under correct conditions with ring numbers written down and eventually compared with future results.

How many widowhood cocks do you have and how many stock birds?

This year I started with sixty-three widowhood cocks, mostly composed of pigeons of two years and older. It includes only a few yearlings. I have twenty-five yearlings that are raced purely to the perch as single unpaired birds. I currently have twenty pairs of stock birds.

The Ratio

Are these numbers enough to compete in all the big International races and the build-up races you have to compete in before you get to the long-distance ones, or would you like more?

I would definitely not like to have more pigeons. I would prefer to have fewer. Numbers such as these are at the limit of my capacity to manage them well and keep the quality as high as I can get it, but as you know there are far more pigeons bred than actually survive to compete at the top level. The ratio between pigeons bred and pigeons that eventually compete in top-level long-distance races is the most important ratio in pigeons. We are not talking about 'Champions' here, just good reliable pigeons that comprise the bulk of any team of long-distance pigeons, pigeons that are likely to have good races and perhaps occasionally an excellent race. I have to breed many in the first place in order to find the pigeons that will compete in the long races. The whole thing is very difficult. I suspect it will never be completely solved, but trying to even partially solve this issue makes the sport of pigeons endlessly fascinating. This ratio problem and the overall results of the loft should be at the centre of everyone's attention.

Good Breeders

Which are the good breeders that have been, or still are, the most important in your colony and have made the largest contribution?

I tend to change the pairs each year, but this year I have put some of the same couples together once again because they were producing top pigeons. The cock in one of the couples that I have re-paired together is from 1992. He was a good racer, making 295th International Barcelona in 1997, and I have seen he was a good breeder much later. From his

Picture of '271' the five times to two per cent champion.

Ecaille Sprenkels
NL 2393715.91
5 x Bare 5 x Perpignan

Noir Macot
F361057.98
Brother 953.94 – 2 x Nat
Barcelona 97 and 98

F 810434.92
Very Good Producer

F515689.02
Half Brother 681271.00
689 prize Barcelona and
Perpignan 05

Bleu Sprenkels
F536912.93
6 nat Perpignan 96

Ecaille Claire
F 411503.96
Mother of 54 nat Barcelona
01

NL 1737311.89
v.d. Eynden
Super Ben g. mother
5 x Barc 5 x Perpignan

The '271'
F00-681271
3rd Internat Dax '05 11,898 p
21st Internat Dax '03 19,400 p
113 Internat Dax '04 17,526 p
326 Internat Perpignan '03
17,338 p
157 Internat Dax '06 11,517 p

Cor Groenleer
Holland
Strain – J Steketee

NL 2351283.96
Cor Groenleer
Holland

Cor Groenleer
Holland
Strain – J Steketee

'271' Is a pigeon that has
been times in the top
2 per cent in
International races –

Pedigree of '271'.

number, 720/92, you will see that he was one of the pigeons that survived the theft in 1993, along with 134/92, 104/92 and 117/92. 1992 was a good breeding year: all these pigeons scored at least once in the top 2 per cent of international races, some of them more than once. 720/92 was the best breeder.

Which were the most important pigeons for racing?

The 'Super Ben', of course, and there was 719/99, which flew Barcelona many times and was 54th in 2003 and 170th in 2005. Another of my favourites, though not especially a Barcelona pigeon and also good at shorter races, was a black one named 'Noir Macot' (057/98), a brother to 719/99 and 953/94 (52nd Int Barcelona 1999). 'Noir Macot' had prizes at Limoges, Barcelona, Perpignan and other places. He is the father of 271/00, which won 326th Perpignan in 2003, 21st Dax in 2003, 113th Dax in 2004 and 3rd Dax in 2005. He was a very good pigeon and is now a very good breeder.

Can you imagine life without pigeons?

When the race goes badly I can imagine it all too well, but that soon passes when the next race is good. I used to prefer pigeon sport in the days when we used to compete without prizes. Pigeon sport is gradually getting worse. In Calais, for example, it is difficult to keep a loft of pigeons because of the law. Calais' economy is not very

International pigeons in the top 2 per cent since 1997

Date	Race	Entry (birds)	Pos	Ring	Velocity (m/min)
1996					
04/8/1996	Perpignan	12,551	13	90104.92	1,024.73
04/8/1996	Perpignan	12,551	44	536912.93	973.75
04/8/1996	Perpignan	12,551	67	90117.92	959.42
04/8/1996	Perpignan	12,551	170	752134.92	924.78
1997					
05/7/1997	Barcelona	24,908	52	229953.94	808.89
05/7/1997	Barcelona	24,908	163	229958.94	
05/7/1997	Barcelona	24,908	295	810720.92	
09/8/1997	Perpignan	12,367	21	752134.92	930.16
1998					
25/7/1998	Marseilles	19,968	275	90104.92	851.64
1999					
This year the Ben loft did not have any pigeons in the top 2 per cent International largely because the winds were against French pigeons that year. Nevertheless, Robert was 1434th from Barcelona, 1974th from Pau, 1,140th from Dax and 1,412nd from Perpignan.					
2000					
05/8/2000	Perpignan	18,426	119	361048.98	877.32
2001					
25/6/2001	Pau	7,841	26	361029.98	
08/7/2001	Barcelona	25,760	44	361048.98	1,108.79
04/8/2001	Perpignan	20,859	206	361048.98	1,101.00
2002					
07/7/2002	Barcelona	26,928	470	361023.98	994.35
2003					
04/7/2003	Barcelona	20,204	20	361048.98	958.83
04/7/2003	Barcelona	20,204	54	268719.99	933.54
12/7/2003	Dax	19,400	21	681271.00	962.90
02/8/2003	Perpignan	17,338	3	361048.98	941.08
02/8/2003	Perpignan	17,338	181	361044.98	959.06
02/8/2003	Perpignan	17,338	326	681271.00	1,041.26
2004					
26/6/2004	Pau	8,270	159	268713.00	1,167.07
19/7/2004	Dax	17,526	113	681271.00	1,002.00
19/7/2004	Dax	17,526	265	331445.00	970.10
19/7/2004	Dax	17,526	347	515692.02	955.35
2/7/2004	Barcelona	24,913	5	361048.98	1,241.50
07/8/2004	Perpignan	17,570	21	361048.98	1,032.70
07/8/2004	Perpignan	17,570	69	236819.99	982.34
07/8/2004	Perpignan	17,570	193	373698.98	953.46
2005					
01/7/2005	Pau	8,421	21 (1st Int Hens)	268713.99	998.67
03/7/2005	Barcelona	25,815	170	268719.99	946.47
17/7/2005	Dax	11,898	3	681271.00	1,051.52
06/8/2005	Perpignan	17,653	378	509353.02	840.64

Distances to the Ben loft

Pau	862.342km	Barcelona	1,066.918km	Marseilles	891.613km
Dax	795.925km	Perpignan	918.174km		

Note: The famous 'Super Ben' (361048.98) scored seven times in the top 2 per cent. 'Super Ben' is now owned by Mr Hiroshi Kijima of Tokyo, Japan.

strong at the moment and there is 16 per cent unemployment.

For my final question, can you identify the particular quality that has made you so successful with pigeons?

I think it is because I have an objective. This is most important in the sport of pigeon racing. My objective is to do well in long-distance International races. I do not buy pigeons everywhere, only from places and lofts where I have conducted my research. Everything must build towards my objective. I also prepare the season in advance with my objective in mind. I recognize that my objective is difficult, but that also can be turned to your advantage. The few consistent pigeons that succeed in this type of competition are unquestionably very good, so it is important to set your aim to include the best competition available in your initial plans.

Really good pigeons of world class only arrive when the competition is the best possible and is also of world class. You can base your whole decision-making, the breeding, the racing and the management on races such as this. If you do consistently well you are entitled to think your entire management, including the initial selection of your stock, was also good. If you fail, of course, then your management or the pigeons are not good enough and you have to start again, but it is better to fail trying for the top class than to fail at a lower level. It is all a matter of where you are likely to get the most satisfaction.

CONCLUSION

Robert Ben's role in pigeon lore is to confound all our entrenched and preset views about pigeons. We are forced to rethink our opinions and almost everything we thought we knew. Robert Ben has turned pigeon sport on its head. The supposed need we have all felt, from time to time, to own hundreds of pigeons and house them in palatial lofts is no longer necessary. It is no longer the only way to good results.

Most of us have been seduced, perhaps unconsciously, into having photographs from the early days of the sport imprinted on our minds. These old photographs of palatial 'Grand Château' lofts have become synonymous with success in big races. The working man developed a kind of complex trying to compete against such establishments. He has always seen himself to be at a disadvantage. He has even accepted as fact that, should a big win occur to a loft of modest circumstances, it was only a 'lucky strike', a one-off that would soon right itself in favour of the safer and easily understood natural order of the 'Grand Château'. Big lofts with many birds were perceived as the kind of establishments that were supposed to win the big races. Their wealth and buying power demanded it should be so.

The Robert Ben contribution has somewhat debunked this image. His success has not come from palatial lofts, independent means and a personal fortune, but from a greater understanding of the true statistics of pigeon sport. In a way he has democratized the sport. His achievements have taken away any justification we might have for citing our own circumstances as an excuse for failure, the 'if only' justification. Despite his circumstances, Robert Ben has made it because he has applied himself to defining, analysing and knowing where he is going. He has developed to a greater degree than ever before the need for a clear objective as a guiding force. He has proved that having a clear objective is even more essential to success than anything else. A clear objective should now become the normal procedure in establishing a loft of long-distance pigeons chosen in the first place to do well eventually. Robert always had a plan, a guide, a fully thought-through system despite his modest circumstances.

Objective

It is impossible to creep up and steal someone's objective. An objective cannot be stolen, copied or used in any way other than by its original creator. When it comes to 'objectives' you have to provide your own.

This rather upsets our own thinking. Having a clear objective uncluttered by thoughts of fame or what might be sold is almost bad-mannered in today's sport. It is certainly unusual. A clear objective eliminates lesser goals in favour of the one big goal. That is its strength. Robert states that he preferred the sport when there were no prizes. This gives us a clue to the idealistic nature of his objective, but he is still notoriously difficult to pin down. We first have to suffer the indignity and the pain of being horribly wrong. We have to follow how his objective has developed and then perhaps get a clue as to how it has worked for him. This is always difficult. The false ideas we have all entertained from time to time have to be cast aside. They may prove to be at best merely skimming the surface of what he is all about and at the worst a closed door to our understanding. Robert Ben from Calais demands that we all re-examine our prejudices.

When we meet him and discover what he has

achieved, and the circumstances under which he has achieved them, it is disturbing for those interested in the breeding and racing of pigeons, and the methods by which we can get them to do well at International level. Such enthusiasts have much to learn, but those motivated solely by buying and selling pigeons are unlikely to respond. This is a man who politely turned away a Japanese offer of a suitcase full of money in exchange for his famous 'Super Ben', the best international long-distance pigeon in Europe, by quietly saying, 'I don't sell pigeons.' We will return to that story below.

Here we have a humble man of undoubtedly modest circumstances, who cares for his elderly, infirm mother in a tiny house in the heart of Calais. Robert Ben does not drive or own a car. He rides a bike. Robert does not keep strict time because he does not own a watch. From time to time he even forgets to buy pigeon food and it is only when it runs out that he is prompted to ask his daughter to get some more. Yet despite all these lapses this man has devised a workable 'Objective', a statistical method to improve his chances.

Objective and Method

Before his pigeons were stolen Robert Ben had decided where he was going and how he was going to get there. After the theft his determination was doubled. His aim was to achieve consistent results in at least four of the five main Belgian International races. The exception was Marseilles, but even in this race Robert has had some success (275th in 1998 with the cheq cock 104 of 1992, one of the pigeons left behind after the theft). The four main international races that formed his objective were Pau, Barcelona, Dax and Perpignan (of which Barcelona is the furthest from Calais and Dax the nearest). Calais is not in a particularly good location for international racing, being one of the longest flying locations for French national racing. Statistically, for international success Calais should need a bit more east wind to achieve high honours. Calais is not the ideal place, but nevertheless success is possible if the pigeons are of good quality, and if they are happy and fit for the task.

Breeding quality is the most important ingredient in the 'Ben' objective. Robert quickly identified that the greatest improvement to quality could be made through breeding. If he could improve this to the point where he could breed a greater percentage of pigeons to do well Internationally, this would reflect on the loft as a whole. If this ideal were to be achieved then all results would automatically improve. How this was to be done was the next step.

It is generally recognized that on average one pigeon in twenty or thirty of all the young birds originally bred make it to the top 10 per cent of International racing results. In most lofts the performance of the breeding loft in being able to breed International pigeons is a hit and miss affair. Breeding is never certain, nor is it controlled. Some years the breeding loft will not produce anything at all, others there will be a few but never a glut. Breeding is the most difficult of all the disciplines involved in long-distance pigeon racing, yet breeding is more often than not overlooked and sidelined behind actual racing. This is because breeding does not show an immediate effect.

Often we get sidetracked away from breeding by the apparent need to master feeding, training and other requirements deemed to improve performance. The odd top performance bird happens almost by accident in many cases. Top racers acquire a lionized central role in most lofts. It is they who grab the headlines. It is they who are praised and then put to stock, often to breed nothing themselves. Meanwhile the pairs that bred the headline pigeons in the first place are perhaps no longer there at all. We all pay lip-service to having a good breeding pair, but in reality we pay more attention to top racers. There is a charismatic status about owning a star performer. This is almost always in preference to owning a top breeder. So powerful is this preference that breeding has become the most neglected side of pigeon sport. Far more attention is paid to actual racing and racing techniques than to breeding and the performance of the breeding loft, yet breeding is the foundation of long-distance races and long-distance pigeons. We have all made this fundamental mistake and most of us continue to make it. Breeding, by and large, is just not exciting enough for the average fancier.

Lofts with a top breeding pigeon or pair are fortunate. Many lofts are at the top only while a 'Golden Pair' is present and producing good birds, but as soon as they die or are no longer able to produce the loft begins to slide. In so many cases nothing is done about this problem until it is too late. It is only after the breeding pair has gone and their absence is missed that frantic steps are taken to replace them.

Replacing them is not easy, usually ensuing in a mad buying scramble, scampering here and there in an effort to buy another 'Golden Pair'. Time begins to run out, things get frantic and tempers frayed, and all because measured and controlled breeding was not a part of the ongoing policy in the first place.

Studying the menu – Robert Ben and his eldest daughter Verginie confer over the menu – She now has a great influence in the pigeons. Some Widowhood hens are to be kept at her house next year.

More than anyone, Robert Ben is aware of such problems, but because he has the advantage of not being too materialistically minded he recognizes the non-charismatic, hidden side of pigeon sport. His objective compass now comes into use. He concentrates on breeding. That is why the breeding loft is continually tested and updated. That is why the racing section is not relied upon to breed, and why the famous 'Super Ben' was allowed to race over many years despite his success. The breeding loft is there to breed and the racing loft is there to race. The two have entirely separate roles, each doing the job it was designed to do. Having an objective identifies the problems. It also indicates how to overcome them. Without an objective this is not so.

Objective and Priorities

If there is one benefit to being in possession of a clear objective, it is that it arranges priorities. Expensive details, although good looking, will never achieve the same improvement in performance as improved breeding. Driving off from the golf tee with a flourish is eye-catching, but the greatest number of strokes can be picked up on the putting green. The same is true in pigeons: feeding special seeds or tinkering with this or that in the water does not gain as much as improved breeding, which produces a higher return and is easily able to double the performance of any loft. Where there is only one pair producing good quality pigeons, a loft in possession of a breeding plan and a clear objective can quite easily double that to two. A breeding plan will almost certainly also identify the good breeding pigeons much sooner. Robert Ben is aware of this and is not prepared to waste his time chasing much-hyped improvements that at best may be only marginal. He is in too much of a hurry for that. Lofts that are in possession of a clear objective and know where they are going are more likely to improve than those that are not. A modest loft with a clear objective is one that understands the statistical nature of pigeon racing. Such a loft can quite easily overtake one that has the advantage of a greater number of pigeons simply because they can afford them. This is the Robert Ben message.

Objective and Results

The pigeons' treatment at every stage of their development, from when they are born to maturity, is staged in a way able to both educate for success and eliminate failure at each level. In the Ben loft young pigeons, not fully developed, are allowed to make mistakes. They also have their freedom. From this freedom and their mistakes they learn at their own pace, one at which experience can be fully absorbed. Robert warns us to be patient at this stage. It is only later that you must be a little bit strict. Even yearlings, some of whom are not paired but are raced single just to the perch, are still allowed time to develop and mature without pressure. The object of their early lives is to survive and to get the chance to eventually race and do well at International level, until which time they are still maturing and strengthening their bond to the loft and its surroundings. Bonding and performance increases with age, as was shown by the results achieved by 'Super Ben' as he grew older. In many lofts vitality is often equated with results. They believe that a pigeon's top performance occurs while it is relatively young. This is not so in the Ben loft. The instinctive will to race home gets stronger and more skilful with age. It is not unusual for a pigeon to perform statistically better at six years of age than it did when it was two or three. It is not unusual for a long-distance pigeon in the Ben loft to do its best when relatively old. Maturity has it benefits, not least because if a mature pigeon has success this is a sure sign of uncontaminated vitality bred into and part of the pigeon's physique.

No doubt mistakes are made, as they are in every loft, but the owner and the pigeons continue to learn all the time. Robert sees his eventual objective as a guide to everything, even learning. He is constantly learning from his own mistakes and observations. He only admits to having learnt one thing from another fancier: not to race a pigeon that has been ill early in the year. Apart from that everything is self-taught based on observation and knowing where the loft is going. For this reason Robert Ben makes a trip to the Netherlands every year, travelling by train with phrase book in hand to visit lofts and buy pigeons. More important than the actual trip, however, is the research that has been done before he goes. He scrutinizes the International race results to identify the Dutch lofts that have shown the most consistency over a period of at least three years. He only visits those that come out on top. These are not necessarily top lofts of established fame but often what he calls 'second-division lofts that are still up-and-coming', since he advises that it is better to buy from the best pigeons from a second-division loft than the second-best pigeons from a top loft.

By definition these best birds that he buys are bred from the one in twenty or thirty that have made it to international level in Dutch lofts. What Robert is doing is conducting a statistical buying strategy in a gradual effort to acquire for his stock loft pigeons bred from birds that are top ratio pigeons bred by others. His breeding loft is therefore automatically composed of statistically top-quality birds, although still not certain to breed top pigeons. The only certainty about this is that it is composed of the right genes.

Back in Calais the newly purchased raw material undergoes further selection on the basis of how they breed. This buying strategy and the resulting selection continue year after year. The phrase book, the train journey and the research are essential components of the whole strategy.

Without detailed research any buying for the stock loft would have a larger element of luck. Once again Robert Ben has attempted to take some of the chance out of pigeon racing and breeding. A businessman whose time is at a premium cannot expect to carry out the same level of detailed research. That is yet another example of how he can level the odds. The result is a stock loft designed to produce good racers more by design and less by luck or intuition, since as Robert admits, 'I cannot tell if a pigeon is good or not by handling it. All I can do is to tell if it has good results.'

Robert's international results demonstrate the success of this policy, which could not have been achieved without an objective in the first place. Most of the second-division Dutch lofts that Robert has found from his research have gone on to become famous themselves. Some have had huge success internationally, while some have been responsible for breeding top pigeons for others. Success in the Ben loft has improved the reputation of many Dutch lofts.

The eventual aim of an objective, if it has any value, must be clear. In Robert Ben's case this is International success statistically measured by the end product. It is no use having a woolly objective, a 'See how we go' policy ready and willing to alter course at the slightest hiccup. This will surely fail. 'See how we go' thinking usually ends up with 'see how we go pigeons', depending more on luck than on good thinking.

'Super Ben'

We cannot leave Robert Ben, his ideas, methods and, above all, his 'objective' without a mention of 'Super Ben', otherwise known as the '48' or, more formally, F3610848.98. 'Super Ben' is a product of the Ben objective system. The achievements of 'Super Ben', with five international results in the top fifty places (3rd International Perpignan 2003, 5th International Barcelona 2004, 20th International Barcelona 2003, 21st International Perpignan 2004 and 44th International Barcelona 2001), must be judged as a whole. 'Super Ben' did not gradually get worse as he aged, he got better. 'Super Ben' started his racing career modestly. As a young bird he was placed 283rd from 1,996 pigeons in a race from Le Mans (347km/215 miles) and then 1,894th from 21,652 pigeons in a race from Poitiers (497km/310 miles). There was nothing startling about that, nor did he show little of his future potential in his steady progress as a yearling in 1999, when he was 111th from 2,028 pigeons from St Vincent, a distance of 840km (520 miles). At that time he was just a pigeon 'worth keeping', nothing more. He was, of course, destined to improve dramatically. As a two-year-old in 2000 'Super Ben' flew Barcelona adequately to achieve 164th place national and 3,372nd international. This experience set him up for a dramatic improvement later the same year, when he was 119th International against 18,246 pigeons from Perpignan.

'Super Ben' had arrived. From this time he was always 'first marked' or first selected in the Ben loft every time he was sent. If there is one lesson Robert Ben has taught us, it is that we must judge pigeon racing statistically, weighing the good and the bad and leaving nothing out. We must judge each racing pigeon, breeding pigeon and loft statistically. We must attempt to alter the odds in our favour in a controlled way. Only by doing this can we hope to advance and improve. Of course, this requires everyone to identify the area that can be improved and the areas best left alone. That is a matter of judgement based on having a clear objective. A clear objective is what we all have to provide ourselves with. If it is well designed and feasible it will almost certainly reveal more about long-distance pigeon racing than we knew before we started. If it is not clear it will muddle us up even more. Robert Ben, the humble Frenchman from Calais who does not drive and does not possess a watch, has shown us a new way. It is now up to us.

Selling 'Super Ben'

The story of how 'Super Ben' was eventually sold has all the elements of a fairy story. In its own way it is a reflection of a remarkable owner and a remarkable pigeon. There is no doubt that 'Super Ben', with his 'Super International' performances, was a hugely saleable item in great demand by rich pigeon fanciers the world over, but he was never toted for sale, either openly or in secret.

Before 'Super Ben' the city of Calais was hardly known in pigeon circles; after 'Super Ben' everyone knew Calais. It shocked fanciers in England for here was a pigeon, just 34km (21 miles) from the English coast, achieving what was previously thought impossible in the UK. Belgian fanciers were also impressed. 'Super Ben' was achieving outstanding top International positions over and over again, year after year. No wonder people took notice. Regardless of Calais' lack of fashionable glamour, this particular pigeon demanded special attention as it was beginning to create pigeon history.

In 2004 'Super Ben' was six years old and at the height of his powers: 5th International from Barcelona from 24,900 pigeons and later 21st from Perpignan from 18,192 pigeons. Performances like this were unheard of in any pigeon, let alone a six-year-old that had already scored four times before in the top fifty places.

The news obviously spread. Not long afterwards

Author John Clements(left), Robert Ben, his two daughters and a grandchild, 2006.

Space is so limited at the 'Ben' establishment the widowhood hens have to live separate in the cellar of the house for the few short months of the racing season. Next year there is to be a big improvement. They are to be kept in the garden of his daughter's house nearby.

Hiroshi Kijima arrived from Tokyo at the door of the Ben household with a suitcase full of cash. He was, of course, invited into the house to discuss his offer to buy this famous pigeon, but although Robert appreciated the offer it was nevertheless politely refused. Robert Ben did not want to sell his '48', nor did he have much of a disposition to sell pigeons at all. Mr Kijima left empty-handed.

But, as happens in life, things didn't stop there. Robert's eldest daughter, Virginie, pointed out that it was a great deal of money and the pigeon, although a very good one, could still die the following day. Perhaps her father should reconsider his decision. Taking his daughter's advice, Robert contacted Mr Kijima and told him the pigeon was now for sale. There appears to have been something unique about the relationship between the man and the bird, reflected in the original refusal to sell the pigeon. The ideals behind such a decision were still alive and even now it seems he could not bring himself to take money from a bird that had given so much pleasure. A moral compromise was reached by which the proceeds of the sale were divided equally between his two daughters. It was they and not Robert who were to benefit financially.

This is a fitting end to the story of a talented bird that had flown its heart out. Robert did not benefit directly from the sale. There is a kind of moral hidden in here, perhaps relating to the quality of mercy and being twice blessed. Perhaps it is about feeling sufficiently blessed by the life and career of such a pigeon that to profit again could be considered insultingly ungrateful. Whatever it is, the story of a great pigeon, its owner and his two daughters is only likely to be repeated once every hundred years, statistically that is.

CHAPTER 6

Alan Darragh

Cullybackey, Co. Antrim, Northern Ireland

BACKGROUND

In mainland Britain Alan Darragh is hardly known; in mainland Europe he is not known at all. His name is known to only a minority of investigative fanciers who, in their wisdom, have made it their business to identify the best fanciers based on what they have achieved and the place they fly. Being good but unknown is not unusual, but a regular phenomenon in modern Britain and a symptom of our system. Most fanciers everywhere receive their vital information not from results but from advertising and publicity. Alan Darragh does not publicize, though he maintains an informative website. He is in pigeon racing purely for pleasure, and this makes him a revelation to those who find him.

Alan Darragh, a busy man.

For more than forty years Alan has been building a family of pigeons based on the best long-distance performance pigeons that Ireland can produce. We use the word 'produce' but do not infer a production line. Only a meagre number of good pigeons fly successfully from France into Ireland every year. They are rare pigeons and Alan knows all about birds of this quality. Even though he is an all-round racing man, from the start he has based his work on the testing of pigeons to meet the Irish need for long-distance performance. Long-distance pigeons are still the basis of his strain and still win at all distances.

From a Small Island

Ireland is still relatively small enough for those who live there to know who is who and who is doing what. Nevertheless Ireland is rich enough in talent to produce outstanding pigeons of world class. The route the pigeons fly is probably the most difficult in Europe since they have to cross two stretches of

'Swallow Brae Surprise', Winner of the Old Bird National Fourges 2003, flying 502 miles. Photo: © Copyright Sid Collins

Independent Ranger; INFC King's Cup winner 1986. Photo: © Copyright Sid Collins

sea to get home. Difficulty of this kind induces brave and determined pigeons.

Ireland has another advantage that has largely disappeared on the British mainland. Irish pigeon racing is big and united. Both the Irish National Flying Club for the whole of Ireland and the NIPA (Northern Ireland Provincial Amalgamation) for Northern Ireland ensure hot competition and a regular supply of champions. It is remarkable that Irish pigeon racing has been able to keep it this way, despite the location rivalry that tends to split clubs in other parts of the world. Ireland has been able to

Swallow Brae Dawn 1st Section 2nd Open Irish National Flying Club Redon 2002. Photo: © Copyright Sid Collins

produce outstanding pigeons and outstanding fanciers largely from raw material inside Ireland itself. Alan Darragh and his pigeons are undoubtedly good examples.

THE INTERVIEW

The Start

How old are you and when did you first start playing with pigeons?

I am now fifty-eight years of age. I flew my first race in 1961, that is forty-five years ago, while I was still at school. The gist of the story was that my father brought home two pigeons and said they were mine, but in truth he had an interest in them as well. He had just come out of the Royal Marines after serving for twenty-two years. Since he had joined up straight after leaving school, he was still a relatively young man when he came out. He then joined the Post Office here in Northern Ireland and did another seventeen years in a second career. He ended up with two pensions, one from the Marines and another from the Post Office. When he left the services I think he was more than ready to settle down and have a hobby connected with home. Of course, there is nothing better than racing pigeons to keep you connected with home. That was how he was thinking at the time, even though by necessity we started as keen, but absolute beginners, feeling our way step by step.

In our house 'pigeons' became something to be talked about, a topic of conversation. I was the one with ambitions to move on. I read all I could and studied all the theories current at the time, 'eye sign', 'feather quality', 'wing theory', 'yellow and buff feather' and all the rest. I think I was the curious one.

Pigeons for Fun

When you first started with pigeons did you go immediately to long-distance birds or did you start with sprint pigeons?

I still like to race pigeons for fun, both short and long races. My view of the different type of racing is that if it is a 320km (200 miles) race I know I am going to clock. I may be late or I may be early, but I am almost certain to clock. It's different when it comes to racing from France with sea crossings as part of the course. After crossing first the English Channel and then the Irish Sea, just to see one coming home brings joy and a deep sense of satisfaction. Just to get one and know you are in the clock with a pigeon that has done such a thing is a relief and thrill at the same time. When you 'Are

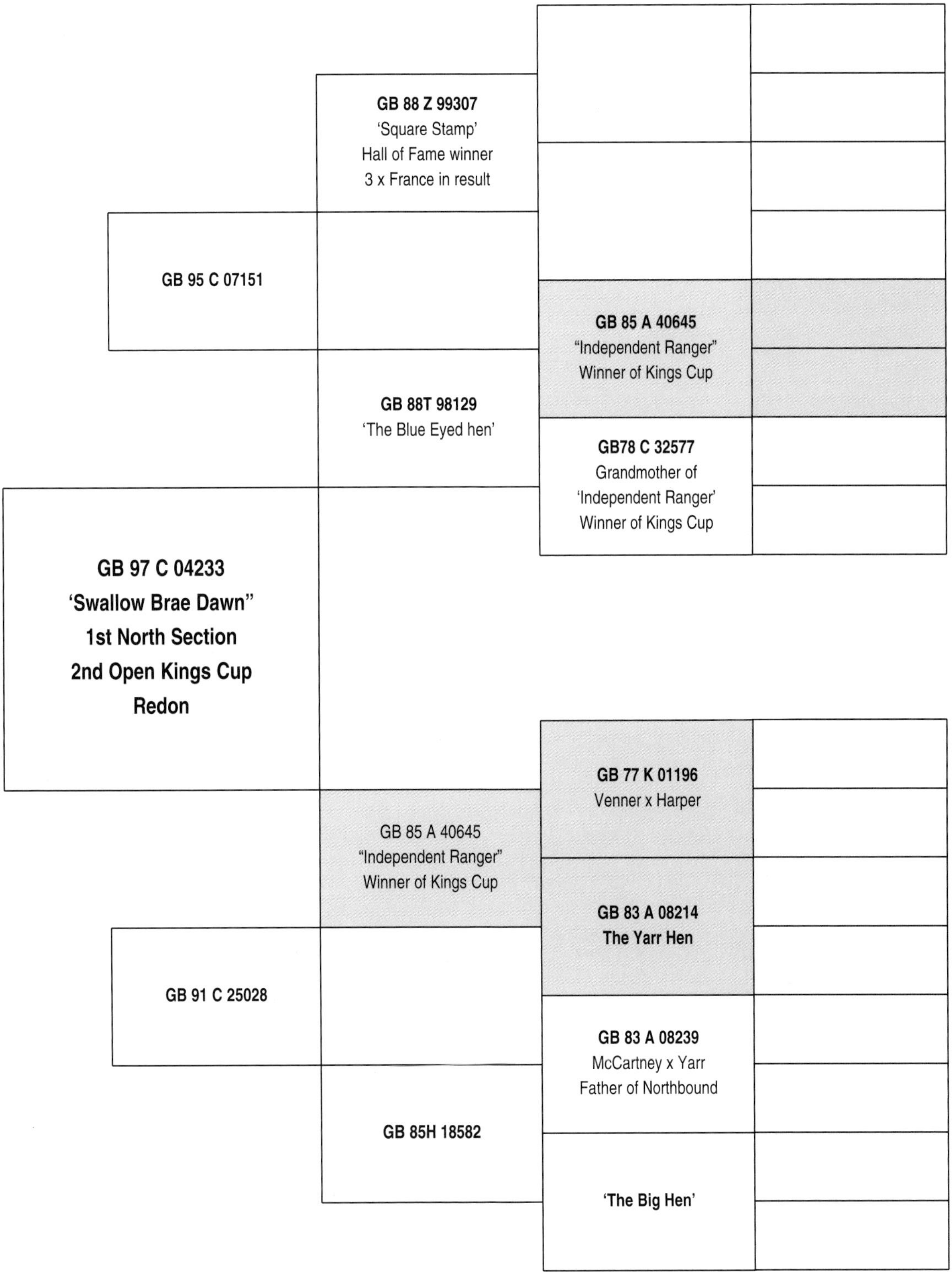

GB 97 C 04233
'Swallow Brae Dawn"
1st North Section
2nd Open Kings Cup
Redon

- **GB 95 C 07151**
  - **GB 88 Z 99307**
    'Square Stamp'
    Hall of Fame winner
    3 x France in result
  - **GB 88T 98129**
    'The Blue Eyed hen'
    - **GB 85 A 40645**
      "Independent Ranger"
      Winner of Kings Cup
    - **GB78 C 32577**
      Grandmother of
      'Independent Ranger'
      Winner of Kings Cup
- **GB 91 C 25028**
  - GB 85 A 40645
    "Independent Ranger"
    Winner of Kings Cup
    - **GB 77 K 01196**
      Venner x Harper
    - **GB 83 A 08214**
      The Yarr Hen
  - **GB 85H 18582**
    - **GB 83 A 08239**
      McCartney x Yarr
      Father of Northbound
    - **'The Big Hen'**

Pedigree Swallow Brae Dawn.

The Swallow Brae range of lofts has been built up over the years to equal the ambitions and development of the strain. Photo: © Copyright Sid Collins

In' you then want to see how early you are. If you are really fortunate, perhaps another pigeon comes to double your pleasure. There is a deep satisfaction to this type of endurance racing, but I get fun out of both types of racing and enjoy both in their own particular way.

The Stock

When did you buy your first long-distance stock?

The very first pigeons that came were long-distance stock – we were long-distance orientated from day one. They were from Old Irish stock, a pair of late breds from a Mr French off his super pair of pigeons that had just won 1st and 2nd from Dinard in the Old Bird Derby race. These were the original pigeons my father bought for me. Other pigeons came from Sam Moore and the Moore family. They were local pigeons from Ballymena but had certainly done well from France. Later I also had pigeons from Billy Erwin that were direct children from his pigeon 'Moonlight Mannequin', the 1968 King's Cup winner from Nantes. You could say that at this time I was collecting together the best pigeons I could from the local area. There is still a trace of 'Moonlight Mannequin' in my pigeons today. She was another 'purple' pigeon. She flew sixteen-and-three-quarter hours on the wing from France the night she won the Kings Cup. All these were truly great individual pigeons.

Yarr and McCartney

After all this I actually bought myself, with no help from my father, an inbred son of McCartney Bros of Moira 1959 King's Cup winner from Redon. I also bought a direct pigeon from Yarr's of Crumlin number one stock hen. In those days I couldn't have afforded such a pigeon. Just to tell you the story, Stanley Calvert was a multi-millionaire builder who had a burning ambition to win the King's Cup. He went to Yarr's and gave them four or five hundred pounds, a lot of money in those days, for their top stock pigeon. Unfortunately Stanley Calvert fell downstairs and was killed. Following this fatal accident all of his pigeons were then offered for sale by auction. The hen he had previously given so much money for was nine or ten years old by this time. I bought this hen at the sale.

The auctioneer, Jack Irvine, who was himself second in the King's Cup, said to me, 'Alan, you have bought the best hen in the sale. If you had not bought her I would have done so, even though she is so old.' I think he did not bid against me because I was young and enthusiastic. That is how I came to buy her, but the story does not end there. This nine-year-old hen I bought at the 'Calvert' sale is the grandmother of my 1986 King's Cup winner 'Independent Ranger', the pigeon that has had the biggest breeding influence in my loft up to this time.

Good Blood

So in the early days of your loft you brought all these good pigeons together and bred from them to form a family. Did you pair them in any particular way? Did you have a plan to develop them or was it just a haphazard joining together of good pigeons?

In those days we were always arguing about things like 'eye sign'. Nowadays I don't have so much interest in it, but I do know all about it. There is one thing I can say about this early stock. All the pigeons carried great feather quality, they all carried good wings and all had great balance. They were just good pigeons. Also at this time we had a pigeon that was very well bred down from these basic pigeons. To be honest I was not in love

'Champion 05', 1st Open NIPA Inland Derby 1988 from Skibbereen. Photo: © Copyright Sid Collins

with this pigeon, but my father said we should keep it because of its breeding. The upshot of it was we sent it to France and it came home a week or ten days late. The following year we sent it again. It was a very hard race and there were only eight pigeons on the day. Next morning my father shouted to me while I was still in bed, 'It's good weather, there could be pigeons this morning.' It made me laugh because this blue cock was the only one we had entered in the race and I had written it off even before it was sent. Suddenly a shadow crossed my bedroom window. I shot out of bed and sure enough it was this blue cock. Our pigeon was 9th open, the first to be clocked the next morning in the Friendship National from France. That cock was a grandson of the French pair of late breds we originally started with. Even though this pigeon was not the best of handling he was still perfectly bred. I always maintain that blood will sooner or later come out. It may miss a generation but, sooner or later, if you have the good blood it will come out. Possession of good blood is more than just important. It is absolutely essential.

Proportions of the Cross

Since those times have you used different birds for a cross, and have you tried any more imports?

I suppose I am like any pigeon man. I love trying different pigeons but I always keep my basic family intact. Within my basic family I have about five or six pairs that go together regardless. These pairs I usually pair Uncle to Niece or Aunt to Nephew to keep the family going, but if I read about someone who has had a great performance I usually try to buy a late-bred hen of such a pigeon for an experiment. The first of this cross is of course half and half, 50 per cent mine and 50 per cent the import, but I love to eventually have a mating that has three-quarters of my own basic family and a quarter of the cross. I have discovered over the years that five or six of my top racers that have flown and scored up to 600 miles are of this proportion. If afterwards I breed from these pigeons then the proportion goes down, with only an eighth of the cross left. This means you have the benefit of hybrid vigour but not the dilution of good qualities. In time the cross has largely disappeared and has been absorbed into your own family. This breeding system of crossing into an already existing family of known good-quality pigeons is a super way of breeding. Providing the basic family is always superior in numerical strength it allows your breeding policy to be ongoing and almost last forever. That is, of course, providing regular testing takes place to ensure the survival of the fittest within the colony. Performance and testing is at the heart of everything: if momma trots and papa trots, the baby has to trot. My best performance pigeons go to my best performance pigeons. If at the same time I happen to be mating aunt to nephew or uncle to niece that is even better.

The Sea Test

Obviously Northern Ireland is a special place and the conditions for long-distance pigeons are extreme. Would you try pigeons from other places, perhaps from England or the Continent?

Over here if I get a pigeon that has flown long distance into Ireland I know that this particular pigeon will stick its head into the sea, but if I bring in pigeons from England, the Netherlands or Belgium then 75 per cent of these pigeons will not take the Irish Sea. Some may take the English Channel, but when pigeons are tired and have to tackle the sea from the Bristol Channel to Ireland most turn back towards the land and will not tackle the extra crossing. If a pigeon turns up at three or four o'clock in the afternoon ready to fly on and he knows (I believe they do know) that he has 100 miles of cold water to fly, it takes a pigeon with super guts to attempt it.

Van Wildemeersch

So would you say that most of your successes, most of the great pigeons you have had over the years, have come from Irish pigeons?

I have tried many English, Belgian and Dutch pigeons – mostly hens from the good pigeons, I might add. Almost all have failed, but the one pigeon that did succeed was a direct pigeon I got from Van Wildemeersch called 'The Blesse Cock'. The first year we bred from that cock we took four of his youngsters to the Channel as young birds and all four came home. We have never done that before or since with any of our other Continental breeds.

Do you have any preference whether the pigeons you import or try to cross with your breed are hens or cocks?

I have no preference – a good pigeon is a good pigeon. To me it makes no difference. I race hens and I race cocks.

How long would you give a new cross before you decided it was no good and you had to clear out the lot?

As a rule I don't let that many in that I have to clear the lot out. Most of the time I am working with one pigeon, so nine times out of ten I am

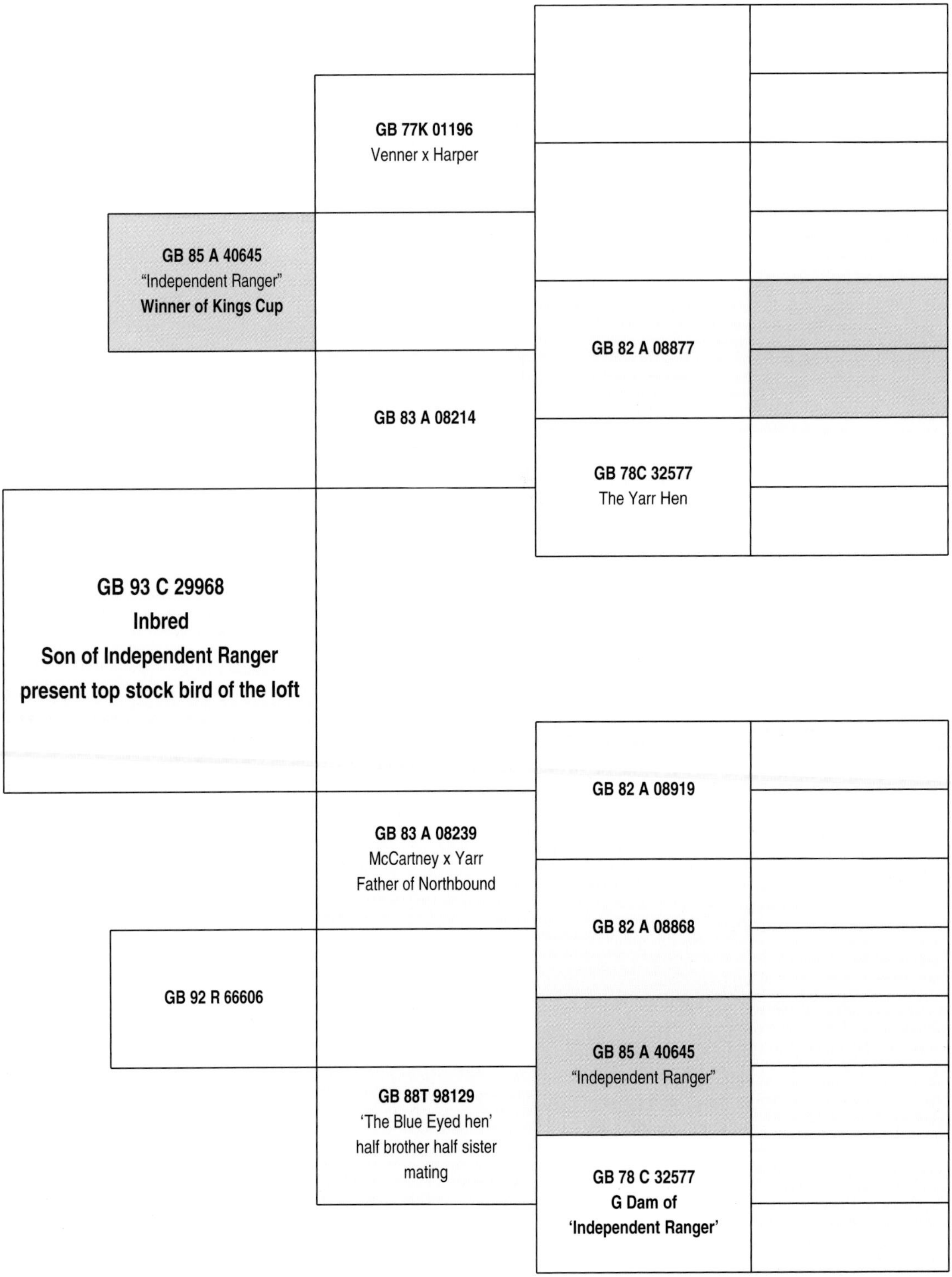

GB 77K 01196
Venner x Harper

GB 85 A 40645
"Independent Ranger"
Winner of Kings Cup

GB 82 A 08877

GB 83 A 08214

GB 78C 32577
The Yarr Hen

GB 93 C 29968
Inbred
Son of Independent Ranger
present top stock bird of the loft

GB 82 A 08919

GB 83 A 08239
McCartney x Yarr
Father of Northbound

GB 82 A 08868

GB 92 R 66606

GB 85 A 40645
"Independent Ranger"

GB 88T 98129
'The Blue Eyed hen'
half brother half sister
mating

GB 78 C 32577
G Dam of
'Independent Ranger'

Pedigree of son of Independent Ranger.

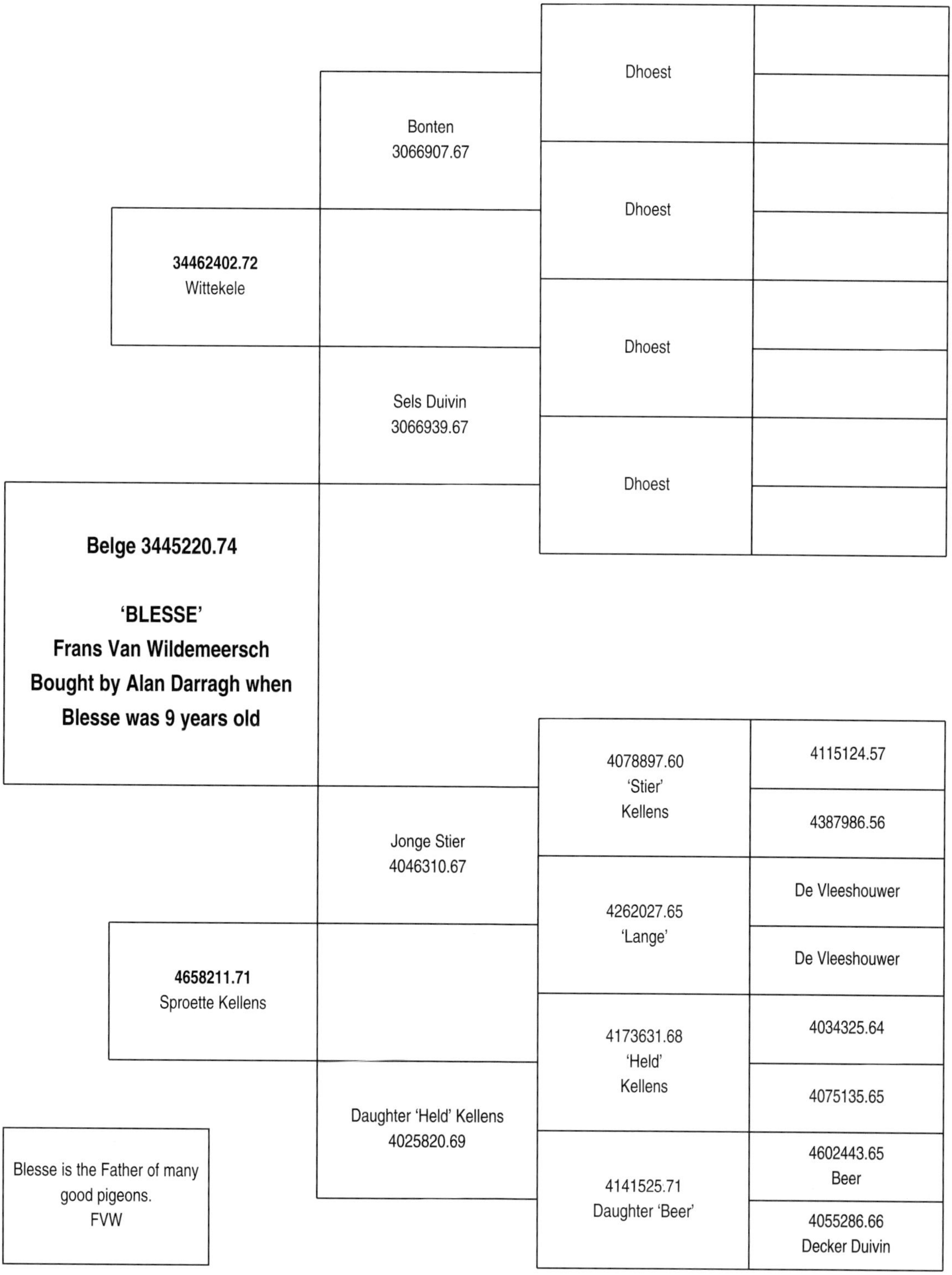

Dhoest

Bonten
3066907.67

Dhoest

34462402.72
Wittekele

Dhoest

Sels Duivin
3066939.67

Dhoest

Belge 3445220.74

'BLESSE'
Frans Van Wildemeersch
Bought by Alan Darragh when
Blesse was 9 years old

4078897.60
'Stier'
Kellens

4115124.57

4387986.56

Jonge Stier
4046310.67

4262027.65
'Lange'

De Vleeshouwer

De Vleeshouwer

4658211.71
Sproette Kellens

4173631.68
'Held'
Kellens

4034325.64

4075135.65

Daughter 'Held' Kellens
4025820.69

4141525.71
Daughter 'Beer'

4602443.65
Beer

4055286.66
Decker Duivin

Blesse is the Father of many
good pigeons.
FVW

Pedigree of the Wildermeersch pigeon Blesse.

working with a new import that is crossed with mine. So in the first year of racing as young birds, if four or six from such a mating are taken to the Channel, and if they don't come back, I don't have to bother about clearing them out. Racing does it for me. On the other hand, if they do come but they are not early, I mark it down as a fault of my own. I tend to think it is up to me to get this particular pigeon in better order the next time I send it.

If a pigeon were brought in to cross with your own family, how old would they have to be before you could judge the cross to be worthwhile?

When we bought 'The Bless' it was out of the Wildemeersch stock loft and was ten years old. We will not say how much we paid, but the next year a fellow fancier from here in Ireland paid a four-figure sum for a daughter of this pigeon.

Pigeons Past their Best

Presumably you have made mistakes over the years. Have you bought pigeons that have done you little good?

That is a fact, but a lot of my best imports that have bred some of my best breeding pigeons have been nine and ten years old when the loft that bred them and sold them to me though they were too old and no longer useful. Sometimes I have only managed to breed four or five youngsters off these relatively old pigeons, but in many cases one of those four or five have turned into a goldmine for stock. You could say I was just buying as good a blood as I could get, regardless of age.

Racing

How do you treat young birds in the year of their birth? What is expected of them at this time?

2nd Open INFC Young Birds. Photo: © Copyright Sid Collins

The best way I can describe it is this: if they don't go to school when they are young they are not worth much to me. They must learn when they are young. The young birds must go to every race and all of them must go to a race of 400km (250 miles) plus. Nine or ten of them go to Penzance, which is 530km (330 miles). At least half of my youngsters will go to the Channel as youngsters. The other half will go to Skibbereen, a race point down in the extreme south-west of Ireland. It is a distance of a little more than 250 miles to my loft.

Expectations

You have already told me you do not breed many late breds. Is that to fit into your policy of testing the birds when young?

I only breed the occasional late-bred when it is of very exceptional breeding. Most of the time I do not entertain them. I might buy the occasional late bred off top performance pigeons to experiment with as a cross, but usually you will not see a late bred in my loft.

What do you expect of the yearlings?

I expect the yearlings all to do well on the channel across the Irish Sea. Here we have six or seven channel races from England or France. I expect the yearlings to be in two or three of those races every year. Some will go to the Yearling National from Sennen Cove in Cornwall over 480km (300 miles). If they don't perform well and come across the channel at that stage, then they are not likely to come when they are two and three years of age out of France.

What do you expect of two- and three-year-old pigeons?

As I said earlier, I am one of those fanciers that wishes to race from day one. I am not one whose sole objective is to race the channel or to perform only in the long races. A typical situation might involve two brothers: one is set up to race early in the season in the shorter races, while the other brother, bred in exactly the same way and given the same work as a two-year-old, might be given only a couple of inland races and set up to race from France from 800 or 960km (500 or 600 miles) in June or July.

So does the same family of pigeons do both the short races and the long races?

That is correct, but that is more down to the management and how I treat them than it is due to the individual pigeon.

'West Bound Lady', 1st West Section 9th Open SNFC Nantes (600 miles) for G. Rankin of Blantyre, Scotland – One of numerous examples of a Darragh pigeon winning for other fanciers. Photo: © Copyright Sid Collins

Do Looks Matter?

Is there any physical attribute you particularly look for in a mature pigeon? Are you looking at the wing, the throat, the head, a particular shape of the body or what?

If you pay attention to the ten-point 'International standard' of judging a pigeon and use that as your guide, you are likely to make better selections. I am not saying that a pigeon with all ten points in the International standard is necessarily a better pigeon, but if you take this standard as your guide it will be easier to get a good race from a pigeon with ten points.

When examining a pigeon in your hand and it is deep, or has an ugly head or some feature that does not comply to the generally accepted sense of good looks, do you dismiss it at once or have any other thought?

A pigeon must have good feather. Good feather makes a good pigeon. Feather quality is essential in all pigeons.

You said you were into 'eye sign' at one time, but have since gone off the theory. What is your present opinion about such things?

Over here there are a lot of pigeons with good eyes, but in my experience unless a pigeon carries that hard brittle eye it will not come in the cold weather and fly for fifteen or sixteen hours. On the other hand, the rubber ring is not very heavy and we have clocked both big and small pigeons, so they come in all sizes and shapes. Good pigeons do not fit a regular format, but they must all have 'good balance', regardless of size. The wings and the tail must fit on the body of the pigeon in a balanced athletic way or they are not going to stay on the wing for fifteen or sixteen hours. The eye is another thing. I like the eye set in the head at least in line with the line of the beak or even higher. The best two eyes in the loft are your own.

Respiratory

Do you look down the throat of a pigeon to assess its respiratory condition?

For a start you shouldn't have to, but if you have respiratory trouble and have also studied 'eye sign', as I did forty or more years ago, the eye will be able to tell you if the pigeon has a respiratory condition. The eye always tells you. When a pigeon has such a condition there is always a bubble. Most people will tell you it is 'One-Eyed Cold', but when that bubble is at 9 o'clock, at the front of the eye close to the beak, then it is a respiratory condition. Respiratory trouble is down to bad ventilation in your loft. If the ventilation is OK then you will not have respiratory trouble. If an eye sign glass has any use at all, use it to see the health of your pigeons. The eye of a pigeon will tell you long before you will see it anywhere else in the bird. A bird will always have a bubble at 9 o'clock when it is having trouble breathing.

The Wing

Would you please tell us about some pigeons with outstandingly long wings that only mature later in life when such a pigeon has gained enough body strength to power the wing?

All pigeon fanciers like to see a good wing, but those of us who prefer long-distance racing like to see a lovely flowing wing that is perhaps a bit longer than normal, with a nice spread of the flights at the end of the wing. Some fanciers like the three end flights level with each other, though I prefer to see the end flight shorter.

Do you place a great deal of importance on the secondary feathers?

Oh yes, secondary feathers in the wing are very important. The secondary feathers have to be well covered – that is a must. If the wing is not well covered you are wasting your time. The cross-section shape of the wing is curved in a bow shape,

"Swallow Brae At Last" winner of 1st Friendship National 2006. Photo: © Copyright Sid Collins

where the bend of the bow is on top. It is this curve that gives drive and lift to the pigeon. You are wasting your time unless this part of the wing is efficient with good secondary flights without gaps. The pigeon will not be able to sustain flights over many hours.

Immunity and Treatment

Do you consider a high degree of natural immunity essential in long-distance pigeons?

You are asking me about illness. My father was a believer that if a pigeon were ill it must be killed. I believe that also.

Even though in modern life more potions and medicines are used than ever?

What you say is true, but I have to say most are wasting their money. I watch folk buying for worms; I watch folk buying for coccidiosis. All those things are easily cured. If your loft is dry you don't have coccidiosis to start with – it only comes in damp. As for worms, in the winter after the moult I throw all the drinkers out. I shut the doors of the loft and I don't go back for three days. The pigeons have neither food nor water. A worm of any kind can't live without being fed. You only have to do that and you don't have to treat for worms because there are none.

The only thing around here that is treated, and I consider it essential, is canker. A pigeon is only as good as its last drink. I have no control over where a pigeon drinks when it is coming back from a race or even around the loft. If a pigeon drinks from a puddle or from contaminated water it can catch canker. I would not go to a national race unless I had treated for canker beforehand. The minute the pigeons return from a race they are treated for canker. I often use five or six different canker treatments in a single year because of the different strains of Trichomonas, the canker protozoa. There is only one treatment that kills all known strains. It's made for humans, not for pigeons, and is called Flagyl. I prefer Flagyl S, a new one on the market for human use, but I also use other brands just in case.

Do you clean out the lofts on a daily basis?

I clean out twice a day. As you know, I am a joiner. The work van leaves here every morning at 7.45am. I get up at 6 o'clock every morning. I let the widowhood cocks out at this time. While they are exercising I go in and have my breakfast. After that I scrape out the widowhood cocks' loft. I take the flag down, and set out the feed, water and whatever else there is to do. I then put the hens out. My wife then lets the hens in at 9am. They exercise for an hour and a quarter. The same procedure happens at night, when the cocks are out again from 5pm while I clean out the lofts. The hens go out between 6pm and 7pm. This didn't happen tonight because I was meeting you at the airport. Unfortunately your arrival upset the routine a bit, but I can forgive you for that.

Happy Pigeons

Do you consciously work for contentment among your pigeons by making the environment something they are happy with?

Oh yes, that is essential. The environment must be a happy and comfortable place. If I go in the loft

Widowhood boxes – the lofts are cleaned out every day.

and see a pigeon that is not content, then I know that pigeon is not going to race. Generally the loft and the situation around the loft must be conducive to the contentment of pigeons – if not, the pigeon will tell you and make up its mind to move. It certainly won't race. The pigeons here have to be content, and content with you as the manager, or you are wasting your time.

Do you have any pigeons in your team at the moment that are wild or you just don't get on with?

I have pigeons here that would cut the face off me, but I still get on all right with them. They are only wild because they don't want me catching them or handling them. I respect that in their temperament. That is the way they are. Of course, I have to catch them to race them, but that is the only time I do it. Any other time I refrain from handling them at all. They are not frightened of me. It's just that they don't want me to handle them. Providing I respect their wish they will race, but if I tried to force them then the whole of their trust would go out of the window and they would no longer race with commitment. That would be the waste of a good pigeon. That is one of the reasons I would like the adoption of automatic timing, then I wouldn't have to catch pigeons. I always allow pigeons to have space. I have a rule of thumb for space: my formula is one pigeon to every four square feet of floor area.

Vaccination

What conditions do you vaccinate for annually?

Paramyxo, of course. I do not immunize for pox because here in Ireland we have not had pox for the last ten years. As for paratyphoid and illness caused by salmonella, you will only have that if you have a dirty loft. I do not have a need to vaccinate against paratyphoid.

If illness broke out in your loft, either from a stray or when the pigeons come back from a race, would you suppress the infected individuals, try to cure them or take another action?

Touch wood it has never happened. In order for strays to do any damage they must be there for at least five days. Because the widowhood pigeons are locked up except for exercise, this just does not happen. As for pigeons returning from races, quite often here in Ireland we get pigeons coming back from France possibly a week or two weeks late. Those pigeons are then put on a light diet and brought back to fitness. If after two or three days such pigeons do not respond and are not absolutely bouncing with health after their effort I want to know the reason why. The only thing those pigeons would come back with to annoy me would be canker. To answer your question more fully, even though I haven't had it, if it did happen and a pigeon returned with paratyphoid or a salmonella condition, the only thing to do would be to kill the individual and wipe out the illness before it took a hold. If you cure they will only breed youngsters that will breed it again.

Advice for a Novice

What advice would you give a novice attempting to build a team of long-distance pigeons?

Well, I really class myself as a novice (I'm still learning to this day), but if a new starter wants to begin to build a family of pigeons that has the potential to go on and race from the long distance then what he wants is some late-bred pigeons from a good racing loft. He should first of all choose pigeons from lofts in his own area that are performing the best.

Building a Strain

Should he go to one loft or more?

If he manages to become friendly with one loft and gets to know the breeding and methods of that loft he should go there. It may take him a couple of years longer to get success this way, but when success comes it will be more sustainable. This is the ideal, but in my experience new starters are generally overcome with enthusiasm, going here, there and everywhere wanting to soak up as much experience as they can in as short a time as possible. Enthusiasm is not a bad thing. It should be encouraged, but patience should also be encouraged. So unless the novice is an unusual person with an old head on his shoulders, and can cope with his own enthusiasm and exercise a little patience, perhaps it would be better to go to five or six lofts and get the best late breds he can from those lofts and try to build a family himself. He can then sit back and have a full sense of achievement. In my own case I get more fun out of actually breeding pigeons than I do out of racing them. My pigeons blended over forty years are 'Darragh's'. I don't have to run about shouting that my pigeons are Van der Espt's, or Busschaerts or something else. They are mine. I think that is where most of the fancy go wrong by wanting to sell other people's names. They want to buy and sell 'Brand Names'. Most are not interested in building a family of their own, but if they did they would get a greater sense of achievement. Instead of being on the commercial catch-up rollercoaster they would be creating something of their own.

BUYING PIGEONS

Is there anything you would advise the novice to avoid?

I daren't say it because you might write it down. I would go to racing lofts every time. If the loft has clocked out of an International race last year or the year before, I would want a youngster that's directly out of a pigeon that has raced and had a good performance. You are always better with pigeons directly off a performance pigeon, even if that pigeon is 50th in the race. Racing fanciers are interested in what happens to their pigeons after they have left their loft.

PATIENCE

Where should the novice be with his team of pigeons after three years? How long should it be before he can clock from France, for instance?

I have clocked in pigeons from France as yearlings but of course the novice can't afford to do that. He will not have the necessary strength in depth in his loft after three years. He must wait until he is in a position where he can afford to lose the pigeon he's sent. No fancier should ever send pigeons to any race, and never to France, when he can't afford to lose the pigeon. If a novice breeds thirty young birds and after the yearling stage he has fifteen left, then he is doing well. If he is on line with figures like this he can afford to send half of those fifteen pigeons to France as two-year-olds, preferably leaving a brother or a sister of the ones he has sent at home. A novice has only two years at the very least before he can send to France, but on the other hand a novice has to learn how to send them there. He has to learn how to condition the pigeons for such a journey. That is not easily learnt.

SYSTEMS

You fly both widowhood and pigeons on the nest. Do you have a preference for any particular system?

I fly 'Widowhood', I fly 'Natural' and I fly 'Roundabout'. I will fly a pigeon anyway I can get it to race. Widowhood pigeons, both cocks and hens, come into top order more easily. They eat less and are generally lighter, so when it comes to long-distance racing they are easier to prepare. But it is possible to mix systems and get the best from both. A pigeon is paired up, then put first on widowhood to gain fitness and can later be re-paired on the nest. From this it is possible to calculate whichever nest condition the particular pigeon prefers. This adds extra motivation to the overall good condition gained while the pigeon was on widowhood.

A perch that is only large enough to allow one pigeon to stand on it at a time. Alan Darragh opens this 'One Pigeon' hinged perch in the widowhood section the morning the birds are basketed. The cock that manages to claim it as his own is usually the first pigeon back on the following day. A useful method of choosing your pool pigeon. The perch in this photograph is in its 'open position'.

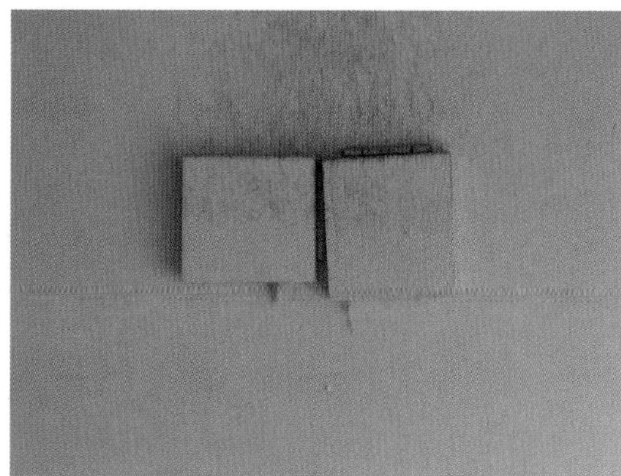

The same perch in its 'closed position', as it is every day except the day of basketing when it is used as an inducement for a dominant cock to show his dominance.

Yearlings are raced on widowhood as well. It is easier for me to race widowhood. I can let the widowhood pigeons out for an hour in the morning and an hour at night – they are never taken for release by car and yet they are ready for racing.

Are the hens you race on the nest?

No, they are also on widowhood. The only time my pigeons are on the nest is when it comes to the long races, when they are paired after first being on widowhood.

Preparation for the King's Cup

Can you give me some idea of the treatment you would give to a pigeon that is earmarked for the longest of races, such as the King's Cup or something equally difficult? What would you do during the run-up to such a race?

If I were getting an older pigeon ready for France, say a pigeon that's three, four or five years old, I would realize there is no point in starting with such a pigeon in the first two or three races. Experienced pigeons such as these have to be held back. What you then do is bounce them in at 200 or 250 miles for their first race. This you can do with experienced pigeons. The experience of this direct jump to 250 miles shocks them a bit, but the work they have to do just to get home brings them into condition. I then bring them back and toss them or race them regularly from 100 miles. Experienced pigeons treated in such a way can then be sent to France with confidence. They are fit. They are motivated. They are in good condition, but nothing has been taken out of them.

Carbohydrate Loading

Do you use herbs such as garlic?

I do use garlic – I like garlic myself. I use garlic after the pigeons return on Saturday, Sunday and Monday. How I do it is this? I press two cloves of garlic into a drinker with a garlic press. I push the cloves under the water while holding the press. That way all the goodness goes into the water.

What do you do in the final week before basketing for a long and important race? Do you give peanuts or what?

My pigeons love peanuts, they will run after peanuts just as most pigeons will. But I do the reverse. Five days prior to basketing I feed them barley or depuritive for two days. At the five-day stage they are near enough ready for the race. They do not work, they just rest. At this stage I do not want the muscle extended or hurt at all. They then get barley for two days. After the barley I load them for three days with carbohydrate.

I suppose you mean maize?

Maize is something everyone talks about, but it doesn't have to be maize. You can feed carbohydrate seeds if you wish. When pigeons are fit and ready to go to a long race they will not eat, but if I feed my pigeons depurative for two days they become hungry. They are then hungry enough to eat as much as they can for three days. It is this store of strong food that fuels them for the race.

After the Race

When a pigeon returns from a long race, do you give anything to aid its recovery.

The sooner you bring them back up to good condition the better. They get glucose. They get honey. They are fed groats. I have Volumen and honey mixed in the water at the same time. When a pigeon has done sixteen hours on the wing, or perhaps twenty hours if they come next morning, I give them as much as I can to get them over their ordeal and back to fitness.

How long is the hen allowed to sit with the cock after such an effort?

After a race like this I never take the hen away again for the whole season. The pigeon has done its job for the year. Most of my pigeons that go to the last race are already paired. Be it cock or hen, they have raced widowhood for most of the year but have been paired up for the last race. If it is a widowhood cock that has been raced and he returns a bit down, then I allow him to have his hen overnight and have it taken away the next morning. It all depends on the effort and the condition of the pigeon.

Winter Treatment

Are the pigeons separated during the winter?

I can't get my pigeons separated quickly enough. I want them through as good a moult as quickly as I can – I want them ready for the next year. The moult is the most important time of the year. They must have a good set of feathers for the following season. The feather I grow in September and October is the feather I have to race with the next year.

Is there any special feed you give them to help the moult?

I am a great believer in barley. Barley grows great feather. So when pigeons are moulting it is essential there is barley in the mixture.

Pairing Up

When do you pair up?

I would like to sometimes pair earlier, sometimes later, but my pigeons are always paired in December. The whole lot, apart from a few odds and ends, are paired in December, including the pigeons that are earmarked for France in July.

Here is the trick. When the youngsters are fourteen days old I take the hen away and the youngster away. I put the hens and one youngster in the Young Bird loft and let the cock feed the other youngster in the widowhood loft. The hen rears one youngster in the YB loft and the cock rears the other in the nest box. You are now interviewing me in May and my widowhood cocks haven't dropped a flight yet. They will begin to drop their flights when I want them to begin. When the big races are coming around my cocks will all begin to drop their first flight feathers, but if you let the hen lay after rearing that starts the moult immediately. The secret to this is not to let the hen lay. So my cocks are further bonding to the box by feeding a youngster and I have done nothing to start the moult. This means my cocks will not see another youngster until they feed a late bred or they are feeding a youngster prior to going to a long-distance race. After the cock has fed the youngster the nest box is scraped out; the bowl is turned over and the cock is on widowhood from then on. He then starts to fly. He wants to rake the skies, he wants to get fit – and it saves me money on petrol going up the road.

Is there any special food you give them before pairing up?

My pigeons are fed mostly barley during the moult, but for a fortnight to ten days before pairing they get some good strong food, mostly a breeding mixture.

What to Look for When Pairing Pigeons

What physical characteristics do you look for or want to compensate for when pairing up the birds?

I like the eyes to be balanced. Because I inbreed a bit in my family of pigeons the hens tend to get smaller and the cocks tend to get larger, so I try to take that into account and compensate for it. When I am pairing the pigeons I go as far out in terms of relationship as I can. Now as regards 'eyes', the classic method is to pair a 'violet' to a 'yellow' eye, but in a whole lot of cases I often pair a yellow to a yellow or violet to violet. If I get the pigeons I like and the performance I like, then I pair them together regardless. Performance matters above everything.

The Environment

How did you manage the construction of your lofts? What was in your mind when you built them?

Well, all my lofts used to be flat roofed. 'Widowhood One', as we call the main loft around here, is fully insulated. The walls and roof are insulated and when the sun hits that loft it is approximately 60° Fahrenheit. If it gets warmer than that, I open a small ventilator in the bottom front of the loft. In the other lofts I have used pan tiles on the roofs. These are mainly young bird lofts and July racing lofts. The form comes later in these lofts. To race early and have good form you must have a steady temperature. I used to have three lofts, but I sold two of them when I moved. The two fanciers who bought these lofts from me have since become good fanciers. I think I contributed in part to their success, but you are never satisfied with the lofts or the construction. You always wish you could do something to improve things. If I were going to build lofts again I would go back to glass-fronted lofts with one small ventilator in the bottom.

The magnificent view from the lofts across the countryside. No doubt the pigeons also love the environment at 'Swallow Brae'. Photo: © Copyright Sid Collins

The 'Ventilation Grill' which controls the temperature in the loft.

The thermometer, which tells Alan when to use it. (The average loft temperature is 60 degrees Fahrenheit.)

Numbers

How many pigeons do you have in your race team and how many at stock?

I have sixty pigeons in the race team and twenty pairs of breeders. Every year I breed ninety to a hundred young birds for myself.

Would you like to have more pigeons or are the present numbers enough?

I would like fewer pigeons. Really the numbers have crept up on me. I would like to go back to where I once was. It takes two hours in the morning and two hours at night. I work for eight hours at my job, so my day is taken up completely. I have little time for anything else.

Testing

Considering you are line breeding and have a team of related pigeons, is it necessary to have a minimum number for genetic variety?

When you are line breeding or close breeding it is essential to race them. You have to conserve the stamina and the vigour. Men tell me that close breeding multiplies the good qualities and so it does. That gives you a great advantage because a good pigeon can breed you a lot of good pigeons, but this breeding policy also multiplies the weak qualities. I had a successful loft for years using fewer pigeons. Now when I see that some pairs are not working out I try to compensate by breeding out that bit more so that they improve, but in truth you would do better with less and only breeding off the supreme one or two pigeons. If you turn up an absolutely top breeder by chance, that breeder will provide the loft with good pigeons for ten years and you don't need to find another for eight or nine years. But most fanciers get greedy, they oversell and often sell the one pigeon that could have been their next top breeding pigeon.

How many good producers have you had in your lifetime?

I would say I have been very fortunate. I have had champion '05' – nine or ten years ago he had bred over a hundred first prize-winners in this part of the world. After that I had 'Ranger' and 'Swallowbrae Lad'. They bred a pile of good pigeons. I would say over the last number of years I have had ten or a dozen good breeding pigeons. This is very fortunate, more than one can expect and more than most people get in a lifetime.

The Main Birds

Which birds have been most important to the development of your loft?

'Independent Ranger', 'Swallowbrae Lad' and 'Champion 05' are the best three. I suppose the top breeding pigeon today would have to be the inbred son of 'Ranger' from when 'Ranger' was crossed with the 3rd Open Lamballe hen, which was herself a daughter off 'Ranger'. This inbred son of 'Ranger' would have to be one of the best stock pigeons existing in the loft at the moment.

3rd Open 2nd Section Lamballe 2001.
Photo: © Copyright Sid Collins

Have you had any good racing birds that haven't bred anything?

Nearly all of my top pigeons have bred first prize-winning pigeons. This may be because they are line bred and go back to an aunt or a niece that is also inbred. I really can't answer that because the breeding policy of the loft is basically 'line breeding'. If this loft were a loft that relied exclusively on cross-breeding then of course I would come across pigeons that raced well but didn't breed at all. This is because those pigeons were the result of a cross and would not cross further. That happens in a cross-breeding loft but it does not happen here. Here I make sure that I conserve the basic good blood so that good related blood is always flowing through every pigeon. This means I can always cross the blood of good racers back into good related blood that is already there. The effect is to further reinforce it. I just don't get breeding 'dead ends' or breeding 'blind alleys'. I try to get a smooth upward progression of gradually improving pigeons and, I hope, more of them. Once a good racer is put to stock in this loft they all become pretty useful.

Pigeon Personality

Have any of your great pigeons had any behavioural traits?

Going back a few years I had a pigeon called 'Granddad'. This pigeon was a direct son of 'The Bless' of Van Wildemeersch. You asked if I kept late breds, well, this pigeon was a late bred. I decided to race him as a two-year-old. The first race he had a night out. The next race he was my third or fourth pigeon. The next race he won. I then moved house. I then won two NIPA sections with him to where I moved. I moved again and he won again. Each time I moved I broke him within two or three days. In each location he won. At his last location I showed him a peanut and he jumped out of his nest box and bit my young son Richard on the ear. He then came to me, I gave him the peanut and he went back to his nest box. When this pigeon jumped from Richard to me he was ready to race: he won the section at seven years of age on this system. This pigeon took over the whole loft. You could see the personality in him, he was just bursting with energy. Here was a pigeon that knew what he wanted and was prepared to race for it.

Family Life

How do you fit pigeons in with your family life and your job?

I say I'm just a fancier. I just like pigeons for fun. I'm not dedicated in any way.

[At this point Mrs Betty Darragh could not hold herself back. 'He's not just a pigeon fancier, he's a pigeon fanatic and has been so ever since I met him', she said with a laugh.]

The first ever article on this loft was written by my wife after we had won the National. When I let the hens out for their exercise, it's my wife who gets them in after I've left for work. I could not manage the pigeons without my wife and I couldn't imagine life without pigeons. My daughter was the secretary of the Irish National Flying Club. I should think the whole family has been connected with pigeons and pigeon racing at one time or another, but we are still a very strong family despite it all.

The Irish Contribution

Pigeon racing, especially at long distances, is an even greater challenge in Ireland than for those in the rest of the United Kingdom. By its very nature we can never know everything, but you have been more successful than most fanciers in the sport, so would you please tell us a bit about your personal philosophy, what governs your actions and why you do things?

I am a great believer that what you put into something is what you get out of it. I do not believe in luck in any shape or form. There is no such thing as luck. Luck is a superstition and I don't believe in superstition of any sort. Therefore I believe hard work, including the study of the subject, takes you some way to where you want to go. If I send to a 800km (500-mile) race and get a pigeon on the day I am delighted with it, but if I get one a week later I am equally delighted with that one, for I believe that late pigeon has perhaps worked even harder than the one I clocked.

A lot of people condemn a late pigeon. I don't. I say to myself, if I work harder on your condition next year and get you in better shape, you will come earlier next time. I honestly think that 90 per cent of pigeon fanciers don't give the pigeon enough credit and are reluctant to blame their own shortcomings on themselves. The long-distance pigeon is a kind of miracle in nature. No other animal can do what a pigeon does. A pigeon is less than a pound in weight, probably closer to 14 ounces. Some at their racing weight are only 13 ounces. There is no other animal or bird that can fly for sixteen hours and cover more than 500 miles in one day. Think of how a pigeon races from France to here. First he or she comes up the Cherbourg peninsula and crosses the English Channel, landing round about the Isle of Wight. The pigeon then has to cross England to somewhere near the Bristol Channel, from where there

'The 123', NIPA Bird of the Year 2003.
Photo: © Copyright Sid Collins

is about 480km (300 miles) of the cold Irish Sea to cross. Here in Ireland we reckon that every mile over the sea is equal to a mile and a half over land, because over the cold sea there are no thermal currents to provide uplift. The pigeon has to work by pure effort from its own resources to make land on the other side.

I have discussed this issue with the Belgians and the Scots. The Belgians once held a race from Skibbereen in Ireland to fly back to Belgium. The Scots did a similar thing. They tried it once and never came back when they discovered what the cold Irish Sea could do to them. We here in Ireland have no choice. We have been forced to breed pigeons able to cross the Irish Sea. All this tells me how nature has to be marvelled at and that it is able to rise to any occasion in certain individuals. Nature is able to gradually overcome such obstacles and be better for it.

I told you that my pigeons have Logan/Van Cutsem in my pigeons. Mr Carr of Dublin, known as 'Mr Carr the Brewery man', brought the Van Cutsem pigeons into Ireland in the early 1940s. He paid over £100 each for them – that was big money in those days. When these pigeons came off the boat at Dublin he took the ring numbers and then tossed them. He told Van Cutsem that he would only buy the pigeons that made it back to Belgium. By this strategy he made sure he had the right raw material to breed from here in Ireland. That is why the Van Cutsem pigeons have had such a big influence here in Ireland. A good friend of mine in the South of England told me you need 'Iron Pigeons' to fly into Ireland. What he said was right. I would say that 75 per cent of long-distance breeds or strains imported for stock into Ireland fail to leave their mark. Many thousands have been tried.

What You Put into It

Can we sum up by saying the pigeons give as much to you as you give to the pigeons?

Yes, every time. It is interesting to see how they progress every year and what influence your breeding and management has had on them. I would say any French race brings super performances just to get here at all. I think I have here in the loft now sixteen pigeons that have been in the top fifty places from France. I can show you two first-prize pigeons, five second-prize winners, thirds and fourths and so on. I am grateful to every one of them. They are all super pigeons.

CONCLUSION

Irish fanciers will no doubt read some of the other breeding ideas in this book and remark 'That wouldn't work here in Ireland' or 'That would have no chance over here'. They would be right, for the basic quality of successful pigeons that fly from France to Ireland is higher than in most other places. There are also not so many of them at any one time.

When it comes to getting pigeons to fly from France to Ireland very good pigeons are needed just to stand still. The pool of top-quality pigeons found in Ireland is not as large as that found on the Continent. Mainland Europe can expect huge races such as the International Barcelona. Huge numbers can also be expected to fly the course successfully. For these reasons, if they are so inclined, fanciers can use these numbers statistically in their quest for candidates for continuous

The Darragh family home.

George Barr and Jimmy Greer with Alan in the centre. George and Jimmy are frequent Saturday visitors to 'Swallow Brae'. When it comes to a bit of 'Banter'; they give as much as they get. George Barr timed a Darragh bred pigeon ahead of the man who bred it.

The NIPA Gold Medal – gained for timing in the same pigeon four times from France. The number of pigeons that have earned this medal is still in single figures. Photo: © Copyright Northern Ireland Provincial Amalgamation

crossing. Ireland does not have this luxury. It is for this basic reason that Alan Darragh and other fanciers use the 'line breeding' method, based on what they know about high-quality pigeons in their location that, in his words, 'will stick their heads into the sea'. The statistical method of analysing huge results is just not available to him, so he has no choice but to use the line breeding method.

This is not as bad as it sounds. In Ireland line-bred strains of pigeons that have emerged over the years build upon each other to produce more line-bred strains, which in their turn produce more line-bred strains. The best, or the ones that last, stand up to the testing over a difficult course. This is in effect using a history of fifty or sixty years of successful Irish strains to produce future Irish strains. This is real generation gene building, the survival of the fittest, in which over many years the fittest strains have quite often been related to those of similar quality.

Alan cites the original Van Cutsem pigeons and others as highly influential. An appreciation of the history of Irish long-distance pigeons is therefore essential if one is to grasp the full significance of breeding in Ireland, for history is the resource upon which they build. Where Robert Ben can study international results over three years, the same effect is achieved in Ireland by studying results over a generation.

It is probably for this reason that Ireland has always played a unique role in producing perform-

Northern Ireland Provincial Amalgamation

THE GOLD
FRENCH DIPLOMA

This is to Certify

that

A. DARRAGH, Cullybackey

obtained the following positions

1998	10th Open	2nd Sect. B	Dinard
1999	96th Open	16th Sect. B	St. Malo
2000	27th Open	4th Sect. B	Sartilly
2001	74th Open	12 Sect. B	Lamballe

"GOLDEN DREAMS", BLUE COCK, GB96C 03786

The 'Gold French Diploma Certificate' awarded to 'Golden Dreams' bred and raced by Alan Darragh. Photo: © Copyright Northern Ireland Provincial Amalgamation

The '465', winner of 25 first prizes and three times 1st section NIPA. One of the great pigeons Alan Darragh has owned and one that crosses in well with the long-distance pigeons. Photo: © Copyright Sid Collins

ance livestock, whether horses, greyhounds or pigeons. Pigeons are probably the latest example. When the rest of Europe finds out just what has been happening to Irish long-distance pigeon breeding, the value of top pigeons produced here will rise dramatically. Not that the likes of Alan Darragh are doing it with money in mind. It is the thrill of the chase, a particularly Irish turn of mind coupled with jesting against each other, that powers everything here. In Ireland you have to take a joke or you are a lost man.

How has he done it? What are the underlying factors at play here in the tiny village of Galgorm? One answer is that strain building cannot be done overnight, nor can it be done without a joke. Enjoy it. Relish the thought of clocking from France. It's this spirit that has contributed to what makes this part of the world special: it's called the survival instinct.

CHAPTER 7

Hagens Brothers

Achthuizen, The Netherlands

BACKGROUND

Ad and Rinus Hagens live on the island of Overflakkee, just south-east of Rotterdam. The area comprises a series of islands created by a wide delta of rivers idling their way across the flat plains of South Holland and Zeeland before finally flowing into the North Sea. A large part of the island of Overflakkee is below sea level and is protected from the North Sea by man-made dykes. On the night of 1 February 1953 the dykes broke and large parts of the island were submerged. That night many throughout Holland died. It was a disaster the people of Oude Tonge, Middelharnis and the surrounding villages will never forget. Ad and Rinus live in a small modern house in a tiny village called Achthuizen, a few kilometres from Oude Tonge, which was particularly affected by the disaster. They are ordinary people aware of the danger of flooding and also aware that they have to carry on with their lives. Pigeon sport plays a big part in the lives of the Hagens brothers. Long-distance pigeon racing always seems to sit comfortably with disaster: people who sense that their lives are under threat, for example in mining areas and fishing ports, seem to be attracted by the freedom of the pigeon and pigeon racing. Ad Hagens and his wife Sonja spoke to me and answered my questions at their home, where they keep the stock pigeons.

Outstanding Results

The Hagens Brothers have won more top prizes than most. If ever an ordinary family captivated the attention of the pigeon world it was the Hagens Brothers. They won the International Perpignan with 'Sonja' in 1996, 1st International Tarbes in 1998 with 'De Bauer 014', 1st International (hens) Barcelona with 'Sarina' in 1999 and 1st national St Vincent 2001 with 'Maxima'. In the course of six

The Hagens' family L to R – 'Rinus Hagens' – 'Ad Hagens' – 'Lucinda' his daughter holding their dog and 'Sonja Hagens' Ad's wife. It is easy to see the inspiration behind the names of some of their famous Hens. Photo: © Copyright Peter van Raamsdonk

'Sarina' One of the Hagens Brothers' famous hens – 1st International Barceona hens 1999. She flew Barcelona twice more and Perpignan twice. In the prizes each time she was sent. Photo: © Copyright Peter van Raamsdonk

'Sonja' – Another successful hen, this time 1st International Perpignan against 12,483 pigeons in 1996. Sonja is, of course, named after Ad's wife. Photo: © Copyright Peter van Raamsdonk

years they won two International races: 1st International hens (3rd International Barcelona) and the foremost annual Dutch National (St Vincent). It is a formidable collection of early prizes. The Hagens loft has been called the 'loft of miracles'.

Those who studied these things and sought to emulate their exceptional results quickly realized something special must be going on in Achthuizen. This was not a huge loft backed by tremendous resources. As International lofts go it was a relatively small affair, managed by ordinary men with ordinary families. The question of how an ordinary loft could produce such outstanding pigeons in such a short time attracted much attention. Good results always attract attention; super results demand it. The Hagens Brothers' results shouted to the world of long-distance pigeons, 'pay attention!' And the world did.

The Start

Ad Hagens was fifteen years of age when he and his younger brother Rinus started with pigeons. Ad is now fifty-four and Rinus is fifty-one. They started with short-distance flights from 70 to 700km (45–450 miles). At that time they had pigeons from a local man, Jan Nobels of Achthuizen. These were of two Belgian strains, those of Jos van den Bosch from Berlaar and Louis van Loon from Poppel. The Van Loon pigeons came from Jan Rozier from the university town of Leiden, Rembrandt's birthplace.

After a very successful period with this kind of racing the brothers began to look for a further challenge. In 1984 they bought their first long-distance pigeons from the Lalieu-van Dooren

'Bauer 014' – Another international first. 1st International Tarbes 1998 against 3,040 pigeons. Photo: © Copyright Peter van Raamsdonk

partnership of Thorn. These were a whole round of late youngsters from the breeders and came directly from the International 'ace' Jan Theelen of Buggenum, on the other side of the country near the border with Germany. Gradually the shorter flights were abandoned, the pigeons were sold and from 1989 the loft concentrated solely on long-distance racing.

Building for the Long Distance

In 1989 the brothers went to the Van de Weerdt brothers of Meersen and bought some late youngsters off the best pigeons they had. These pigeons were paired together in the stock loft and the offspring raced. The pigeons descended from the Van de Weerdt stock included such renowned names as 'Carcasonne', 'Gianni', 'Rijs' and 'Orlano'.

The Van de Weerdt and the Theelen pigeons

'Carcasonne' – the father of 'Sarina' – Carcasonne is a racing widowhood cock bird with many prizes. Photo: © Copyright Peter van Raamsdonk

'Olano' – a pigeon of the Van de Weerdt line.
Photo: © Copyright Peter van Raamsdonk

were then crossed. The result of this cross was unbelievably magic. 'Sonja', the International Perpignan winner, came from the cross as did 'Sarina', the Barcelona Hens International winner. 'Bauer 014', the Tarbes International winner, also came as a result of the cross between the Van de Weerdt and Theelen pigeons, as did others too numerous to mention. Undoubtedly the amazing results of this cross were more than could reasonably have been expected by even the most optimistic of fanciers. They were beyond the wildest dreams of the Hagens brothers or anyone else. International speculation was rife, offers were made and some of the best pigeons were sold.

The question on everyone's lips was whether the Hagens Brothers had sold their best pigeons and would they be able to replace them. Similar stories involving fanciers and the sale of champion pigeons have been told and re-told many times, with speculation over whether the loft would be strong enough to stay at the top once its best pigeons had been sold. Every story of this kind is fascinating, but the outcome is not always the same. The Hagens Brothers did not sell their best breeders.

Further Introductions

In 1996 the Hagens Brothers cooperated with the Brothers van Doorn of Someren. Pigeons that resulted from this included 'Pantani', '*Julio*' (3rd Nat St Vincent from 8,556 birds), 'Melinda' and 'Lisa'.

Still trying to strengthen the loft, the Hagens Brothers next went to the famous Brugemann Brothers of Assendelft. They bought sixteen pigeons, two of which were put directly in the stock loft. The remaining fourteen were raced and, of the nine Brugemann pigeons that were entered in the Barcelona International of 2003, five won prizes, so the introduction looked promising.

In 2005 the loft entered fourteen pigeons for the Barcelona International: by 17.36 on Sunday, the day after liberation, they had eleven pigeons home in the following times: 11.11, 11.37, 11.50, 11.53, 11.58, 13.11, 13.46, 14.18, 14.38, 14.53 and 17.36. In the Dutch National they were 34th, 74th, 106th, 118th, 127th, 317th, 424th, 531st, 598th, 663rd and 1443rd from 7,489 pigeons. The first pigeon home was from the line of the Brugemann pigeons, but many were the grandchildren of 'Sarina' and the Theelen pigeons. In the International 'Angelo', which had been 48th in 2003, was 236th, while the first arrival was 'Shafira', a Brugemann Brothers cross, with 71st place in the international result from 25,815 pigeons. Many of the others were children and grandchildren of 'Sarina', following the line from the likes of 'Rooie Kweker', 'Carcasonne' and 'Kweker 42', so the old blood still retained its power.

The strains of the Hagens pigeons since they first started with long-distance racing may be summarized thus:

Jan Theelen – (Kuypers Bros – Van Wanroy – Oude Champens – Hofkens – Oude Van Tuyn – Hermans etc)

Bros van de Weerdt - (Tossens Warsage – Emiel Matterne – Oscar Devrindt – Hector de Bou etc)

Bros Van Doorn – (Bros Kuyper Neer – Jan Theelen Buggenum)

Brugemann Brothers – H. Oostenrijk – G. vd Kuruk – Vertelman and son – Wim Muller – J Moerman

'Gianni' – a pigeon of the Van de Weerdt line.
Photo: © Copyright Peter van Raamsdonk

'Julio' – a three-times performer at national level.
Photo: © Copyright Peter van Raamsdonk

THE INTERVIEW

Selection and Early Training

Have you made any mistakes when you have bought pigeons?

Not everything has been successful. Despite taking every care in our original selection there have been a few mistakes. As soon as we find out imports are not working for us then the whole lot go, regardless of reputation.

When you start off with youngsters from imported stock, how much work must they do as young birds?

It is essential they go to races of 300km (185 miles). It does not matter whether they win a prize, but they must have the experience of the basket.

We do not breed late-bred youngsters. Everything must be bred early enough to experience the basket that year. We just cannot afford not to test our pigeons. Testing is the cornerstone of our policy.

How much work must the yearlings do?

The yearlings must eventually have two long-distance flights. Here in the Netherlands we have special long-distance races from Bordeaux and Bergerac for yearlings only. Bordeaux is approximately 840km (520 miles) and Bergerac is approximately 812km (505 miles). All the yearlings must go to these two races. I am pleased if they do well, but they do not necessarily have to win a prize. Providing they come back to the loft in a reasonable time they are allowed to stay and have another year. The long yearling races act as a kind of test to measure the breeding loft and also to test new pigeons. They can be difficult testing flights for yearlings. At this stage everything is a test of the blood. We are testing the stock loft as well as the race pigeons.

How do you treat two-year-old pigeons and what work is expected from them?

When the pigeons get to be two years old they are still not absolutely mature but their range is taken further. At the two-year stage they go to two long-distance races. They go to St Vincent, which is the main race in the national programme, as opposed to International races, and for the other there is a choice between Dax, Perpignan and Marseilles. A very few two-year-old pigeons will go to Barcelona. That is the longest and possibly the most difficult race. Barcelona is a race for really mature pigeons.

Is there any physical attribute you particularly look for in a mature pigeon? Are you looking at the wing, the throat, the head, a particular shape of the body or what?

We like soft silky feather on a medium-size pigeon; to us this is a sign of quality. We like to think the pigeon is well muscled. But all of this is not enough, so after we have looked at the pigeon we like to see it perform. The basket and how a pigeon breeds are better guides than supposed ideas about looks when it comes to selecting. Of course we like to study the pedigree, but a really good pigeon can be entirely unlike its brother or sister. One can be good but the other useless. That is not to say breeding has no purpose. It has, but it must be taken side by side with the results from the basket. If a pigeon is well bred and races well then it is likely to breed well. If a pigeon races well but does not have a good pedigree, then it is probably doubtful – either that or the pedigree may be false.

'Shafira' – a cross of the Hagens and Brugemann lines – 1st pigeon from Barcelona in 2005.
Photo: © Copyright Henk Kuijlaars

Everything has to be tested the whole time if only to spot our own mistakes. It is to be hoped we find we have done good things as well.

Medical Treatment

For what conditions do you treat the pigeons?

We treat the young pigeons for paramyxo. That is essential. For paratyphus we use a paratyphoid cure in the winter, but not vaccination. We treat all the pigeons for ten days with Parastop. There are some other things we do as well. For instance, when the pigeons have been sitting on eggs for six or seven days we treat them for trichomoniasis for seven days. We use a veterinary specialist for pigeons who lives in Genk in Belgium. He checks the pigeons and supplies all the advice and products we need for health and condition. We stick to his programme. The main thing is not to overuse medicines and, above all, not to treat unless they need it, but we do give a treatment for respiratory two weeks before really long races providing it is possible in the time; we do this sparingly, perhaps only once a year.

Do you clean out the lofts every day?

Yes, we do clean, but we have also covered the floor with beech wood chippings. We use this to keep the loft dry, but it also has other uses. Although we clean the nest boxes and perches, we do not have to scrape the floor. The time saved allows us to spend more time observing the pigeons and noticing anything that is going on socially between one pigeon and another in the loft. Observation is one of the main reasons for success in all lofts, but you must have time in order to do it.

What ideas do you have about ventilation and the environment?

We have double windows so that the pigeons are not exposed directly to the outside. The air in the loft comes in from above the heads of the pigeons through an 8cm (3in) gap between the wall and the roof.

Do you have any advice for a young fancier starting with pigeons?

He must first look for a local man who has been racing well for a long time. From this man he must buy a round of late breds. He should race these pigeons and also breed off them. After three years racing and breeding, and after he has gradually increased the distance he is flying the pigeons, he should then go to someone else who has a number of years' experience competing Nationally and Internationally and buy some more late bred pigeons. He should do the same with these as he has done with the first pigeons. After he finds which are the best he should cross some of them, but not all of them. After five or six years he should be ready to compete Internationally for the first time. The whole exercise is to build up two families of pigeons gradually, while at the same time learning how to race them. He will make some mistakes, but if he is observant and patient he will gradually improve to the point where he has some pigeons he can rely on. Of course, the pigeons must be tested at every stage of their lives, both for breeding and also for racing. That is the only way. If he is lucky he will find one pair of excellent breeders by crossing the two families. If he is very lucky he will find two pairs. If he does that he will be very successful for the next few years both nationally and internationally.

Do you fly both the 'natural nest' system and widowhood?

From 1989 to 1999 we flew both systems in tandem. At that time we had forty racing widowhood cocks and thirty racing couples on the nest. Although we have had a lot of success on widowhood with pigeons such as 'Carcasonne', 'Gianni', 'Rivaldo' and 'Bauer 014', we have now abandoned the widowhood system and are completely 'natural' with everything on the nest. We did it because by using the natural nest system we could race both hens and cocks. This not only tested both sexes but also provided us with double the number of pigeons. With our particular strain hens play a big part and can win early prizes. Examples of hens doing well include 'Sonja', 'Lucinda', 'Sarina' and 'Maxima'.

'Rivaldo' – Bordeaux specialist – 2nd and 7th Bordeaux 1998 and 1999 against more than 10,000 pigeons each time. Photo: © Copyright Peter van Raamsdonk

Maxima sister to the international winner 'Bauer 014' and herself a national winner. Photo: © Copyright Peter van Raamsdonk

The Yearly Routine

What is your yearly routine of pairing and splitting up?

The race loft on the 'natural system' is paired on 1 April and the breeders are paired in the middle of January. The race birds are allowed to rear one youngster per nest. After this has been reared and they are again sitting on eggs, the pigeons that are scheduled to fly in the first 'Fond' (long-distance race) are separated. It is calculated when these pigeons will be in a nest cycle where they have six- or seven-day-old youngsters for the first long-distance race. They are then paired accordingly so that they are in this nest position for their first race. Other pairs that are scheduled for later races are treated much the same. Sometimes it is necessary to send pigeons that are sitting about eight days. While they are at the race we put the eggs in an incubator and replace the ones they are sitting with pot eggs. After they return, as soon as we feel they are sitting once again we replace the pot eggs with the real eggs from the incubator. This rather complicated process is designed so that the hens do not lay many eggs during the season.

After the season is over the nest couples are allowed to stay together until early December. Then we separate them, the cocks staying in the compartment with the nest boxes, and the hens are put in a separate section with perches. In the cocks' compartment the nest boxes are closed at this time and perches for them to sit are hung in front of every box. They stay this way until 1 April when the nest boxes are opened once again and the pairs are allowed to mate. During the period of the moult they are given a lot of baths and have Tee (a herb mixture) defused in the water every day in order to encourage the growth of the new feathers, but herbs such as garlic are never used even in the racing season.

Training

Can you tell us how you exercise the race team and how long they must exercise?

The nest system of flying pigeons is time-consuming, but if you have the time and make the effort it is possible to get the hens and the cocks very fit. For instance, at 6am every morning the cocks are exercised around the loft for an hour. After the hour is up they are called in for their food and the youngsters go out from 7.30 until 9am. At 1pm in the afternoon the hens are exercised for an hour. After they have flown for the hour they are allowed to come into the loft on their own. In the evening at 5pm the cocks are again exercised for an hour. After the hour they are called in and fed. This routine lasts the whole of the racing season.

Breeding Numbers

How many youngsters do you breed each year?

About 80 early youngsters are bred and about 30 youngsters from the second or third rounds are bred. The early ones are expected to race up to 400km (250 miles). Generally we follow the 'Peeters of Genk' system of racing and training. Norbert Peeters is a vet from that area. When the pigeons return from a long race, for example, we give them a 'Peeters' recovery medicine to get the tired pigeons back to normal as soon as possible. The sooner they are normal the sooner they will be fit enough to train and be sent to further races. Another example of using the 'Peeters' methods comes before pairing, when they are given special stuff in the water for six days to get them into the

A modern racing hen 'Lorena' – 17th International Dax 2005 against 11,898 pigeons. Photo: © Copyright Martin Kwakernaat

best possible condition of fertility for breeding. We also use the 'Peeters' high-quality brewers' yeast on the food as part of their build-up for the long races. There are no secrets about any of this, all we are trying to do is give our pigeons the best possible ingredients for health and fitness when they are required to make their greatest effort.

Race and Stock Numbers

Can you tell us how many you keep?

Next year and, as far as I can tell, into the future we expect to race only on the nest. That is the natural system. We will have sixty nest couples including yearlings. That is 120 pigeons for racing. We have twenty-two pairs of stock pigeons here at the house. We breed 100 youngsters to race every year. That is the sum total of our whole structure and what is needed to fly long distances in the way we do it.

The Programme

Would you please give us some idea of the programme you race?

The long-distance programme is massive. Not only are there the home Nationals of the Netherlands but International races as well. All these races are at least 800km (500 miles). You need a lot of pigeons for such a programme because our loft is competing against thousands of fanciers from the Netherlands, as well as those from Belgium, Germany, France and now England in the International races. Competition is very hot. Some of the lofts are much bigger than ours and are better placed. Some are smaller than ours and specialize in one or two big races per year. Some, of course, fly much further than we do, so you can say they are in a worse position. But wherever you live it is always difficult and you can always fail when competing in such high-class competition. In a competitive situation like this it takes a great deal of effort just to stand still and even more effort to do well continually. There is no time to switch off and relax. The wind plays a part, of course, but even when the wind is not good for us we still expect to get pigeons. Good pigeons will always do well regardless of the wind. They may not be right at the top of the list but they will still do well. For instance, when 'Sonja' won the International, flying 1004km (625 miles) from Perpignan, a French pigeon was second flying 926km (575 miles) and a Belgian pigeon was third flying 899km (560 miles), so regardless of the wind, which could not have been good for all of them, they still did well because they were good pigeons. Even a German pigeon far to the east of us in the Ruhr was 8th International on that day. All these pigeons were good birds because they had the ability and fortitude to navigate on their own regardless of wind or the company of other birds. The whole purpose of our loft is to find birds of this quality. So far we have had more than our share, but it is a difficult thing to do and more difficult to keep doing it.

Which individual breeders have had the most effect on the foundation of your family of pigeons?

The 'Rooie Kweker', the Jan Theelen basic pigeon, cannot ever be underestimated. His contribution has been enormous, for his presence is in the pedigree of most of our top pigeons. He is the grandfather of 'Sarina', 'Lucinda', 'Bauer 014', 'Rivaldo' and 'Ricardo'. He is an absolute top stock bird that also breeds stock birds. I should also mention the pair '111' of 1989 and 'Sproetje 74', also of 1989, which bred 'Carcasonne', for here again we have a breeder that bred other breeders. 'Carcasonne' bred 'Sarina' (3rd int Barcelona and 1st hen), which has in turn bred a load of successful pigeons to perform right through to Barcelona.

There are others, of course: the '319' was mother of 'Rivaldo' and grandmother of 'Bauer 014' and 'Maxima', so she too was a breeder who also bred breeders. Up to now I would say these are the main ones, but we have others coming up that have yet to make the kind of history these have made. I hope they can do it. If they are half as good they will be very much worthwhile. We would say all the good breeders have bred pigeons for other fanciers, who in turn have raced well with them. Fanciers who have done well with our pigeons can boast five or six 1st National wins at the last count.

The Rooie Kweker – a foundation Theelen pigeon. Grandfather two international winners – Bauer 014, and Sarina. Photo: © Copyright Peter van Raamsdonk

NL 74 447636
De 636
Jan Theelen

78 934635
De 635
Jan Theelen

NL 76 584144
De l44
Jan Theelen

NL 84 180230
De Rooie Kweker
Jan Theelen
Grand Father of 'Sarina', 'Lucinda', 'Brauer 014', 'Rivaldo' and 'Maxima'

NL 67 857834
Ref 'C' Jan Theelen

NL 75 1472183
Klein d Oude 34
Jan Theelen

NL 71 1414252
Ref 'N' Jan Theelen

Pedigree of the Rooie Kweker.

'Britt' – one of the latest winning hens.
Photo: © Copyright Martin Kwakernaat

My pigeons are in the pedigree of this year's International Barcelona winner for Gerard Van Tuijl, for example. We are pleased how our pigeons have gone to other lofts and influenced the breeding in those lofts. It is good for us that our pigeons can travel and do well.

Which have been your best racers?

Well, 'Sonja' and 'Sarina' (1st International and 1st International hens Barcelona) were two of the best hens it is possible to have, but there have been many others, such as 'Rivaldo', 'Bauer 014', 'Maxima', 'Rijs the Goede 47' and 'Olano' to name but a few. I almost forgot Lucinda, which was 6th National Barcelona and 23rd International. Some of the latest ones are 'Britt' and 'Angelo' (NL 00.1764077), which has twice been high in the list from Barcelona. 'Lynn' (NL 00.1919549) is one of the really good red pigeons with Theelen in her. The cross with the Brugemann pigeons are now coming through. 'Shafira' (NL 02.1584714) is one of them. A lot of my good pigeons have been hens.

Did you notice anything special about these good pigeons when they were young or was it only their good performances that attracted your attention?

I think in the young pigeons I notice really good health and vitality. I don't think I notice anything else worth speculating upon. Speculation is very heavy on the nerves: it is better to leave it to the basket and actual racing than to special signs intended to show hope for the future. I am not that good that I can see exactly into the future.

How do the pigeons fit in with your family life. Are your wife and daughter interested in the pigeons?

[At this point Sonja Hagens answered] Lucinda and I are interested, but we don't do anything.

- **NL 95 1877800**
  'Sarina'
  1st Golden Barcelona ZLU
  1997 1998 1999
  1st Internat Barcelona Hens 6419p
  3rd Intenat Barcelona
  28,095p
  - **NL 91 2131301**
    'Carcasonne'
    13th nat Carcasonne 94
    1371p
    49 nat Pau 95 2156p
    52 nat Bordeaux Old 93
    - NL 89 1926111
      Bros Van de Weerdt
      Father 'Sonja'
      - **NL 82 1567890**
        Bros Van de Weerdt
        3rd nat Marseilles
        47 nat Lourdes
        - **N:84 313881**
          De Favoriet
        - **NL 84 314096**
          'liskouie
      - **NL 84 313862**
        Bros Van de Weerdt
        - **NL 73 1533348**
          'Oliepit'
        - **NL 78 1125854**
    - **NL 89 192674**
      Sproetje 74
      Bros van de Weerdt
      - **B 85 030**
        Zwarte Tossem
        Tossem Warsage Belge
      - **NL 81 433632**
        Bros Van de Weerdt
        - **NL 77 1927140**
          'De Pernienan'
        - **NL 73 1533330**
          Bros Van de Weerdt
  - NL 94 1357139
    Sister of 21st nat Barcelona
    93
    - NL 84 180230
      De Rooie Kweker
      Jan Theelen
      - **NL 78 934635**
        De 635
        - **NL 74 447366**
          De 366
        - **NL 76 584144**
          De 144
      - **NL 75 1472183**
        G Dtr oude 34
        - **NL 67 857834**
        - **NL 71 1414252**
    - **NL 88 1765025**
      M Van Geel
      Mother 21 nat Barcelona
      - **NL 87 8793062**
        Son of Mooi Oogie
        Martha van Geel
        - **NL 83 15951**
          Manke Poot
        - **NL 83 705045**
          Mooi Oogie
      - **NL 87 8793043**
        Half sister Vlekje
        Martha van Geel
        - **NL 79 1445731**
          M Van Geel
        - **NL 80 8009266**
          Dtr Dolle
          M Van Geel

Pedigree of Sarina.

NL 92 1120350
'Sonja'
1st Int Perpignan '96 12,551p
18th nat San Sebastian '95 1125p
35 nat Marseilles 944601p
94 nat St Vincent 11822p
109 nat Perpignan 4342p

NL 89 1926289
Bros Van de Weerdt
Father 'Sonja'

NL 83 1221695
De Kleine Blauwe
3rd nat Barcelona 89
27 nat Perpignan 87
42 nat Barcelona 87 etc

NL 82 1568065
Bros Van de Weerdt

De '500' E Matterne

NL 67 1001110
Father 1st nat Barcelona

NL 77 1927174

NL 81 433485
Dikke Rooi
Van de Weerdt
Flew Int Perpignan 7-14-99

NL 77 1927140
De Perpignan
3 x Perpignan

NL 67 1301812

NL 73 1533330
Bros van de Weerdt

NL 67 991325

NL 84 180237
Mother 'Sonja'
Jan Theelen

NL 78 934634
'G Son Oude 34'
Jan Theelen

NL 72 580548
De 548
Jan Theelen

NL 75 2003692
Dtr Oude 34

NL 78 934639
'Golden Breeder
Mother 'Dolle Greet'

NL 76 584099

NL 73 1355135

Pedigree of Sonja.

- **NL 96 2216014**
  'Bauer 014'
  1st Int Tarbes '98 – 5034p
  Brother of 'Maxima' 1st National St Vincent 2001- 31,537p
  - **NL 93 2627932**
    Father of Maxima
    Flew himself
    6 x National prizes include
    32 nat Dax 4620p
    - **NL 90 2441047**
      "De Goede 47"
      Brother of Rijs – Carcasonne etc..
      - **NL 89 1926111**
        Bros Van de Weerdt
        G Grand Mother
        'Bauer 14'
        - **NL 82 1567890**
          Bros Van de Weerdt
        - **NL 84 313862**
          Bros van de Weerdt
      - **NL 89 1926274**
        Sproetje 74
        Mother of Britt
        - **Belge 85030**
          Black Tossem
        - **NL 81 433632**
          Bros van de Weerdt
    - **NL 89 1241090**
      Mother of 9th Nat Tarbes 96
      20th nat Carcasonne 32 nat Dax
      - **NL 88 1764661**
        The Super 61
        25 nat Bordeaux
        - **NL 84 180248**
          Jan Theelen
        - **NL 84 180238**
          Jan Theelen
      - **NL 84 180247**
        Jan Theelen
        - **NL 00 584179**
        - **NL 00 934453**
  - **NL 95 1877718**
    Mother of
    Maxima Half sister of Rivaldo
    2nd Nat Bordeaux and 7th nat Bordeaux 32nd Nat Montauban
    - **NL 84 180230**
      De Rooie Kweker
      - **NL 78 934635**
        De 635
        Jan Theelen
        - **NL 74 447366**
          De 366
        - **NL 76 584144**
      - **NL 75 1472183**
        G Dtr Oude 34
        - **NL 67 857834**
        - **NL 71 1414252**
    - **NL 91 2131319**
      "De 319"
      52 Nat St Vincent 11822p
      173 nat Bergerac
      - **NL 84 180230**
        De Rooie Kweker
        - **NL 76 934635**
          De 635
        - **NL 75 1472183**
          G Dtr Oude 34
      - **NL 84 180237**
        Mother "Sonja"
        Mother of 1st Internat
        Perpignan 96 12551p
        - **NL 78 934634**
          G Son Oude 34
        - **NL 78 934639**
          Golden Stock pigeon

Pedigree of Bauer 014.

- **NL 99 2303041** **'Maxima** **1st nat St Vincent** **Sister of 'Bauer 014'**
  - **NL 93 2627932** **Father of Maxima** Flew himself 6 x National prizes include 32 nat Dax 4620p
    - **NL 90 2441047** "De Goede 47" Brother of Rijs – Carcasonne etc..
      - **NL 89 1926111** Bros Van de Weerdt G Grand Mother 'Bauer 14'
        - **NL 82 1567890** Bros van de Weerdt
        - **NL 84 313862** Bros van de Weerdt
      - **NL 89 1926274** Sproetje 74 Mother of Britt
        - **Belge 85 030** Black Tossem
        - **NL 81 433632** Bros van de Weerdt
    - **NL 89 1241090** Mother of 9th Nat Tarbes 96 20th nat Carcasonne 32 nat Dax
      - **NL 88 1764661** The Super 61 25 nat Bordeaux
        - **NL 84 180248** Jan Theelen
        - **NL 84 180238** Jan Theelen
      - **NL 84 180247** Jan Theelen
        - **NL 00 584179**
        - **NL 00 934453**
  - **NL 95 1877718** Mother of Maxima Half sister of Rivaldo 2nd Nat Bordeaux and 7th nat Bordeaux 32nd Nat Montauban
    - **NL 84 180230** De Rooie Kweker
      - **NL 78 934635** De 635 Jan Theelen
        - **NL 74 447366** De 366
        - **NL 76 584144**
      - **NL 75 1472183** G Dtr Oude 34
        - **NL 67 857834**
        - **NL 71 1414252**
    - NL 91 2131319 "De 319" 52 Nat St Vincent 11822p 173 nat Bergerac
      - **NL 84 180230** De Rooie Kweker
        - **NL 76 934635** De 635
        - **NL 75 1472183** G Dtr Oude 34
      - **NL 84 180237** Mother "Sonja" Mother of 1st Internal Perpignan 96 12551p
        - **NL 78 934634** G Son Oude 34
        - **NL 78 934639** Golden Stock pigeon

Pedigree of Maxima.

Sometimes I clean the breeding loft if Ad is busy with something else, but generally I provide the back up and do the work on the computer without which everything would be so much more difficult. If there is a social event down the club, a tombola for instance, I go with my husband to be friendly with the other fanciers, but it is up to the men to do the hard physical work. It is they who understand the pigeons and how to get them in good condition. I don't think I can claim any responsibility for the results, good or bad. I keep out of it. I can't imagine a life without pigeons in this house, since they are so much a part of everything we do.

Do you have any further ambitions and what do you think of the sport today?

As regards further ambitions, we have already had a very fruitful career in pigeons and we are grateful for that. I hope our success has not taken our feet off the ground and that we continue to try to do our best and perhaps continue to learn as we go along. We are always trying to understand the pigeon in an attempt to get the best out of what we do.

The future of the sport is another big question. At a local level in our club the sport is in decline, but I still believe the sport has a future on the International stage. The fact that thousands of pigeons are liberated in far away places and manage to return to their home lofts is still an incredible natural phenomenon that impresses not just to those who race pigeons, but also thousands of ordinary people who know nothing about the breeding and conditioning of pigeons. I think this will continue in some form or another and I hope my brother and I will remain part of this sport for years to come. This sport, however, serves another function in that it is still possible for the ordinary man with an ordinary family and limited wealth to get to the top. It gives hope to everyone who applies himself that he can do likewise.

CONCLUSION

The Hagens Brothers have one of the best records in the Netherlands and also possibly in Europe. They have won two full international races, an international hens race and National victories. Their record is amazing.

They do not have a massive palatial loft, nor are they the richest fanciers around – rather the contrary, they are inclined to be modest in both manner and disposition. On the surface there is nothing unusual about the Hagens brothers except the results of their pigeons. It is results that concern us here, for how could such an unassuming loft be so very good?

THE OBVIOUS ...

The obvious things are easy to see; they have quality pigeons that are well looked after. Like all the other top lofts in this book they stress the importance of testing the strain at every stage to keep the quality high, but that still has not answered the question of why they are so good. The secret may lie not in what they say but in what they do. Their race team has always included a high proportion of hens flying to the nest.

... AND THE NOT SO OBVIOUS

During my interview Ad Hagens announced that the following year the whole of the race team was to be turned to the 'natural' nest system of racing pigeons. Sixty couples (120 pigeons in total) were to be raced using this system. Previously they always had thirty cocks racing widowhood and perhaps forty couples racing to the nest. They now intended to jettison widowhood altogether. This was a major move. Here we had a major European loft that has won International races calmly announcing that they were to abandon what is conventionally believed the best system of racing pigeons (the widowhood method), a practice that is used by the vast majority of successful international fanciers. Are they going back in time?

Something new is happening. Top lofts do not

'Angelo' A modern double international performer. Photo: © Copyright Martin Kwakernaat

change on a whim or fancy. The Hagens Brothers are not likely to make a major change without a lot of thought. At first sight the reasons for change are not so obvious.

A Type of Mind

Ad Hagens shows that he is the type of man that understands pigeon basics. He may not be the most expressive and opinionated man but he certainly understands pigeons: his whole life and the life of his family revolve around them. The family cannot imagine life without pigeons. So why have the Hagens Brothers embarked on such a fundamental change? They are certainly not intending to go backwards, that's for sure.

Hens versus Cocks

When questions like this come up the solution invariably concerns improving the chances of the loft statistically. The reasoning goes like this: if major success at international level has been with hens raced naturally, then surely if the numbers allotted to this procedure were increased and more resources were put into racing natural hens, then everything must improve. The thought goes even further, for we may indeed unlock a previously untapped resource by racing hens, particularly those whose main effort and claim to fame is in marathon long-distance events.

It is well known that in shorter races natural hens cannot normally compete against widowhood cocks, but when the races get longer and more difficult, natural hens can, and often do, beat widowhood cock birds. There are some reasons why this might be so. Hens tend to relax more and fight less in the basket on the way to the race. Hens seem to have greater tenacity and more determination over a longer period than cocks. As in everything to do with pigeons, however, there is a downside, since hens are much more difficult to manage. Egg laying and all that goes with it interrupts the progress of a hen pigeon on its way towards peak fitness. With cocks that problem does not exist. It is generally thought that the simplicity of racing cocks makes widowhood racing more efficient. Cocks just get fitter and fitter as the season goes on, flying further and training harder as condition improves. It is true there are problems managing the widowhood hens, while the fact that only one sex is raced cuts the potential team in half. Nevertheless most fanciers opt for the easy male widowhood method and are prepared to accept the fact that widowhood hens are wasted as the price they pay for greater efficiency. Nevertheless hens can come into their own in the longer races. If the more irksome problems of racing hens could easily be overcome then hens might even surpass cocks, especially in the longer races.

Ad Hagens in thoughtful mood.

A New Idea

Very few new ideas are introduced into pigeon sport. Almost everything has been tried before. The 'It's already been done' attitude pervades the sport to the extent that it inhibits new thinking, yet it is the new thinkers who take the sport forward. It is they who win, for it is they who are thinking ahead of their time by refusing to accept existing methods automatically. That is why racing hens on the natural system against the conventional thinking of the day may well add to our existing knowledge. It may not seem a drastic chance, but in the hothouse atmosphere of International racing it is indeed a major change.

For the natural system with hens to work it is necessary to set time aside in the middle of the day to train the pigeons. Ad Hagens tells us he exercises the hens every day for an hour between 1pm and 2pm. This is the time when the hens do not want to get back into the loft because the cocks are sitting and they are thus free to exercise without pressure. This is also the time that many fanciers who work away from home are unable to give. By making this time available for hens, they can come into their own and get into better condition than they would by normal means.

Something else is also happening. Ad Hagens likes to send his hens to important races sitting on a youngster of about a week when the hen is not immediately expected to lay. With this in mind it is not hard to calculate that approximately twenty-four days can be set aside from the initial

The Hagens Brothers performances in the top 2 per cent from the international races from Marseilles, Pau, Tarbes, Barcelona, Dax and Perpignan. Most of the top performances have been with hens.

Date	Entry	Race point	Position	Distance (km)	Ring Number
1996					
04/8/1996	12,551 birds	Perpignan (Sonja)	1	1,004.991	1120350.92
1997					
26/7/1997	15,740 birds	Int Marseilles 97	100	940.614	1357140.94
09/8/1997	12,367 birds	Int Perpignan 97	232	1,002.991	1877753.95
09/8/1997	12,367 birds	Int Perpignan 97 (Orlano)	244	1,002.991	1877752.95
05/7/1997	24,908 birds	Int Barcelona 97	58	1,153.084	1877706.95
05/7/1997	24,908 birds	Int Barcelona 97 (Sarina)	95	1,153.084	1877800.95
1998					
27/6/1998	7,520 birds	Int Pau 98 (Gianni)	49	997.946	2216041.96
04/7/1998	24,139 birds	Barcelona 98 (Sarina)	136	1,153.084	1877800.95
26/6/1998	3,045 birds	Tarbes (1) 98	102	996.795	2216014.96
1999					
02/7/1999	28,095 birds	Int Barcelona (Sarina)	3	1,153.084	1877800.95
09/8/1999	17,574 birds	Perpignan 99	326	1,007.990	2525670.97
2000					
09/7/2000	26,597 birds	Int Barcelona	477	1,161.137	1464122.97
05/8/2000	18,426 birds	Perpignan	183	1,007.990	1464103.97
05/8/2000	18,426 birds	Perpignan	214	1,007.990	1464001.97
05/8/2000	18,426 birds	Perpignan	235	1,007.990	1156116.98
05/8/2000	18,426 birds	Perpignan	249	1,007.990	1156150.98
05/8/2000	18,426 birds	Perpignan	269	1,007.990	1464079.97
05/8/2000	18,426 birds	Perpignan	324	1,007.990	1156131.98
2001					
04/8/2001	20,859 birds	Int Perpignan 01	200	1,007.990	2303154.99
2003					
12/7/2003	19,400 birds	Dax 03 (Britt)	221	937.463	1919565.00
12/7/2003	19,400 birds	Dax 03	379	937.463	1834301.01
02/8/2003	17,338 birds	Perpignan 03	147	1,007.991	1834232.01
04/7/2003	20,204 birds	Barcelona 03 (Angelo)	48	1,166.144	1764077.00
04/7/2003	20,204 birds	Barcelona 03	246	1,166.144	1919549.00
04/7/2003	20,204 birds	Barcelona 03	255	1,166.144	1764084.00
2005					
03/7/2005	25,815 birds	Barcelona 05 (Shafira)	71	1,160.200	1584714.02
03/7/2005	25,815 birds	Barcelona 05	154	1,160.200	1764076.00
03/7/2005	58,15 birds	Barcelona 05	219	1,160.200	1584708.02
03/7/2005	25,815 birds	Barcelona 05 (Angelo)	236	1,160.200	1764077.00
03/7/2005	25,815 birds	Barcelona 05	258	1,160.200	1919508.00
17/7/2005	11,898 birds	Dax 05 (Lorena)	17	972.668	1584601.02

Stock hens.

laying of the eggs until the youngster is a week old, when intensive training can take place. This is the maximum time a hen can be free of laying. It is the time a hen can be brought into super condition. There is little doubt a natural hen played in this way can be brought into the best condition of the season. If the pigeon is also of good quality there is no telling what can be achieved. Perhaps Ad Hagens has discovered a new and more fruitful way with pigeons that utilizes both sexes but gets the hens into better condition than could normally be achieved when racing both widowhood and natural at the same time. It certainly worked with 'Sonja', 'Sarina' and 'Lucinda'. Now that everything in the racing loft is fully on the nest it may well create even more famous pigeons.

CHAPTER 8

Mark Gilbert

Windsor, England

THE INTERVIEW

The Start

What age were you when you first become involved with pigeons?

I was fourteen years old at the time. My father kept some pigeons, which he used to race jointly with a partner. I think it was a bit out of sympathy for me, and also in recognition of my enthusiasm, that they allowed me to look after the stock pigeons. I used to race home from school as fast as I could to do the job. This was probably the start of the pigeon bug.

The Magic Word 'National'

When did you first begin to race with long-distance pigeons?

I think I was sixteen when I first clocked from Pau with the National Flying Club. I was 173rd Open at my first attempt. It was I who trained and set up the pigeons that year. The fact that I had clocked a pigeon in such an important race at my first attempt gave me such a thrill. I think it took a time to sink in but when it did another bug hit me. This time it was the 'National' bug. The 'National' bug is still with me to this day. I don't think you ever lose that kind of thing. It's the build-up, the breeding and training of the pigeons, and anticipation of a huge event all combined that makes it memorable.

The Gilbert family. Geoff, Mark's father at the back – in front Mark and his two daughters, Melissa on the left and Abigail on the right. Photo: © Copyright Bryan Siggers

Sprint racing does not have the same kind of build-up and expectation. It does not have the magic word 'National' attached to it, either. The thought of competing against the best long-distance pigeons in the country is still special to me. Of course, at that time the thought of actually winning a 'National' never entered my head. Another great thing about long-distance racing is the finality of it all. If you fail from the longest race there is not another chance to succeed until the following year. In these circumstances, success, if it arrives, is a double or even a treble dose of 'long-distance' excitement. There is nothing quite like it. I think you would have to be emotionally dead not to respond to the romance of a small pigeon flying long distances.

The Air Freight Business

After I left school I started full-time work in the air freight business at Heathrow, London's main airport. I was managing huge exports and equally big imports from all over the world. I felt pretty good doing a job like this, it gave me a feeling of being important, doing important things at the heart of an important international airport. It was not long before I got married. My wife and I bought a house in Egham, not far from my job at Heathrow.

I suppose I suffered from the natural arrogance

of youth, for I was just as ambitious in my job as I was with the pigeons. A work colleague and I naturally thought we could do the air freight business better, cheaper and more efficiently than the firm we worked for. It seemed natural for us to start working for ourselves rather than work for someone else. This did not go down too well with our former firm, but we stuck to our guns and started up in business on our own. It was pretty difficult at first, working hard to build up the business, but eventually we had success. My colleague and I have since gone our separate ways. We are still good friends and both of us have a successful business in this field. He is doing well and so am I, although I am better at pigeons. He completely fails to understand this side of my life.

The elation I experienced after my initial success at Pau was still with me. Once my business was doing well and I could relax a bit, pigeons came to the fore again. I decided to seriously set about developing a team of long-distance pigeons to race National races. I studiously scrutinized the results of all the National races and the fanciers who were doing well at Pau.

Geoff Cooper, who lives and competes near Bath in Somerset, seemed to me a good man and a good place to go. I was determined to visit a fancier who was doing what I wanted to do. I visited him with the idea of buying a few pigeons and also learning as much as I could. I did buy some pigeons, but in part I also failed.

Incomplete Understanding

For some reason my understanding of his system was not complete. I could only get his pigeons to fly and win up to about 560km (350 miles). I was probably doing something really wrong. I suspect I was feeding incorrectly, for he was getting them to fly Pau quite regularly and I wasn't.

The feeding system I was using at the time was to bring the birds down after every race by feeding barley and then build them up again in time for the next race. This Continental feeding method was popular at the time, but obviously it was not good enough for pigeons expected to fly from Pau to England. It seemed it had its limitations. Using this system 350 miles seemed to be the birds' limit – above 350 miles the wheels fell off. I think I only ever got one home in a race above 350 miles. Nevertheless these birds were still winning at shorter distances. I think I won seven first Federation prizes in very strong local competition. They were in fact very good birds, but in my case were not being used correctly.

Are these Cooper pigeons a part of your present colony?

No, they are not. Over the years I have bought different pigeons and for various reasons the original Cooper pigeons disappeared. I think I won the SMT Combine with one from Nantes, but times moved on and I moved on. I was continually busy with my business and my family.

I moved house again, this time to Windlesham in Surrey. Moving house forces you to evaluate your pigeons. You also have to re-evaluate yourself at the same time.

Original Deweerdts

Geoff Cooper had told me about the Deweerdt lofts and how good the Deweerdt pigeons were. I decided to take a trip and see for myself. After this I started to introduce original Deweerdt pigeons, just as Geoff had done soon after he first started.

Once again events took control. This time it was the unfortunate death of Eric Cannon of Godalming in Surrey. Eric was a brilliant National fancier with a record second to none. After his death his pigeons were sold at auction. I thought here was a chance to invest in original pigeons that had actually done some winning. I bought one cock that was 6th and 12th National Pau. This particular cock was a brother to his famous 'Culmer Bess', one of the all-time best Cannon pigeons. I bought nine children off his merit award winners. Out of all these pigeons came my two National winners, 'Night Flyer' and my 'International Dax' winner. They both have Cannon blood in their pedigree.

The Search for Further Improvements

All these pigeons have been good but it is the area

The Racing Loft.

of extreme distance and the breeding of such pigeons that I would like to improve. My aim would be to improve the ratio of pigeons I am breeding to the amount of really good long-distance pigeons I produce. What I am really saying is that even though I have had some outstanding individual results I do not consider myself anywhere near to where I would like to be. I want to improve my breeding. I want to produce an improved, reliable family of pigeons that can fly the long distance on a regular basis. That is my aim.

I am now looking at reducing the numbers of stock pigeons I have. I want to refine the stock loft to the point where I can concentrate on the ones that are breeding the good ones. From these good ones I want to create a family. Even though I recognize that nothing is ever absolutely certain in pigeons, I would like to move in a direction where my breeding ratio of good pigeons compared with the number I breed improves.

Defining Attitudes

Have you ever thought of what kind of person you need to be in order to be successful with pigeons? Should you be relaxed, dynamic, ruthlessly ambitious, considerate or what?

I use the same kind of attitude in my business as I do with pigeons. I definitely think you have to be realistic with both pigeons and business. You should stop dreaming about both of them. You have to admit to yourself what can actually be achieved and, perhaps more to the point, also accept your shortcomings and failures so that realistically you can do something about it. A lot of people think they are 'superstars' in the pigeon sport, but in actual fact they are no such thing. I think I am quite good at being realistic with myself. I know sometimes I have bad races just the same as everyone else. I know where I have had success, but I also know that success is far from certain. This is being realistic. When you attempt to evaluate the loft of another fancier you can only ever see about 20 per cent of what is really happening. You see what he wants you to see. You probably miss some of the good things but overlook whole areas of failure. You have to work hard being realistic in pigeons, both with yourself and with others,but realism, if you can accept it, pays great dividends.

Mark in his Trophy Room.

Would you say you had a scientific frame of mind?

No, I don't think so. I just think if you send them and you have done your job to the best of your ability they should do theirs, but of course they don't always do it, nor do you always do yours. I try to understand this aspect of the sport and not fool myself. I know there are still things to learn. I am also aware that I don't know everything there is to know, of that I am absolutely sure.

The Complications of Crosses

You have bought in various pigeons to compose a family: the original Cooper pigeons, those direct from the Deweerdt brothers in Belgium, the Cannon pigeons, the Van Elsacker pigeons, and now the Biss pigeons as well as some others from the Massarella stud. Are there any more?

My theory is that there are only so many good pigeons because there are only so many good races. The best pigeons are the ones that are consistent in good class races. If possible you have to buy as near those best pigeons as it is possible. The pigeons I want are pigeons that are going to be consistent and win prizes over 500 or 600 miles in the best races. This is, of course, a tall order. I am aware of this, but this is still what I am aiming at. Of course when I bought pigeons from the late Eric Cannon's final sale and the late Jim Biss's final sale I had the opportunity to buy original pigeons that had actually won at this distance, but the downside to all this is I have acquired quite a few crosses in the pigeons. To be honest, the more crosses you have the more difficult it gets. I am at the stage now of trying to get the best of them to form themselves into a family. This is the basis of my thinking. Very few fanciers ever achieve it or even come close. I am still trying to get there. I aim to do so by being as honest with myself and as realistic as I am able.

I have been told over and over again in the course of my research for this book that the ideal situation is to have a basic family of related pigeons of high

quality and then to cross into them individual top pigeons from a similar but unrelated family. Do you agree with this?

Yes, I think I do. I have probably gone over the top with my crosses but I am still learning. I recognize that this is the time when it is getting harder to make decisions about breeding. If it were not difficult then it would not be worthwhile. It is this kind of decision-making that makes the sport so fascinating. I hope I eventually manage it.

Cocks or Hens

Do you have any preference for either cocks or hens for breeding?

No, I don't think so. As well as my best breeding pigeon, the 'Red Deweerdt cock', I have a hen that has bred three pigeons to win the Federation up to 350 miles. She is off a Louella cock called 'De Bergerac', bred and raced by Gurbe v d Schaaf of the Netherlands. The father of my hen was 1st Dutch National Bergerac from 36,737 pigeons, 7th National Ruffec and 106th National St Vincent all in the same season. This hen is bred in the purple, down from 'Invincible Spirit' (1st International Barcelona) on the hen's side and down from the world famous Jan de Weerts '131' on the cock's side. There is a smattering of Janssen Bros of Arendonk in there as well. I am looking forward to testing these pigeons at a greater distance some time in the future.

The Problem with Importing Mature Birds

When you import pigeons how long do you give them to find out if they are doing the business or not?

That is the problem with long-distance racing. By the time you have found out the quality of your stock in terms of producing top birds, they are dead. That is how I have found it. If I decide I like the pigeon then I like to carry on with it. What usually happens is I buy mature pigeons at the age of two or three or even four years of age. By the time I have had them paired with two or three cocks they are usually six or seven years of age, and by the time the offspring are flying in long races the original pigeons are not filling their eggs or have stopped laying. What I do is I breed off the imports. I race and test those I breed. The good ones that race well at National level will then replace the mature pigeons I originally bought. In short I am trying to create my own 'National' family from pigeons I have bred and raced here at my own loft. That is how I try to do it. I hope it works.

Russell Bradford holding Red Deweerdt brother of Raldo and father of 'Night Flight'.

How do treat young birds in the year of their birth?

The hens have three Channel races. I normally give the cocks five 'inland' races and then stop. The youngsters are all raced on the 'Darkness System', which imitates winter conditions by darkening the loft and thus shortening daylight hours. This delays the moult until later in the year when the racing is over. If young pigeons are obliged to use energy renewing their feathers at the same time as racing their performance suffers.

Do you ever breed late breds and have you had any success with them?

Yes. I have bred late breds and have had success with some of them. The one that was 7th National St Nazaire in 2005 was a late-bred cock of the previous year still carrying two nest flights at the time of St Nazaire. As a part of their education late breds are trained through the winter regardless of the weather. They are usually trained from about twelve weeks of age, but only over relatively short distances.

The normal youngsters go to the 'Saintes' National as yearlings. The whole idea is to test cocks that as youngsters have had a pretty easy time. It is from these that I expect my future long-distance pigeons to emerge.

Two-year-old pigeons, of course, probably have some wins under their belt by the time they get into long-distance racing. What do you do with them?

I tend not to bother too much about prizes at the yearling stage. Providing yearlings are consistent and do not have too many nights out, I keep them. I have had some pigeons that have made an absolute hash at the yearling stage of their lives but have subsequently made good two-year-old pigeons. I try to get the two-year-olds into a 800km (500 mile) race if I can. This race is from either Pau or Biarritz, either with the National Flying Club or with an international organization.

- **Belge 96 3273682**
  'Red Deweerdt'
  Brother to Raldo, Xena etc..
  Father of 'Night Flight'
  1 NFC Saintes/Pau 03
  - 89.3316150
    Aldo
    5th-Poitiers I,107b
    Nest bro Emiel
    1st Internat Bordeaux
    - Belge 83 3324036
      Barto
      118,145,260,290th Nat
      Cahors
      - Belge 75 3300141
        Bartje
        Dark Cheq
        - Belge 66 3449253 Keppe
        - Belge 67 3402125
      - Belge 80.3402024
        BC
        - 78 3483403
        - Belge 71 3302068
    - Belge 84.3200297
      Sister Kristof
      1st prov 2nd nat Perigueux
      - Belge 77 3402159
        Filip
        18th nat Brive 7,700b
        10th nat Cahors
        - 72..3302046 **'Mannix'**
          6th nat Tulle
        - 75.3445175 Dtr 'Keppe'
      - Belge 78 3402200
        Cheq
        - Belge 75 .3445222
        - Belge 30006.72 **Eliza**
  - Belge 92 3317158
    Red
    4 x Barcelona winner
    Half sister Zaina and Boris
    - Belge 91 3313199
      Red
      - Belge 88 3316250
        Gerard
        1st Chateauroux 572b
        2nd Dourdan 395b
        - Belge 3331121
          Limoges
        - Belge 84 3243491
      - Belge 89 3316304
        Daughter **Varazur**
        - Belge 85 3329089
          Varazur
        - Belge 82 3294274
    - Belge 89.3316084
      Sister Emmy Lou, Fix,
      Resso
      - Belge 83 3325181
        Kouros
        4lh Int Perpignan
        - Belge 80 3402021
          Stany
        - Belge 82 3429379
      - 87 3321082
        Emmy
        Co winner 1st Gen nat
        Champion KBDB
        - Belge 81 3339510
          Mirko
        - Belge 86 3158213

Pedigree of 'Red Deweerdt'.

NL 74 527 Line Old Fabry
x Cheq of '61

NL81 1008087
100 per cent Old Janssen
Blood

NL 76 578
Line Bred to Wondervos of
45

NL 87 1017546
'De Bergerac'
1st Nat Bergerac 36,737b
7th Nat Ruffec-106th Nat St
Vincent bred and reared by
G vd Schaaf Nuis Gr

NL 76 2557935
Line bred to the 55 of P v d
Eyden and the J an de
Weerdt '131'

NL 86 709361
Dtr of '080' G G Dam of
1st Dutch nat Bergerac
1991 J Ernest

NL 80 8015080
Half brother Half sister
mating

NL 74 2451943

NL 74 2381961

GB 00 E 87109

Blue Cheq Pied

NL 86 17
Son of De Joop 86269

NL 88 8840569
1st Int Barcelona 1992
42nd Int Barcelona 1991
3 x Barcelona

NL87 8755301 half sis to
Regenworm winner of 1st
'ace' pigeon Netherlands

GB 94 K 70924

NL84 326948
De Barcelona
1st Dutch nat Barcelona

NL 90 M 39811
Line bred v d Wegen
To Oude Doffertje of '58'

NL 91 9169541
87 2744390
Full sister to 1st Dutch nat
Barcelona

Pedigree of '109' son of 'De Bergerac'.

Do Looks Matter?

Is there any physical attribute you particularly look for in a mature pigeon? Are you looking at the wing, the throat, the head, a particular shape of the body or what?

I don't like pigeons that carry a lot of weight. I like them narrow, I would say. I don't mind if they are big or small or have strong backs or not. I don't like the ones that are round like apples and appear to be muscular. You never get long-distance athletes that are muscular. To me they have to be like Zola Budd or Paula Radcliffe, as skinny as they come. I don't look at the eyes, the wing, down the throat or have any fads of this kind. I don't even have a fancy for good-looking heads. Some of my cocks that have flown well at the distance are quite hen-looking. I think most of my pigeons have good feather. I don't mind good feather. Yes, thinking about it, I think feather quality is quite important.

Cultivating Immunity

Do you consider a high degree of natural immunity to illness essential for a long-distance loft to perform well?

I think you have to try to avoid routine treatment, but sometimes treatment is essential. My youngsters never get treated. I want to build up their immunity early in their lives. I race all of them and those that survive I am happy with. I do not worry about losses at the young bird stage. When it comes to the 'Old Birds', I do use treatments. I treat the old birds before any major long-distance race for respiratory conditions and for canker. This is only once a year but not before every Channel race. When the old birds get to 500 miles I treat them using Linco Spectin for respiratory and for canker I use Tricho Plus.

The Widowhood hens are kept in aviaries at the back of the Widowhood sections.

The young ones are vaccinated for paratyphus between six and twelve weeks old, and later for pigeon pox and paramyxo in one combined dose before they start training.

Do you clean out your lofts on a daily basis? If not, what is the reason for this?

The young birds I don't – I only clean the perches perhaps twice a week – but the old birds I clean out twice a day, morning and night.

Is the reason you don't clean the young birds designed to develop natural immunity?

No, I don't think so. I think it's just plain laziness, but I must say since I stopped cleaning the young birds I have had fewer health problems. In truth I learned about it from Bernard Deweerdt. He is of the opinion that youngsters in the early part of their lives should be forced to fight for survival. This is an early way of exposing any health shortcomings they may have. I would never dream of treating for coccidiosis, for instance. The pigeons must develop immunity to such things.

Advice to a Novice

What advice would you give a novice attempting to build a team of long-distance pigeons?

I would advise any novice to go to their best local flyer, to make a friend of him and get the best pigeons he can off this man. One thing I would do is to buy one pigeon of top quality rather than ten of average quality. This applies especially to cocks, because you can get a lot of young pigeons off a cock bird. You can get twenty youngsters a year out of a cock. Obviously there are sharks in the sport who would love to take your money, so for this reason I wouldn't buy off anyone, no matter who it was or whatever the pigeon's pedigree, who was just winning at club level. I want proof of performance. I think this way for the following reasons:

1. You would not know the numbers competing.
2. You would not know whether the seller was in a favourable position or not by looking at his club wins.
3. You are unlikely to know the strength of the opposition.

These are just a few of the difficulties, and for these reasons I would definitely always choose someone who was winning at 'National' level because there quality is known. If there is such a man in your area, go to him; if not, then you must travel to an area where there is someone.

I think some of the studs have been quite good for the sport. They have made it possible to get good pigeons that would not normally be available to the ordinary fancier. Again I must stress the same buying principle applies. Buy one good pigeon that is close to the big winner rather than ten that are off grandchildren or just have an ordinary pedigree. In my opinion a lot of people are making a lot of money out of inland racing and only competing against a few pigeons. Real top-class pigeons are flying against thousands from much greater distances and are distributed over wider areas. It is the long-distance 'National' pigeon that sets the tone and provides the standard for the sport and the country as a whole.

At what stage should the novice be after three years?

I don't agree with the plausible, but wrong, theory that you need to be winning at club level in order to win a 'National'. I would always encourage our imaginary novice to compete at 'National level' from the start. In my opinion there are equally good club fanciers as there are 'National' fanciers. The trouble is they just don't send. It just does not make sense to me. When any fancier moves from 'Club' racing to 'National' racing his pigeons have to learn to break from flocks of pigeons that may not be going in the right direction. National racing teaches this. It also teaches navigation and individuality in pigeons. The pigeons that learn to do this quickly are the ones that should form your family. The sooner the novice gets into this type of racing the sooner he will create something. He should not be afraid of failure, for everyone fails sometime or another. His attitude should always be to be spurred on to great success by competing in big races, important races where the competition is drawn from a wide area. European International racing is the best example of big races over wide areas. Even Polish fanciers now compete from Barcelona. In 2006 Polish fanciers sent 319 pigeons to this race and at least one fancier timed in flying over 1,450km (900 miles).

Systems

Do you fly widowhood, on the nest or both systems?

For the past fifteen years I have only flown cocks on the widowhood system, but I intend to set up a section for racing hens. I have seen a system where the boxes are in three parts: the cock sits in the middle and the hens sit either side. The cock will always be waiting for the first hen to arrive. This encourages the hens to race each other.

The yearlings are on widowhood as well as the old birds. All the cocks are let out twice a day. They mostly fly for an hour each time but they will be flagged if they don't fly an hour. I can honestly say I don't have any problem getting the pigeons to fly after the first couple of weeks – the pigeons fly on their own. I understand that in the early part of the year, when it is cold, some fanciers don't let their cocks exercise in the morning. I'm afraid I do. I'm not saying this is right, but I do it. I am not bothered if the weather is cold or wet or anything.

Preparation for the Long Races

How would you treat a three- or four-year-old widowhood pigeon that is being prepared for the important long race of the year?

Pigeons of this maturity are given four inland races. The first Channel race is the fifth race. They are then given a week off. They then have another Channel race. After this race they are given three weeks off. They do not go training or anything. They just exercise around the loft. At the start of this three-week period they are a given canker and respiratory treatment for five days. At this time I am feeding them Versele-Laga Super Widowhood Plus. Then seven feeds before the long race I introduce Versele Champions Extra Sublime. I also give them peanuts in an attempt to get as much fat content into them as possible. They have vitamins in the water once a week but not other things like brewers' yeast. Once a week I use Johnson's tonic, which they get in the water. I do not use pressed garlic or other herbs.

After the Race

Is there any special treatment you give a tired pigeon when he returns from a long race before he rejoins the flock for normal training?

Nothing, I just give them water. My pigeons have plain water and the normal food. The good ones recover quickly. If they are slow in recovering this is a bad sign.

How long is the hen allowed to sit with the cock on his return?

This depends on the physical effort involved in the race. I normally give them two hours, but if the race has been especially hard I give them only half an hour.

The week before National races I try to allow the hen to be with the cock for most of a day. I find this really enlivens them for the following week.

The Moult and Winter Treatment

Are the pigeons separated for the winter and if so when?

When the pigeons have finished racing for the season I pair them up again and allow them to rear a youngster. After they have done this I split them as quickly as I can so they can get as good a moult as possible. They have a bath every week. I feed moulting mixture at this time. In my opinion separation of the sexes improves the moult.

Pairing Up Stock and Race Birds

When do you pair the birds?

I pair the stock birds on 4 December. I often change the original pairings of the previous year, but once they are paired they then stay together for the rest of the year. The race birds are also paired on 4 December, but I only let them stay with each other until their youngster is sixteen or seventeen days old. The hen is then taken away and the cock finishes rearing the single youngster on its own.

It is important that the hen is not allowed to lay for the second time. If that happens you are in all sorts of trouble. Laying a second round of eggs kick-starts the wing moult in both the cock and the hen. It is really important that the wing moult is delayed so that the race birds have as near a complete wing as possible for when the longer races arrive. There is another aspect to all this. Form or top condition works in conjunction with the state of the wing moult. If a pigeon has to grow big flight feathers while at the same time working hard in racing, it is impossible to achieve top condition.

I don't do anything special or feed anything different before I pair them up. At that stage they are on 50 per cent moulting mixture and 50 per cent barley. I leave them on that until they start hatching out and feeding their young. I then put them on 100 per cent breeding mixture.

Inside the Widowhood Loft.

What physical characteristics do you look for when pairing up the birds? Do you compensate for size, colour, the eye or anything else?

If I have a particularly big cock I look for a small hen to pair it with, but apart from that nothing. I don't bother about colour or the eye or anything other than pedigree and performance. What I am prepared to breed off usually has to be a very good racer or a stock bird that has already proved itself. I may experiment with a cross that has a very good pedigree, but basically the pedigree or performance of the birds is more important than shape or colour.

The Loft

Do you have opinions on the construction and ventilation of the racing loft?

I have made the lofts so that fresh air comes in above the pigeons and stale air is sucked out through the ventilation chimney in the centre of the ceiling. The idea is to keep the temperature stable.

Is the environment of the loft, with the use of an aviary allowing the pigeons to come and go as they please, an important part of the way you do things?

At the beginning of the year when the pigeons are paired they are allowed open access to the loft to come and go as they please. This also happens when they are re-paired again after the season is over and are allowed to have complete freedom.

At the end of the year, after they have reared a youngster, cocks and hens are parted from each other. They are then not allowed out again for the whole of the winter or until they are paired up on or about 4 December. I may be doing a mind trick here or I may be conserving the moulted feathers for the coming year. I may even be doing both, but in my loft the only time mature pigeons fly out is when they have a mate or are on widowhood. It seems to work for me, although we can never really know. They can't speak, although I do believe they communicate with each other in the loft, on the ground and in the air. I don't fully understand their language and how their communication works. I wish I did – the first man to make a proper study of this will become a master fancier.

Are there any improvements you would still like to make to your race loft?

I am always looking to improve. I think I am pretty happy with the ventilation but, as I said, I am looking to race a few hens next year using the three-compartment boxes. They will have to be installed in the winter. I will probably find the snags as I go along. Undoubtedly there will be some. In pigeon racing things tend not to go completely according to plan. There is always a gap between what you expect, what you understand and what you get. In my case it's usually a wide gap.

Numbers

How many birds do you have?

I started this year with ninety-one cocks, of which fifty-four are yearlings. I have thirty-four pairs of breeders and in 2006 I bred 150 young birds. I would definitely like to have fewer pigeons, but when you are building a family you have to keep your options open until such times as you have real information.

Building a family is the most difficult phase simply because breeding is the least certain and least understood part of the sport. Of course, if you wish to compete in National and International long-distance races then you need quite a large race team. This is not wasted effort because competing at a high level in the best competition has another function apart from merely winning. Competing tests the pigeons and the breeding. It also tests your ideas.

I really like this aspect. I like finding out, and being truthful to myself in what I am doing. Like it or not, I like being wrong. You learn more by being wrong than you do by being right. Even if I sent only five or six pigeons to every long-distance race, considering the number of long races there are and the need to test my breeding, I would need a lot of pigeons.

The Main Birds

Which individual stock birds have been essential to the development of your colony?

The most important is the brother of 'Raldo', a Deweerdt pigeon. Another Deweerdt pigeon, a dark cock that came 'off the floor' of the Deweerdt loft, has bred me quite a few good pigeons including the early one I got from Saint-Nazaire last year. He was a grandson of a named pigeon, but because he was a grandson and not a son he was not considered a top pigeon. Nevertheless he has bred some good ones.

This is the beauty of having a family of related pigeons. Good ones often skip a generation and pop up later. Another of my top birds is a daughter of 'Culmer Bess', bred by the late Eric Cannon. This pigeon also had Deweerdt blood in its pedigree via Mick Spencer of Barnoldswick, who won the Nantes National in 1991 flying over 740km (461 miles) with a pigeon that was half Deweerdt. This is a case of the Deweerdt blood taking a circular route before coming back to my loft. I think this happens quite a lot with other breeds and other good pigeons as well. There are probably very few actual basic strains of long-distance pigeons.

I think these have been the three main pigeons, but a pair of Serge Van Elsacker birds, completely unrelated to my others, did really well. I bought them in the belief that I wanted to speed up my pigeons but this turned out to be a stupid idea. I bred only four from them. I gave Geoff Cooper one and kept three myself. One of these three was a hen that won fifteen first prizes. She was also 50th Pau and 30th Saintes in the National. In between these National events she went to a big inland open race and won against 800 pigeons. I put her in the aviary and thought, 'I'm not going to breed out of you because you are not of long-distance blood.' She stayed there for four years. Her parents were used as feeders for the Deweerdt pigeons. As it happened I again moved house at this time. I took the original pair of Van Elsacker pigeons with me. Bill Carr, a local man, called and wanted some middle-distance pigeons. I told him this was a fantastic pair perfect for middle distance. He took them on my recommendation.

The same year Geoff Cooper, who had had one of the original four I bred, won his Federation by 11 minutes and his club by 15 minutes in a race from 100 miles. Although there was a head wind from the north-east on that

Supreme 1st International Dax 2004.
Photo: © Copyright Bryan Siggers

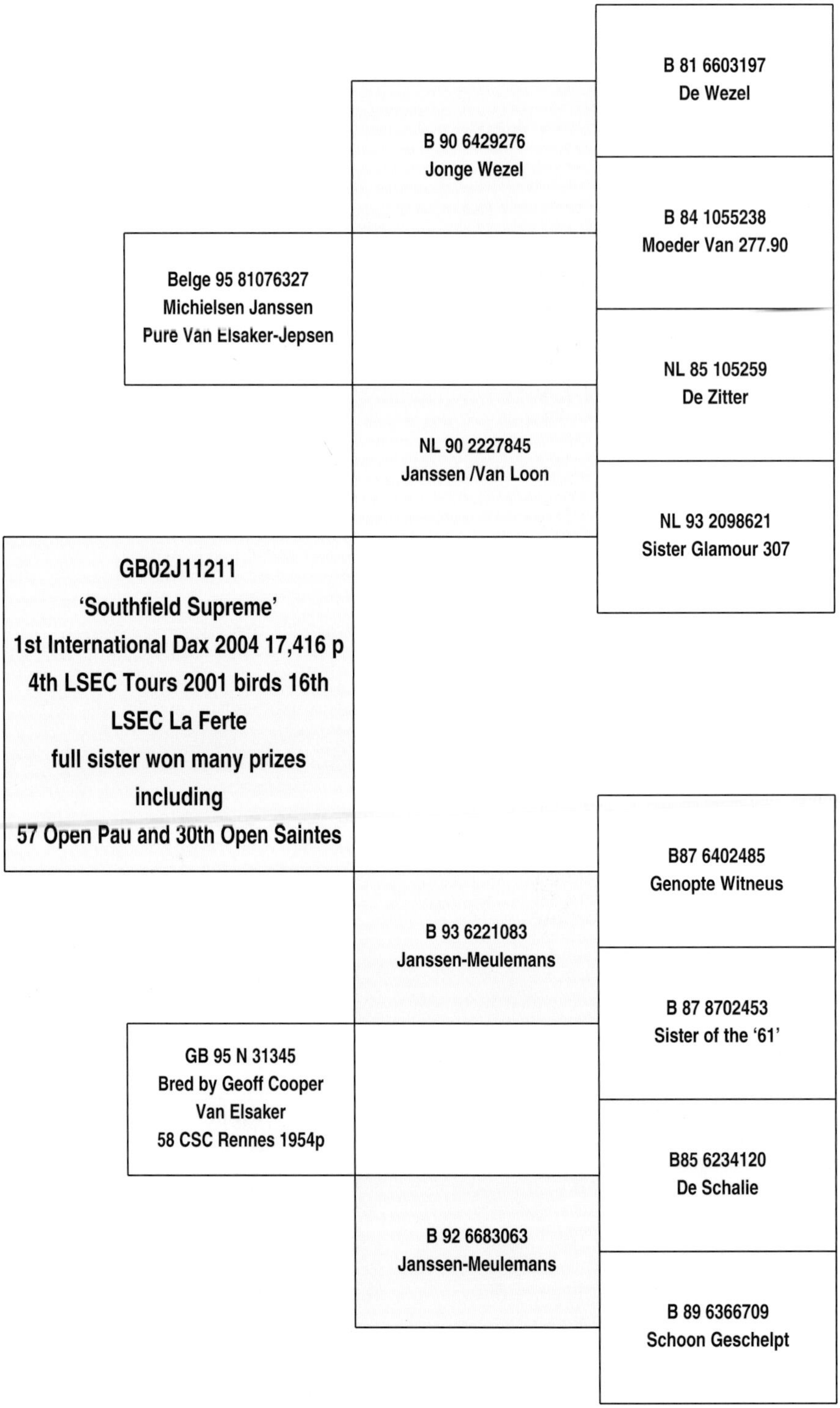

B 81 6603197
De Wezel

B 90 6429276
Jonge Wezel

B 84 1055238
Moeder Van 277.90

Belge 95 81076327
Michielsen Janssen
Pure Van Elsaker-Jepsen

NL 85 105259
De Zitter

NL 90 2227845
Janssen /Van Loon

NL 93 2098621
Sister Glamour 307

GB02J11211
'Southfield Supreme'
1st International Dax 2004 17,416 p
4th LSEC Tours 2001 birds 16th
LSEC La Ferte
full sister won many prizes
including
57 Open Pau and 30th Open Saintes

B87 6402485
Genopte Witneus

B 93 6221083
Janssen-Meulemans

B 87 8702453
Sister of the '61'

GB 95 N 31345
Bred by Geoff Cooper
Van Elsaker
58 CSC Rennes 1954p

B85 6234120
De Schalie

B 92 6683063
Janssen-Meulemans

B 89 6366709
Schoon Geschelpt

Pedigree of Southfield Supreme.

particular day, enough to allow the performance to be believable, he was nevertheless disqualified from winning the Federation on the grounds that it was deemed an impossible speed on the day. Meanwhile Bill Carr, with one of the ones I sold him, won the Federation by 9 minutes against 4,000 pigeons.

The one I had was called 'Southfield Supreme'. He won the International Dax in 2005. This year I have been 3rd and 5th section racing from the north with birds from the same pigeons and 1st LSECC Bergerac also with the same stuff. I can always tell the line of these pigeons by the eye. It is very dark and completely unlike anything else I have. The Van Elsacker pigeons certainly bred fast birds that can fly up to 500 miles. Whether they would go any further than that I don't know, but I have now crossed them with the best of the Deweerdt pigeons. Up to now the jury is still out. The evidence is not yet conclusive.

A Life in Pigeons

How do the pigeons fit in with your family and business life?

I am pretty dedicated to the pigeons. I get up every morning by 5am and am out with the pigeons cleaning the lofts and exercising them. I leave for work about 7.50am, so the pigeon work has to be done before then. I am back home about 18.30pm. I am soon out there again with the pigeons, exercising them for an hour. I suppose I work an eight-hour day and work two hours before work and two hours after work with the pigeons. I think the pigeons are a relaxation from business. If this wasn't the case I don't think I could do it, but, because they are entirely different and use a different part of my brain, I think it works.

My father looks after the stock pigeons. He is now retired so he has time on his hands. We work as a team, not in perfect harmony but he puts up with me. I cannot imagine life without pigeons. I have had them all my life so the thought of being without pigeons seems impossible to me. I think pigeons bring me down to earth as much as anything else in life. Sometimes when I have had a bad race I pretend it would be great not to have pigeons. This thought soon passes and the next week when they have done well it disappears.

Reducing the Odds

Racing pigeons at long distances is always a challenge and full of uncertainties. By its very nature we can never know everything. You have been more successful than most fanciers in the sport, so can you single out the one technique or quality that has helped reduce the uncertainty, shorten the odds and, to some degree, helped produce a successful colony?

Getting the initial good blood helps a lot, but if you are lucky and can find a line that works for you it all becomes very easy. But there is more to it than that. You have to find out how to carry on breeding from your initial success. There are few guarantees. The Elsacker pigeons, with their dark eyes, and the Deweerdt's are the only lines I can absolutely guarantee. The other lines are more erratic. They can produce good pigeons, but not all of them are good. I think that is true with most pigeons. I honestly think getting as near to the good pigeons as possible certainly helps with long-distance pigeons. With long-distance pigeons good blood is a must if you want to reduce the odds. Without good blood you are just permanently banging your head against a brick wall. Good pigeons need not necessarily be direct off the champions, but they certainly must be representative of a good family that has been doing well for years and littered with champion pigeons throughout their pedigree.

Do you have any further ideas and ambitions?

I would like to send a good team to the Barcelona International, perhaps ten or twelve pigeons. I would definitely like to win that one. That is my dream. I want to be more regular and more consistent with my breeding. I want to get a greater number of reliable long-distance pigeons. I am not there at the moment: I have a few good ones, but I want more.

Night Flight, 1st NFC Saintes/Pau National 2003. Photo: © Copyright Bryan Siggers

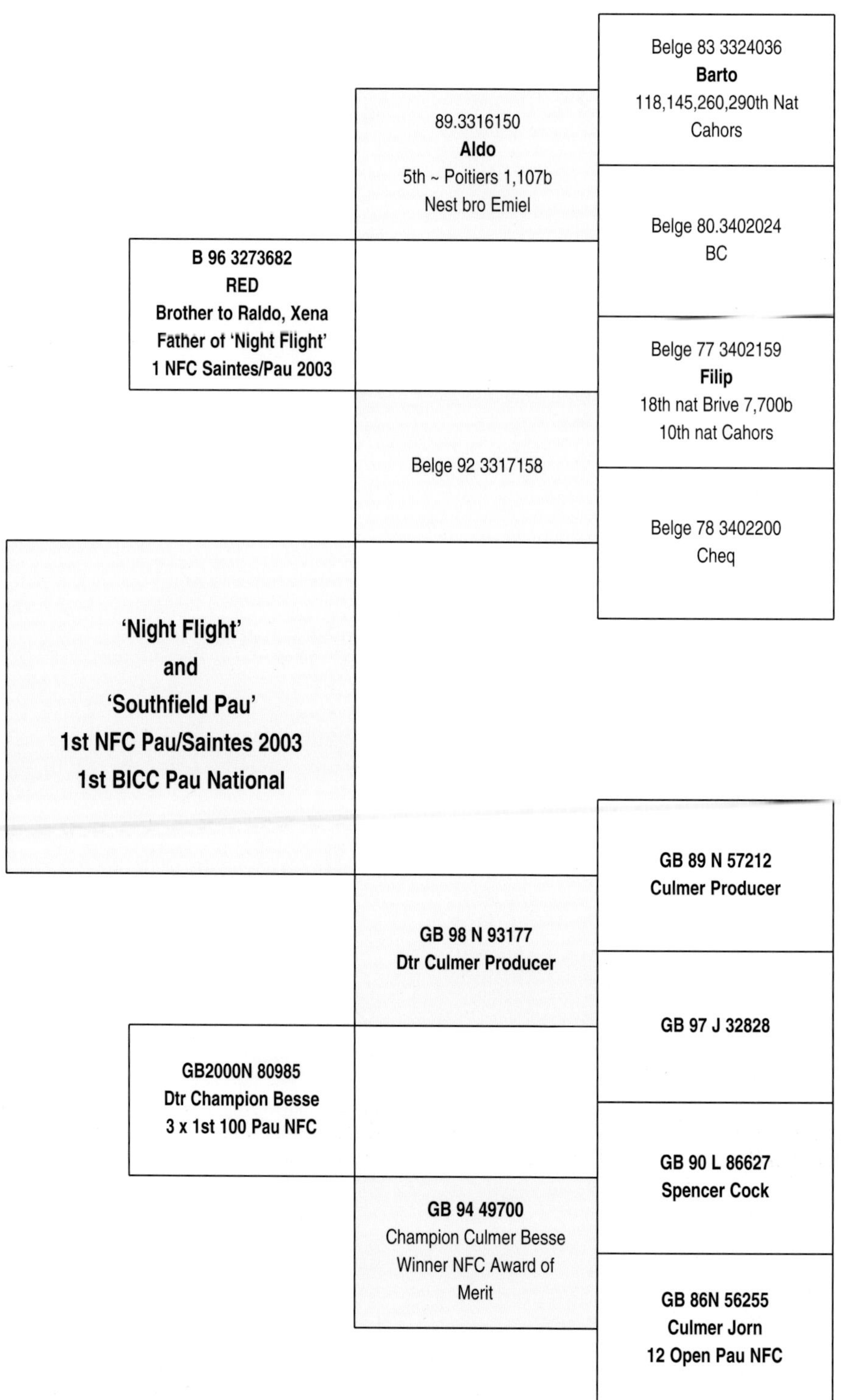

Pedigree of 'Night Flight'.

The Sport Itself

Does the sport have further to go? Are there any procedures you like to introduce into pigeon racing from your business background?

Obviously the clubs could be bigger. I would institute a rule that a minimum number of competing fanciers was required to make a race. That would be a good idea. In Windsor we have a club house that is owned by the members. If this idea were to be expanded in scale so that whole Federations could be housed in the same building, that would also be good. If this happened, rather than a lot of small clubs making up a larger Federation, we could have a large Federation split into sections housed under one roof. This would provide economy of scale. Nationals and Internationals and the other big races could mark and check clocks there. The Federation headquarters would become a 'Pigeon Centre' for pigeon-related events.

If everything was really well organized then whole families could go down there and socialize. They could enjoy something to eat. They could also have events organized on the back of the pigeons and pigeon racing. Some of the grotty places where pigeon clubs often have their headquarters do more damage than anything else in the sport. Wives hate it. The whole thing is anti-social and anti-family. I would like to expand the social side of pigeon racing in an attempt to attract those who, due to circumstances, would like to be fans or helpers in the sport. A thriving social life would encourage all sorts of things to happen that would eventually benefit everything to do with the sport. It is up to fanciers themselves to start the ball rolling.

I definitely think categories within races, as they have in Belgium, would be good. Separate races for hens and separate races for yearlings under the umbrella of a big event would give everyone more chances of winning something.

Why do you think the Netherlands and Belgium have a better standing in the world of pigeons and pigeon racing than we do in the UK?

I think they are not afraid of big races and organizing enormous world-class events. In fact their organization does everything it can to encourage big races that have world significance. It adds to their sporting reputation worldwide. Go down to a Belgian club house and you will find hundreds of fanciers with their families there. There is a buzz about the place.

I think socially we have ruined our sport here in the UK. Successful social events that do take place are generally organized by individuals rather than clubs. When Geoff Cooper and his wife Catherine organized their two garden parties to commemorate the two British International Dax wins it was a tremendous thing. Some fanciers travelled hundreds of miles just to be there, but not everyone there was a pigeon fancier.

The second Garden Party organized by Catherine Cooper at Peasedown to celebrate the UK winning in the International Dax for the second time. Mark is 5th from the left – Brian Sheppard winner of the first UK Dax win is 6th from the left, D. Posey & Son, 1st International hens, are 2nd and 3rd from the right.

In other sports there are social events that revolve around the sport and generate spectators. There will always be people who are attracted to others who are passionate about something. These become fans. They could contribute a lot to the sport.

I don't think the Belgians or the Dutch are any better than us at actually racing pigeons, they just organize things better. Because they export their pigeons and their strains worldwide they earn money. We here in the UK have turned our back on this kind of challenge. It's nothing to do with the pigeons. A lot of their pigeons are just the same as some of ours.

If we could improve the social side I am sure the whole sport would improve and take on a new dimension. Wives would then insist their husbands went to the club and raced their pigeons because it would be an enjoyable thing to do. When I won the International I got a bottle of champagne from the local flyers. That was a good thought – it certainly drank very well. I had hundreds of phone calls congratulating me, of course. I don't think I have ever had an experience quite like it. My pigeon life will never be quite the same again. I would like to think this kind of thing could happen to more fanciers. I would like to think fanciers from the UK could send at least two thousand pigeons each year to International races and the UK could look forward to doing well in those races every year and producing our own world champions. That would be good for everyone's confidence. I know it has been good for mine. I hope it has been good for our local Windsor club and also for the National Flying Club.

CONCLUSION

The Avian Influenza Virus

Early in 2006 restrictions were imposed by the British Government that forbade the release of racing pigeons from France. These restrictions were made in an attempt to inhibit the spread of the H5N1 avian flu virus into the UK. Owing to these restrictions Mark Gilbert decided to turn his entire team of pigeons from their usual route of flying from the south to the north to fly from the north to the south.

Most people in his position would not have contemplated such a thing, deciding to sit it out for a year rather then risk their reputation and their pigeons by sending them in a direction totally new to their experience. These pigeons, after all, represented high-quality stock. Two years ago they had won the English National and a year later an Entente Belge International race against the best pigeons in Europe. Most fanciers would never have contemplated such a bold move. The risk of changing direction with pigeons that were unused to flying from the new direction would have been far too intimidating for most. What made Mark Gilbert do it? What made him undertake such a risk? The answer to this question is at the heart of the 'Gilbert' character and the way he flies his pigeons.

Mark and the president of the Entente Belge Philip Norman, at the Entente Belge International celebration in Belgium.

Fishermen's Tales

Most pigeon fanciers exaggerate a bit. Some, of course, exaggerate a lot.

'Fishermen's Tales' are not confined to fishing alone. Pigeon racing has more than its fair share of expert practitioners in the art of the half-truth or even deliberate untruth. At some time or another we have all left out reference to our failures and talked up our successes. This is normal human behaviour. Most of us take this into account when listening to other fanciers speaking about their pigeons.

Disarmingly, Mark Gilbert does not do this. He is more than frank about his failures and disarmingly indifferent to his successes. What he seems to be more concerned about is where he is going in the world of pigeons and what he ultimately wants to achieve. He is concerned that his assessment of where he is at the moment is realistic and true. He seems to be working on an altogether bigger plan. What in fact makes Mark Gilbert tick? Does he possess a different intelligence? Is his thinking foolhardy or is he superior? He undoubtedly has seasoned followers of the game scratching their heads trying to place Mark Gilbert in some kind of context.

Few Certainties

Mark Gilbert admits to few pigeon certainties. One is the need for top-quality stock. Another is the need for continuous testing of that stock. And then there is the need to do his best to get the pigeons fit.

These basics are partly why he sent his team north to fly south. He wanted to continue testing his birds in race conditions so that he could still eliminate pigeons that were not going to make the grade and thus improve his breeding. He wanted all these basic things more than he wanted superficially good results.

Continuous Testing

Mark decided his testing regime could not afford to take a break. Instead he was going to enjoy the new experience and learn from it by turning a misfortune into a situation from which he could profit. At the time of his decision he fully intended to compete with the North Road Championship Club and race for their coveted NRCC King's Cup from Lerwick in the Shetland Islands. Mark Gilbert was unfazed by such a proposition. He considered the advantages of continued testing and improving the breed outweighed the disadvantages of being new to the route.

As it turned out, government authorities relented somewhat and allowed restricted releases of racing pigeons from France, but only from a distance under 640km (400 miles) into France. This announcement came after Mark's pigeons had already flown some events from the north.

Turning South Again

As a result of the new government decision, Mark turned his pigeons south again to race from France but not before he had suffered one huge loss from the north. Owing to an unfortunate release in appalling conditions of continuous heavy rain, he and many other fanciers from the Thames Valley area lost an enormous number of pigeons in one particular race from Wetherby in Yorkshire. Birds were still returning two weeks after the original release. The race seemed innocent enough, a release from the relatively short distance of 260km (160 miles). No one could have imagined that a disaster would occur, but Mark was to lose forty-three pigeons from the eighty-one birds he originally entered in the race: only five birds made it home on the day of the release.

The London South East Classic

One of the pigeons that had taken two weeks to return from the Wetherby disaster later went on to race from France. After flying and suffering from Wetherby, this particular pigeon was turned south and won a prestigious London South East Classic race from Bergerac in France, flying over 740km (460 miles). The race was for really hard pigeons: only seven birds from a total of 800 entries made it home on the day. This was a fair race for 'Iron' pigeons that were fit and talented enough to fly 460 miles against the wind.

Mark was 1st and 2nd in this Bergerac race. The experience of the disastrous Wetherby race did not seem to have dimmed the courage of the winning pigeon. Indeed, the original thinking that is Mark Gilbert's signature may explain part of the Bergerac success. Mark will readily tell you that at least half the motivation we ascribe to pigeons is false. We just do not fully know how a pigeon thinks. The Wetherby disaster may well have had a stimulating effect on the pigeon's mind, proving that a really fit pigeon cannot be hurt. Fit pigeons, after due rest, are ready to come out again and win once more despite their previous unhappy experience.

Reverse Thinking

The proof was certainly in the pudding, for both Bergerac pigeons were flying against a strong head wind on what amounted to the hottest day of the year. Another aspect of this race, although unrelated, is of interest since it concerns the whole of International racing and the English attitude towards it. That year the International Dax race was held on the same day as the LSECC Bergerac. British pigeons were unable to compete from Dax owing to government regulations that restricted releases to a shorter distance. For this reason Bergerac was as far as they could fly.

The Dax meanwhile proved to be a disaster itself, with no birds making it home on the day of release. If the UK had been allowed to race in International races in 2006 no doubt Mark Gilbert and his Bergerac birds would have taken part from Dax. We can only speculate, but the way his and other birds performed from Bergerac that day suggests that England, and possibly Mark himself, would have once again performed at the top of an International competition. This possibility certainly highlights the need for a revision of traditional British reluctance to International participation. Perhaps we should revise our opinion and substitute keen acceptance for reluctance, then instead of relatively small numbers taking part from the UK there might be sizeable entries. Any increase in the British entry would surely improve British chances.

The whole point of this story is to illustrate how Mark Gilbert thinks. He is scrupulously determined to be realistic and honest with himself. He is resolute in pursuit of his main objective of gradually breeding an improved family of pigeons. He is never prepared to pretend and bluff it out, and admits to being sure of only two things: the need for quality of stock and the need for continual testing. This, of course, ultimately means testing against International competition.

A Challenge

Mark Gilbert examines every challenge, no matter how ridiculous it might appear at first sight, under the microscope of his beliefs. Everything in his life is treated exactly the same. He does not accept anything just because it is accepted opinion, as when he gradually came around to the Van Elsacker cross because it proved itself.

Before 2003 it was generally accepted opinion that Great Britain would never win an International race. Mark Gilbert and Brian Sheppard of 'Groot Brittannie' have blown this conjecture out of the water. Mark firmly believes that on occasion he can beat the lofts from which his stock originated. Most fanciers don't think in these terms, but Mark Gilbert is never going to limit his ambition by negative thinking. The Dutch, the Belgians, the Germans and the French are there to be beaten, providing we all remain competitive and realistic at the same time.

Commercial Thinking

Perhaps because of his commercial career Mark thinks international. His very successful air freight business, Rockwood International Freight Limited, was established in 1989. It operates from Heathrow and Manchester and now has offices worldwide. International thinking is part of his attitude. He accepts 'abroad' as only a flight away from the UK. International sporting challenges are therefore not just feasible, they are a vital part of the testing.

That is Mark Gilbert's bottom line. If any fancier intends to create and establish an improved breed of pigeons it is impossible not to have international testing as a part of the plan. It makes great sense and sounds simple, but it requires a joint effort by everyone.

Mark has also been successful with the best of racing greyhounds, owning a bitch named 'Call Girl' that won the Dorando Marathon over 875m at Wimbledon greyhound track. I suspect that being true to himself is Mark Gilbert's trump card in buying greyhounds, in running a business and in flying pigeons. There are certainly more ordinary dogs than good ones, more failed businesses than successful ones, more ordinary lofts than good ones. For some reason or other, Mark has hit the jackpot in all three.

Mark has avoided the all too human trait of hiding mistakes rather than admitting to them. Stark reality is not generally attractive to most of us, but it is this brand of reality that Mark Gilbert is all about. Whether Britain achieves first-rank status as a pigeon country depends on how this role is understood. When historians of the sport look back they may see the role played by Mark Gilbert more clearly, either as a vital move towards a positive future or as misunderstood and a chance missed. Only time will tell.

CHAPTER 9

Brian Denney

Strensall, York, England

BACKGROUND

Brian Denney is seventy-one years of age. Before he started with pigeons he was a soldier in the Royal Engineers, serving first in Malaya, chasing insurgents up and down the peninsula. He was later in Germany with the British Army of the Rhine at Osnabrück. By the time he came out of the army he was twenty-six, already married and ready to start keeping pigeons. That was in the early 1960s. He never went through progressing from sprint to middle-distance races and finally to the long races. He started immediately to race long-distance pigeons. This was the objective from the start, although many short races have sometimes been won; it was the long ones, the really long races, that mattered.

When Brian was 'nowt but a lad', before he joined the army, he did have a few pigeons although he did not race. Nevertheless the interest was always there and renewed itself while he was serving in Germany. Brian became friendly with some German fanciers who competed in long-distance International races against the Dutch, the Belgians and the French. Brian was inspired by competition over such distances against so many well-known world names. It is no wonder the bug bit. From that introduction there was never any doubt the path Brian was to follow in the course of his pigeon career: he became a long-distance man through and through. No other aspect of pigeon sport came anywhere near to the thrill of competing and owning pigeons that could fly long distances.

Brian Denney.

There have been disappointments, of course. but even these can be turned to advantage if you are driven by the need to solve problems. Brian has always been a 'solver'. That is why the challenge of breeding and racing pigeons to fly huge distances is meat and drink to him. He lives off a challenge.

When Brian came out of the army he looked around before he actually became involved. He began to meet and get to know well-known Yorkshire fanciers, including Albert Witty, who lived close by at Malton, and Derek Smith, the 'ace' of Ayton on the edge of the North Yorkshire Moors. Derek had just won the Up North Combine Bourges race of 1963, a very hard long-distance race: the winning velocity on that day was only 850m (930 yards) per minute. Derek had a tremendous family of pigeons and Brian visited Derek when these were at the height of their power.

THE INTERVIEW

The Start and Inspiration

Did you buy pigeons from Derek Smith?

Yes, I did. I bought pigeons and had some eggs gifted to me from his best birds. That was the start of my long-distance racing, but as far as inspiration in long-distance racing was concerned it was the late

Frank Cheetham of Pontefract who influenced me. Frank won his section in the National Flying Club many times. When the *Racing Pigeon* weekly paper arrived the weekend after the Pau race Frank Cheetham used to be on the top of his section. Frank flew 1,140km (709 miles) from Pau. His achievements were magnificent at the time he flew. The thought that dominated my mind during this time was that I also wanted to do the same. I too wanted to own and train magnificent pigeons that could fly over 700 miles. I have been trying ever since. Fred was a real inspiration for me. He was the pioneer of his day, the man who conquered 700-mile flying into Yorkshire more than anyone else.

You started with the Derek Smith pigeons. Did you put a cross into them?

The introduction of the Van Hee pigeons in 1974 was a major cross. This was probably my most brilliant move. The Van Hee pigeons came from the Louis Massarella stud near Loughborough. I was probably the first to get them. Previously I had bought a cock bird from the same stud in the very early 1960s. This first Louella pigeon bred me my first pigeon to fly Pau. That was in the days when the marking for Pau was at Oxford and you had to send your entries by train. I always kept contact with the Louella stud because of this.

The Importance of the Van Hees

Did you visit the stud again?

Yes. The Van Hee pigeons were a major turning-point in the development of my loft. They were high-class birds. It is probably not possible in modern times to buy a group of such high-class pigeons in one go. You may be able to buy the odd one or two over time, but a group all of which bred good pigeons at the same time is probably not now possible. The Van Hee pigeons were off birds that themselves had been in the International Barcelona result. At that time there was never any hint of drugs or false aids to pigeon health. What you got were pigeons of indisputable quality based on good results – and the Van Hee results at that time were amazing, probably the best in Europe. They were genuine pigeons such as 'Motta', 'Jean Pierre' and 'Napoleon'. 'Madame Motta', 'Splendide' and others were all there in the pedigrees of the original Van Hee pigeons of 1974. They still have great influence today.

I was really lucky because at the time I bought the pigeons they hadn't even been advertised. I also had a free hand in choosing whatever I wanted. John Massarella left me with my basket in the Old Green racing loft to make my choice. I chose a pair

		Bege 70 3110138 **G and M Van Hee**
	'Napoleon' **Belge 73 3104092** G and M Van Hee	
		Belge 65 3100028 **G and M Van Hee**
'The Super Van Hee' **NU74 V 68045** **Blue Cheq**		
		Belge 72 3102513 **G and M Van Hee**
	Madame Motta **Belge 73 3104166** G and M Van Hee	
		Belge 71 3101450 **G and M Van Hee**

Pedigree of one of the original Van Hee's off Napoleon and Madame Motta.

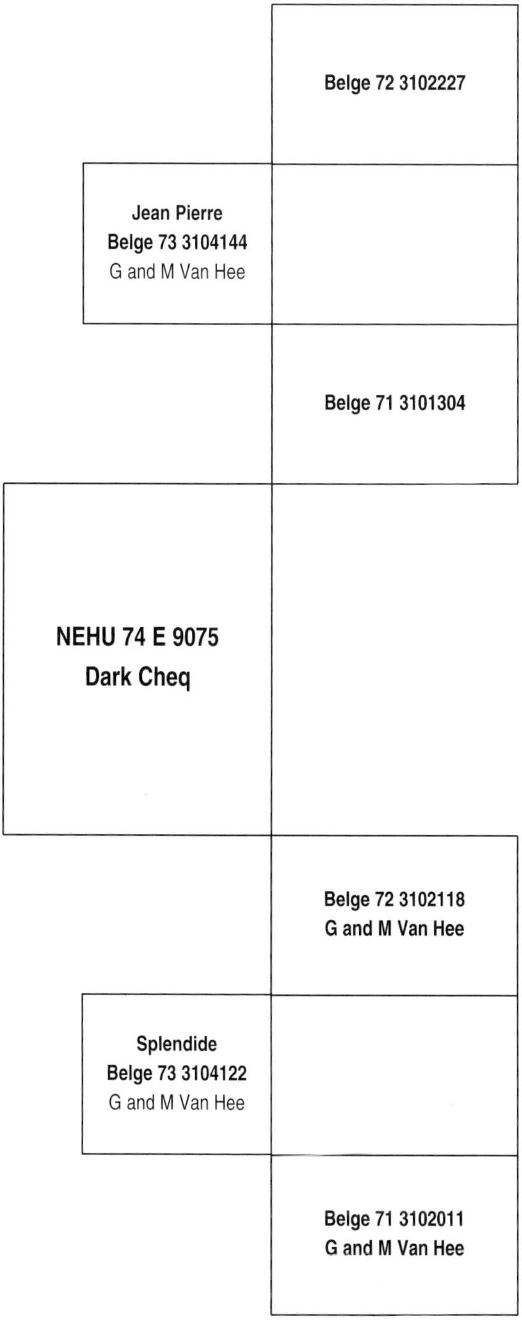

		Belge 72 3102227
	Jean Pierre Belge 73 3104144 G and M Van Hee	
		Belge 71 3101304
NEHU 74 E 9075 Dark Cheq		
		Belge 72 3102118 G and M Van Hee
	Splendide Belge 73 3104122 G and M Van Hee	
		Belge 71 3102011 G and M Van Hee

Pedigree of one of the original Van Hee stock. This one is bred from 'Jean Pierre' and 'Splendide'.

of pigeons off 'Madame Motta' and 'Napoleon' and off 'Jean Pierre' and 'Splendide'. That pair of pigeons bred winner after winner.

I brought the pigeons back on the Saturday. They had paired up in the basket during the journey back and a week later they were sitting eggs here in my own loft. Until the details came through I didn't know what they were off but I didn't care, I liked the pigeons immediately. During their lifetimes that one pair bred pigeons to win thirty first prizes from all distances, including the very long distance races. They were magnificent.

'Dark Peron', A Noel Peiren Pigeon

When you chose them was there any shape you had in mind?

They just stood out. They were wild as anything, but regardless of that they stood out as quality pigeons. My next important breeder after the original Van Hee pigeons, 'Dark Peron', was just as good or perhaps even better. He was chosen on the same basis, on what I felt about him at first sight. My wife and I called in at the stud for a look around on the off-chance after we had been training some pigeons. I noticed this cock bird for sale in a pen for just £15. He also stood out. I asked my wife to stand near the pen and not let anyone else near until I got back, before rushing to call John Massarella to do the deal. The now famous 'Dark Peron' was a pigeon of the blood of Noel Peiren of Zedelgem, who is still a top Belgian champion to this day.

Does it really matter if the breeders are cocks or hens?

Of course I have had good pairs where both the cock and the hen played their part, but I don't think it really matters. There are good cocks and there are good hens, but it is the pair that makes the pigeons.

Disappointments

Have you bought pigeons that just didn't work?

Oh yes, I have. The biggest let-down for me has been without a doubt the Jan Aarden-based pigeons. I had them off the best Louis Massarella owned but couldn't do anything with them. I have had them down from famous Barcelona International winners, all with results anyone would be impressed with, but for some reason I couldn't get on with them. They just didn't act like my own. They had a good opportunity – I even had two sections set aside especially for them with twelve pigeons in each section. I now have only one pigeon left out of the original twenty-four.

'Dark Peron' **GB86V25843** Foundation stock bird Bred by Louella stud	**GB 85 V 42394** Dk Ch Bred by Louella Lofts	**Belge 84 3418953** Bred by Noel Peiren Zedelgem	Belge 813379578 'Donkeren'	'The Limoges'
				'Zwartje'
			Belge 83 3150380 'Zwarte'	Arnold
				Limoges Hen
		Belge 84 3302497 Bred by Noel Peiren Zedelgern	Belge 73 34021112 'Miel' full bro to 1st Int Barcelona Hens	Roosteren Leenaerts
				Sandra
			Belge 80 3491777 David hen Sister to 1st Nat 'Ace' 78	'201'
				'Blue Ijzeren'
	GB 85 V 50735 Cheq Bred by Louella Lofts	**Belge 83 3232067** 'Norella Fandango' Bred by Noel Peiren	Belge 76 3439892 'Sproete Beul'	Jonge Beul
				Van den Black
			Belge 76 3347202 'Blauw Witslag'	Kline Dikken
				Blauwe Witpen
		Belge 83 3232086 'Norella Blauwe' Bred by Noel Peiren	Belge 80 3257248 'The 248'	Blauwen Beul
				Kapoen hen
			Belge 82 3434552 'Blauw'	The 065
				Belge 77 3187874

Pedigree of 'Dark Peron', the Noel Peiren pigeon bought for £15.

'DARK PERON'
(GB 86V 25843)

Bred by Louella and raced by Brian Denney

1988	1st Rugby, 4th Basingstoke, 2nd Sartilly, 4th Basingstoke, 2nd Basingstoke, 2nd Sartilly.
1989	3rd Basingstoke, 3rd Fareham, 3rd Sartilly, 4th Yorkshire Middle Route Clermont
1990	–
1991	2nd Basingstoke, Returned from Sartilly Injured
1992	2nd North East 700 mile club 3rd sect 'K' 33rd Open NFC Saintes 573 miles.
1993	3rd Open Northern Classic Rennes 410 miles, 15th Open N Classic Rennes 410 miles 15th Open northern Classic Niort 533 miles.

Sire of **Whitetail**

1988	1st Basingstoke
1989	2nd Nantes 489 miles
1990	4th North east 700 mile clubs 4th Sect 'K' 51st Open NFC Pau 738 miles
1991	1st North East 700 Mile Club 5th Sect 'K' 234th Open Paul 738 miles

Sire of **'Dark King'**

1997	Flew to 180 miles.
1998	Saintes 573 miles
1999	15th Open Northern Classic Saintes - 53rd Open Northern Classic Rennes
2000	20th Sect 'K' NFC Saintes - 55th MNFC La Ferte 411 miles - 481st MNFC Picauville
2001	18th Sect 'K' 364th Open NFC San Sebastian 742 miles
2002	Flew Pau 738 miles
2003	17th Sect 'K' 296th Open NFC Saintres 573 miles
2004	2nd Sect 'K' 88th Open NFC Pau 3463 birds
2005	10th Sect 'K' 281st Open NFC Tarbes 742 miles
2006	6th sect 'K' 238th Opoen NFC Bordeaux 631 miles 2810 birds.

Grand Sire of **'Tuff Nut'**

1997	2nd La Ferte Bernard 411 miles - 3rd Niort 533 miles
1998	28th Sec 'K' 343rd open NFC Saintes 573 miles
2000	6th Open Northern Classic Saints 573 miles
2001	Flew Pau
2002	1st Sect 'K' 5th Open NFC Pau 738 miles Vel 841. 4085 birds

Compared with the Van Hee pigeons they were poor, but to give credit to the one left he has now flown Pau twice and has won two section prizes.

This experience prompted me to take a second look at International results. I am a bit worried about the fact that some birds might fly at night. Some pigeons that have actually won the International from Barcelona have been timed very early the next morning of the second day. There is a high probability these flew into the night on the first day and because of this secured a false velocity. There is evidence for this because pigeons have been timed in the dark when the race was officially closed. This sort of thing worries me, for it is possible to get an entirely false picture of a pigeon's intrinsic ability because of it.

The Race Team

What work do you expect of young birds in the year of their birth, especially new young birds you introduce into your loft?

I expect any new birds to be as good as my own and to do as much work as my own. I expect my own to fly from the South Coast, a distance of 350km (220 miles). I would train them exactly the same as my own, starting off at 32km (20 miles), then gradually increasing the distance with five or six tosses to 80km (50 miles). At this stage they are expected to start their racing career with actual races. They might have five or six races including the final race from the South Coast. I don't particularly expect these young birds to win prizes in their first year. The only thing they have to do is to survive.

Do you breed late breds?

No, at least not off the race team. Selected stock pigeons that are breeding a nice type carry on breeding until June.

How far do you race your yearlings?

It varies, depending on how many I have and

how good the quality is. Some years the quality is considerably better than others. I don't know why this is, but definitely some years are good breeding years and others are not: 2005, for instance, was a particularly good year. It produced really good yearling pigeons for 2006. All the yearlings went as far as 640km (400 miles), but some went to Saintes (920km/573 miles) and Bordeaux (1,015km/631 miles). Some went to both, but 2005 was unusual because I was blessed with a good team of youngsters. I decided there was enough strength to be bold and test them at a greater distance as yearlings. Up to 2004 the loft had become run down. I had fewer pigeons. Some of the good old pigeons were retired and some were lost, so with this in mind I decided to breed a good team of youngsters to replenish my stock. I think I bred fifty young pigeons and ended up with forty or more that had flown from three races over 320km (200 miles). I really worked the pigeons in 2005. I had everything in absolutely top form. The whole team was really fit so wherever I sent them they flew well. Having said all this, not every year is the same: in 2006, for instance, my youngsters have not followed the same pattern. They have only had one race of 290km (180 miles). As a result of this the 2006 youngsters will be treated entirely different next year [2007] and may only fly from the coast once and have one Channel race. There is no set rule for each year. You have to play every year as it comes according to the raw material you have at hand. But I must stress all long-distance pigeons must be tested sometime early in their career. That is essential to maintain the quality of the loft.

In normal years I would say that the yearling pigeons would have the entire inland programme and at least two Channel races before they moved on to being fully fledged two-year-old pigeons. I am usually up every morning at 5am and have the pigeons out and racing up and down an open sky for at least an hour each for both the cocks and the hens, after which the young birds go out. This is the best time of the day for me and I think the best time for the pigeons. I love clear fresh early mornings; it sets the mood for the rest of the day.

Looks and Fads

Do you have any particular fads when you are looking at a pigeon?

I don't have anything to do with 'eye sign' or deciding the quality of the pigeon by looking at its eye. As soon as I get it in my hand I know pretty much what it is going to be like. I don't like pigeons that are too big. I certainly don't like them deep. I don't like them when they have what people refer to as having a 'weak back', when the pigeon sticks its tail up. I like the pigeon to be a nice-looking pigeon, cocks to be bold and hens to be sweet. I like good silky feather in a pigeon, but I also know there can be pigeons that have hard feather. I like pigeons that are balanced but inclined to be 'long cast' with extra length in the wing.

One of the many things that characterize the Denney loft is plenty of fresh air, but the pigeons can't see outside.

I think my 'Dark Peron' was my ideal shape and style in a pigeon. He overawed everyone who saw him. He was sheer class and he showed it.

Treatments

Do you use any medical treatments or aids for fitness?

Treatments – you won't need much space for this. I have my pigeons tested by a firm called Northern Hygiene. They test for worms and coccidiosis. For quite a lot of years I have had a zero count for both round worm and capillaria (hair) worm.

I usually have a very low count for Coccidia. The last test produced a count of 300. People talk about thousands, so I have no problem there and thus never treat. As for canker, I don't test for it because pigeons get mixed up together with other pigeons in baskets, so they are going to pick something up. Instead I treat them when they are sitting their first round of eggs. After that they are left alone to hatch and rear the youngsters. The youngsters are not treated for anything. They have to race and fly without treatments of any kind. If they get anything wrong with them I just remove them.

When it comes to the long races, after they have been in the basket for two or three days they get a treatment for canker in the drinking water for two days. If they are on a three-week cycle between Channel races they are treated every three weeks after each race. It has been pointed out to me by veterinary surgeons that there is a difference between the canker you can see, the yellow cheesy growths in the mouth area, and the so-called 'wet canker', which is not easily seen. If you get the yellow cheesy variety you are in trouble, but mild forms of wet canker that produce a loss of form can be easily tackled with a two-day treatment.

Respiratory Conditions

What about antibiotics for respiratory conditions or vaccination against paramyxo?

Of course I vaccinate against paramyxo, but I never use antibiotics and I never get respiratory illness because of the degree of ventilation in my loft. It is said that if I ever bought a new loft it wouldn't stay new for long because I would be cutting holes in it. My loft is 'L' shaped. In the centre of the 'L' there is an apple tree that has fruit every year. The ripe apples fall onto the loft roof every September. Ventilation comes in everywhere, particularly around the apple tree. The loft always smells good and clean, but is without draughts.

In my early days I disposed of any pigeons that had respiratory trouble, so now all I have are pigeons with good efficient respiratory tracts and clear mucus-free air sacks.

Also in the old days there was a method of detecting underlying respiratory conditions. All the pigeons used to have their heads dipped into a solution of potassium permanganate for ten seconds. The ones who had some form of respiratory illness immediately showed distress. The ones that didn't flew up to the perch, shook their heads and were fine. This was not a cure but it was a sure method of detecting the ones with an underlying respiratory condition.

If you do have respiratory trouble the old ones are sure to pass it onto the young when they feed them. The youngsters then have greasy wattles and in turn will develop a respiratory condition themselves. I never get any of that. My pigeons have built up a natural resistance over the years to many things: 'respiratory' is one of them. I think I have developed a loft that is ideally ventilated so that it helps keep the pigeons in perfect condition. Even on the hottest of days the loft is cool inside.

The Loft Environment

Do you clean your lofts out every day?

Yes. The lofts are cleaned when the birds are exercising. It becomes easy and only takes a few minutes to scrap out and clean the perches and each nest box every morning.

Do you consciously work for contentment?

Yes, I do. I like to feel that nothing can disturb the pigeons and they feel safe. I have things built so they can't see out of the loft and nothing can see into the loft. When I used to work I didn't have so much time, so at that time I had deep litter. I cleaned the perches and the nest boxes every day, but the floor had deep litter. If your loft is dry I don't think it matters if your loft has deep litter or a clean floor. Either way is just as good as the other, but the pigeons like deep litter so they can scratch about and enjoy themselves. Perhaps they are more contented with deep litter.

Advice to a Novice

What advice would you give a novice attempting to build a team of long-distance pigeons?

He has got to go to a man who has been successful with long-distance pigeons for a number of years. He should buy a team of late-bred youngsters off his best stock pigeons or off his best racers, depending on what he can afford. He should breed as many off them as he can and race all the youngsters. Because he is a new starter he should initially take things a bit easy, but at the same time he should not be frightened of sending and testing them. Pigeons have to be tested at every stage, as young birds, as yearlings and so on. At some time in the life of a long-distance pigeon the bird has to be tested to see if it is made of the right stuff. It doesn't really matter if they are tested in gradual stages or in a big jump, but be tested they must.

It would be good advice for the novice to listen to the chap from whom he bought the pigeons and follow his methods, but he must bear in mind that it is impossible to copy everything. This is because circumstances are always different and what can be done with a mature family cannot be done with a new team of pigeons. As the young fancier becomes more experienced he must learn his own methods, methods that suit his circumstances. Above all he must learn to observe his pigeons critically without bias to a particular favourite or to one that cost a lot.

With the best will in the world no one can tell everything. There are certain things good fanciers do that are habits acquired through a long time of dealing with pigeons. If they are good habits they are in fact essential to the racing of the pigeons. Our novice should observe what works in his own loft and be critical of what does not. Eventually he will naturally learn to do things in a way that helps the pigeons, but even if he is lucky it is often a 'two steps forward and one step back' process. We only ever know in part, we never know everything. But the basis of long-distance pigeons is the old Darwinian adage, 'the survival of the fittest'.

Mature Pigeons

Is there anything special that you do for three- and four-year-old pigeons to get them ready for long races?

The main job is to get them fit. You can only do that if they are exercised and fed correctly. By the time the long races come up they will have already completed one or two Channel races and had perhaps an eight-hour fly and possibly a ten- or eleven-hour fly three weeks apart from each other. The preparatory races are of vital importance. It is because of these races and the exercise they get from flying them that they eventually get fit enough to fly the 1,188km (738 miles) from Pau. You need a bit of luck in the run-up to the long races. Preparation should ideally be accident-free. The preparatory races themselves may be hard, but they must not be so hard as to be termed a smash. On the other hand they must not be too easy. If these races are too easy they do not prepare the pigeon well enough to fly a hard 738 miles. You must always be prepared and the pigeons must be prepared for a difficult race where only one or two pigeons get home in good time. So, race preparation through exercise and actual racing is a vital ingredient for success. Unless the pigeons are in absolutely top condition they will not fly Pau, never mind win at this distance.

As for the food, I feed a widowhood mixture with at least 50 per cent maize in it. I also buy straight maize and add this to the basic mixture as the work they are required to do increases. I buy a bag of hemp seed and use it as a titbit for the longer races. I also buy a bag of red skinned peanuts. They get everything they want as far as widowhood mixture is concerned and afterwards they are topped up with peanuts. They just love peanuts and will eat them at any time, but again they must never be too fat. They still have to be in athletic condition even for the very long races.

I don't use any kind of herbs or garlic, either on the food or in the water. The only thing I have ever used during the last ten years is a Romfried product called Blitz Form. I also use Homoform, which is a kind of small grain mixture saturated with vitamins.

I never give anything in the water: all the vitamin supplement foods such as Homoform are given in the form of food, never in the water.

Is there anything special you do to help really tired pigeons when they return from a long race?

There is nothing special, they just return to the race team and quickly recover themselves. I can't ever remember having a pigeon that was really shattered. The secret is fitness in the first place before they are sent. You can't hurt a fit pigeon. Really fit pigeons are capable of doing much more and flying further than you expect. Good pigeons are capable of fantastic things providing they are fit and well bred. Pigeons in absolutely top form will always amaze. They often amaze you by their good condition when they return after flying for two days. It often seems they could fly more miles if they had to. The good ones shrug off the tremendous effort involved as if it were nothing. Fit pigeons are back to normal very quickly. Mind you, I have had some pigeons that have returned after three weeks. They have had to rough it in the fields and find what food they can. They are often flown down to skin and bone, but in a week or so they have recovered and are back to normal. Good pigeons are notoriously resilient birds. Their constitution and recovery are amazing.

How long do you allow the cock to sit with the hen when he returns from a race?

It can vary depending on the difficulty and length of the race. In the long races like Pau, when you are clocking in all day, I allow pigeons to be together all day and possibly the night as well, but in very short races the cock and hen stay together perhaps only 20 minutes.

Selecting the Type

What type of pigeon do you look for in your team? Do you try to compensate for size, colour of eye or anything like that when you mate them?

I have no big pigeons and I don't have very small pigeons because they were all bred down from the foundation pigeons, which were of medium size. I imagine if I had big ones they would go down and probably so would the little ones. I have no problem as far as size is concerned. As for the eye, I don't even look at them. I concentrate on the line of breeding. I pair the known good breeders together. In a line-bred family like mine the good racers are usually the good breeders, so the basket sorts out not only the survival of the fittest but also the survival for breeding loft as well. 'Dangerman' was a stock bird because he proved himself in the stock loft as being an outstanding producer. He also flew, but not in the very longest races. Having a producer bird such as this is very rare. Most fly and do well in the longest races to prove themselves good enough for stock.

A lot of the yearlings, because they are all of one

family and all have the same bloodlines as many older pigeons, are allowed to choose their mates and to breed and pair themselves. I will take youngsters off such pairs because they are bred well although not proven. The youngsters from such pairs will be tested in races like all the rest. Nevertheless I like love matches within the family. I treat the whole family of pigeons as a unit that has a common blood bond, but this unit has to be continuously tested to maintain quality. Everything is very simple in theory – in practice it is a bit more difficult. Sometimes a wrong decision is made with the best of intentions, but which eventually proves unwise.

Numbers

How many birds would you say you have in your race team on average, how many are there in your breeding loft, and how many youngsters do you breed each year?

I usually have about forty pigeons in the race team and probably twenty pigeons at stock. I usually have one or two decent old cocks that have finished racing; these I like to pair with as many hens as I can during the season in an attempt to maintain the best blood continually passing through the loft.

I have thirty-two boxes in the race sections, so in theory I could have sixty-four pigeons, but I don't use all the boxes. If, for example, I have some young yearling cocks that are spare they are not allowed a box. They have to sit on the floor. Of course, this sets up a rivalry between those with a mate and those without: the ones 'without' are continually trying to usurp the ones 'with'. I think it induces both types to get home a bit faster because of the rivalry for a mate and a box.

Nestboxes – a simple thoughtful design – as are many things in the Denney loft.

As regards young birds, I usually have about forty in my young bird team.

The Main Birds

Which individual pigeons have made a contribution to the founding and sustaining of your family of pigeons?

Without a doubt the cock bird I call the 'SuperVan Hee' was one. He was one of the original stock birds I got from Louis Masserella in 1974. Then there was a pigeon called 'Dangerman' and, of course, 'Dark Peron', the one I told you about that I was immediately attracted to – acquiring 'Dark Peron' was probably the best £15 I have ever spent. The latest cornerstone in the loft today is 'Tuff Nut'. He had a great racing career, being 1st section 'K' and 5th open Pau. A lot of his grandchildren are now coming through to race well. Before the ones I've just mentioned I had a pigeon called 'Continental Queen'. She goes back to the Derek Smith pigeons I first started with. There is also the 'Bordeaux Cock', who was responsible for a lot of good pigeons. The 'Bordeaux Cock' came down from two De Baere pigeons, 'Sheer Pride' and 'September'. The De Baere pigeons have made a great contribution to the family via the 'Bordeaux Cock'.

Did your good pigeons have any particular traits that you can remember?

No, I don't think so, they were just good pigeons. I don't think you can be certain of champions by their looks, although I must say I do have a knack of finding the occasional one. I am forced to say, however, that there has to be something other than looks and that extra something is in their heads. It is relatively easy to breed for physical qualities, but when it comes to mental qualities breeding gets a lot more problematic.

It's a kind of Nature/Nurture thing; nevertheless good pigeons that have flown well have a statistically better chance of passing on some of their mental strength and their physical ability than pigeons that have not flown well. It's more a case of having good healthy genes in the mix and good healthy pigeons to carry them. If you have those two ingredients something will come out. That is why everything has to be tested and above all records have to be kept to let you know where you are going.

I record every race every pigeon has and if it homes on the day or homes the next day. By doing this year by year I can tell immediately which pigeons are the most consistent over time and which pigeons fail the most. By and large the cocks win more than the hens. This is probably the nature of the system, which seems to have an inbuilt bias towards the cocks, but racing hens adds breeding strength to the system.

A Life with Pigeons

How do your pigeons fit in with your family life?

The pigeons are no problem. I have never put my pigeons before my family. We have two daughters and when they were young the children came first, never the pigeons. My work and family always came before the pigeons, but I have had plenty of other hobbies besides pigeons. I think it is suicide not to have other interests; even though pigeons take a lot of your time and are endlessly fascinating they are not everything. I played cricket for years and I play a good game of golf. My golf was mostly winter golf because the pigeons take up the summer months. The priority order has always been family, work and then pigeons, but I couldn't have done it without my wife. She is capable of doing everything with the pigeons. She has always backed me up in everything I have wanted to do.

Can you imagine life without pigeons?

I can imagine it, yes, but I don't think I would like it. I think looking after another animal or bird

Continental Queen 1st Yorkshire Continental club Nantes and 3rd Yorkshire Continental club Angoulême – One of the original base pigeons.

GB79 V 56351
Dangerman

- **Belge 75 3105749**
  G and M Van Hee
  - **Belge 72 3102780**
    G Son of Prins
  - **Belge 72 1215149**
    Black Barcelona
- **Belge 75 3105428**
  G and M Van Hee
  - **Belge 69 3109514**
    Black
    G and M Van Hee
  - **Belge 70 3110141**
    Black 'Yzeren'
    G and M Van Hee

'Prins' Ace
Olympiade
Essen

Pedigree of Dangerman.

species has a civilizing effect in life. You are forced to take a point of view entirely other than your own. You are forced to consider something else that has a life and is living just as we are, but that lives in a different manner to us and has different feelings and, more importantly, a different kind of intelligence. We as humans would be hard put to find our way home over hundreds of miles, for instance. That is a kind of animal intelligence we don't have. We should all consider things like this if we are to be successful with pigeons. We should try to think like a pigeon. It is a mistake to think we can teach pigeons because we are superior. It is they who are superior in their environment and we in ours.

I think I have been lucky in the fact that I have always had pigeons at the back of my house. If I had to go to an allotment every day things would become more difficult. I don't think I would even have started racing pigeons if I had to have them on an allotment, because that would have interfered too much with family life.

If my wife and I are going out, for example, I don't consciously make a decision to be back at a certain time in order to exercise the pigeons. If they miss an exercise then they miss it, but I don't want it to appear that I am casual. I am not. When the main races are happening we put the pigeons first. I really do everything I can to ensure that they are content and in top condition for the longest races. Nevertheless most of the good and important work with the pigeons can be done in the comfort of the sun lounge or even when I am away from the pigeons. I term 'good work' the maintenance of the family's quality, which of course includes the foremost aspect of a long-distance family of pigeons: breeding. I think a lot about breeding. I think a lot about everything to do with breeding. Without breeding there is nothing. Those fanciers who move up from sprint and middle-distance racing have to evaluate upwards the importance of breeding and downgrade the importance of technique. This is often hard for them to adjust, because they tend to think of clever techniques as the main reason for their success. In long-distance racing the secret of success is vitality, breeding and love of home. It is impossible to maintain a family of long-distance pigeons over thirty or forty years without continually testing them, without sound breeding from good pigeons and without good vitality and true contentment. There is nothing complicated about this but many find the patience required to carry out such a policy difficult.

Brian and wife Thelma. Photo: © Copyright Keith Mott

Essential Breeding

You have bred more good pigeons than most and have gone some way towards reducing the odds against breeding good pigeons. Can you tell us your secret and how you have gone about it?

Yes, I can. I have tested them at every stage. Every pigeon I have in the loft has been tested. If I have introduced new pigeons they have been raced. By racing I have eliminated the duffers. By sending them to the distance I have eliminated the ones who can't stand it. By being very strict as far as standards are concerned, I have over the years gradually improved what I have. I am aiming at a situation where every pigeon I send is capable of flying the distance to which it is sent. Every pigeon I have conforms to what I want it to do.

If, for instance, I import six birds from another family of long-distance pigeons, they have to conform to my way of flying pigeons and to the standards I expect. If they don't they have to go. From time to time I have had pigeons that I couldn't make anything of at all. Say, for example, my youngsters have gone off running, flying out of sight for an hour or so while the new ones have swung round and landed on a house. Immediately my suspicions are aroused. I am not prepared to put in a lot of effort to get new pigeons to act like my own. They either do it from the start or not at all. There are others I have had who would rather sit in the field than fly. These are no good.

Every pigeon has to conform to what I want it to do right from the start of its career. I want pigeons that make life easier for me, not more difficult.

When it comes to racing they have to conform as well: if certain pigeons make a habit of coming late then they too are out. By being strict with my selection I have never had too many pigeons, but

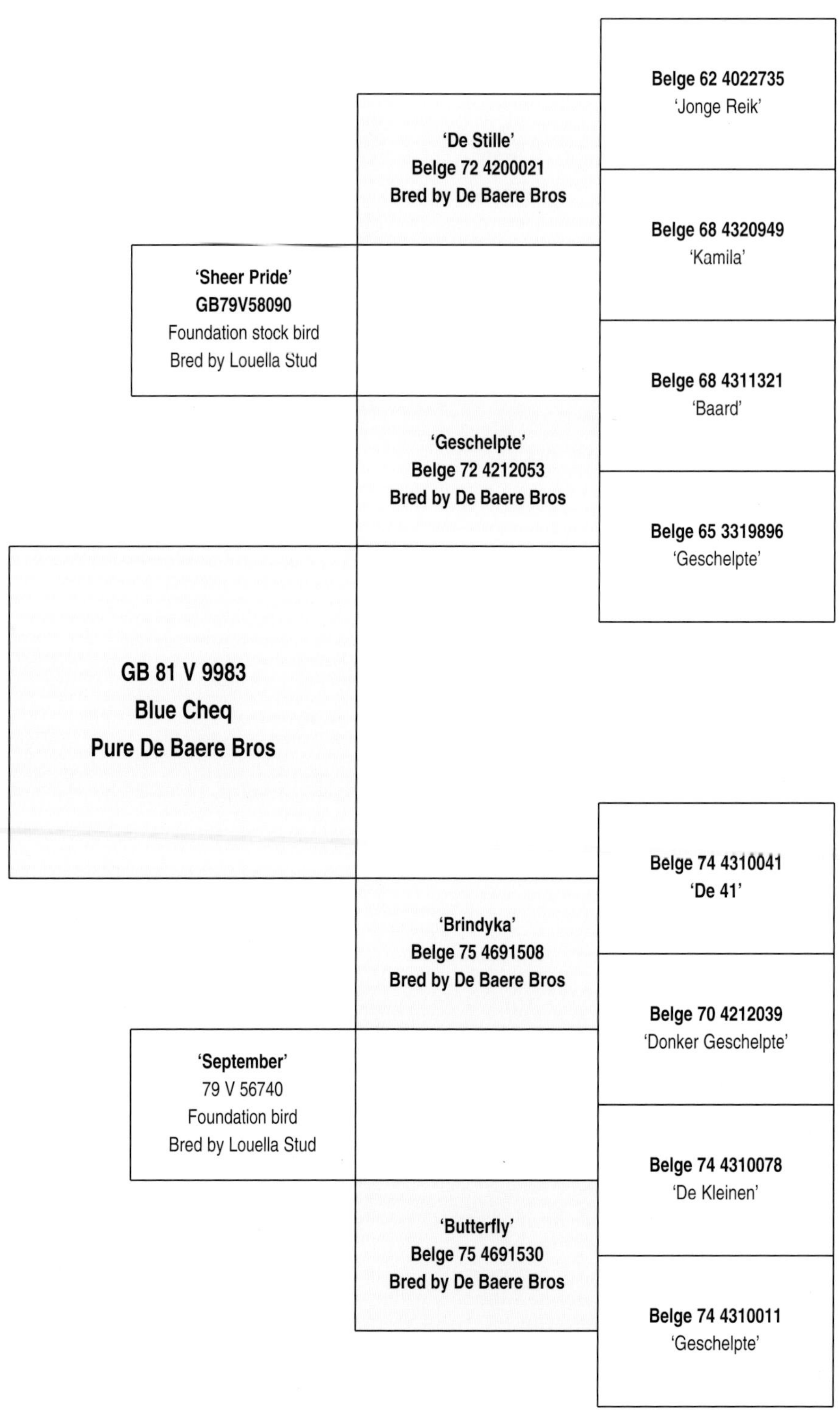

Pedigree of a De Baere pigeon. GB 81 V 9983 off Sheer Pride and September.

have always had good ones or pigeons that have met my standards.

I have set myself a high standard. I am prepared to fly pigeons for seven or eight seasons, including the really long races over 700 miles. I have some pigeons that have done these long races three or four times in the course of their career, and quite a few have flown 500-mile races and 700-mile races twice in a season. By sticking to this standard I never have too many pigeons, for it is only the best that survive.

The ones that are unable to live up to this system are eliminated, but the ones that survive are pigeons that can found a family, or in my case renew and rejuvenate an existing family. After seven or eight seasons you can then put this type of pigeon in the stock loft with confidence. You never have too many of this standard. These are rare pigeons, but it is rare pigeons that are the cornerstones of all good families of pigeons.

I would say that my loft has been created from a line-bred family of pigeons bred down from individual performance pigeons. The old Derek Smith pigeons that started me off were good steady pigeons of high quality that would come from anywhere. The Van Hee pigeons that I acquired from Louella in 1974 were roughly three parts Stichelbaut and one part Janssen. 'Jean Pierre', a foundation pigeon from that time, was half Janssen. Those pigeons, whether due to the Janssen blood in them or not, were exceptionally fast. They would win from all distances, even short inland races where you would not expect long-distance pigeons to make their mark. So they were ideal to go into the sure but steady Derek Smith pigeons.

For the first time in the UK we had a strain of distance pigeons that had speed as well as stamina. The next step from there was the 'Dangerman' and 'Dark Peron' stuff – they were Stichelbaut pigeons. They blended well with the existing Van Hee pigeons, but I was always looking for something even faster. That is why I went for those 'De Baere' pigeons off 'Sheer Pride' and 'September'. It was they who bred the 'Bordeaux Cock' and his brother. They were beautiful pigeons. Their bodies and feather were absolutely super, and as well as being good looking they also bred well. They too came from Louella – I imported six of them young enough to fly out. The result was the 'Bordeaux line', which when paired to 'Dark Peron' made 'Dark King', a pigeon that flew 700 miles four times, as well as Bordeaux and Saintes. These were super pigeons.

Two of the original six 'De Baere' pigeons flew very well themselves. They both went through to

The Bordeaux Cock an outstanding stock bird and racer for Brian Denney flew Bordeaux 452nd Open Pau 109th Open and 133rd Open Saintes NFC. Photo: © Copyright Bryan Siggers

860km (533 miles) but were so good at breeding I stopped them. It's a good job I did because they then started to produce 700-mile pigeons. For years I was crossing 'Dark Peron' stuff with the 'Bordeaux line' and the original 'Van Hee line', and then back with the 'Bordeaux line'. So I now had three lines producing Pau pigeons that easily crossed with each other.

How did 'Tuff Nut' come into this Pau breeding?

I did not breed 'Tuff Nut', it was David Harrison of St Helens. I sold David a son of 'Dark Peron' when 'Dark Peron' was paired to a daughter of the 'Bordeaux Cock' after he had been paired to a daughter of 'Dark Peron'. So in 'Tuff Nut' 'Dark Peron' was on both sides of the father's pedigree. David Harrison in turn paired the cock I had sold him to a Van Bruaene hen bred down from pigeons originally imported by Bobby Mayo, the auctioneer. From this pairing he sent me two youngsters, one of which was 'Tuff Nut'. 'Tuff Nut' is a main breeding influence in my present family. It is no surprise because he was bred in the purple, containing all my best pigeons in his father's pedigree, with the 'Bordeaux Cock' and 'Whitetail' as well as 'Dark Peron'. They are all in there, while the extra cross of the Bobby Mayo Van Braune from the hen's side obviously helped, because 'Tuff Nut' became a wonderful Pau pigeon (he was 5th open NFC).

Provided absolutely top blood is used, the odds against breeding good pigeons are halved. Without

'Tuff Nut'
GB 96 N 27621
1st Sect K 5th Open NFC Pau
738 Miles
28th Section K 343 Open NFC
Saintes
6th Open Northern Classic Saintes
573 Miles

GB 94 N 54680
Bred by B Denney
Sold to David Harrison

'Dark Peron'
GB86V25843
Big Winner to 573 miles

GB 85 V 42394
Bred by Louella
Stud

Belge 84 3418953
Bred by Noel Peiren

Belge 84 3302497
Bred by Noel Peiren

GB 85 V 50735
Bred by Louella Stud

Belge 83 3232067
'Norella Fandango'

Belge 83 3232086
'Norella Blauwe

GB 92 R 96091
Bred by B Denney

87 N 06326
The Bordeaux cock
Bred by B Denney

Cheq Pied
White Tail
51st NFC Pau
Dtr of Dark Peron

GB 90 T 22523
Van Braune
The best of Bobby Mayo

Pedigree of 'Tuff Nutt'.

Tuff Nutt – the latest outstanding bird for stock – also 1st sect 5th Open Pau NFC 738 miles. Photo: © Copyright Peter Bennett

good blood they are multiplied ten-fold or perhaps out of existence altogether. Good blood need not be expensive, but it is the product of tested pigeons and is absolutely necessary.

Ambitions

Do you have any further ambitions?

Yes, I want to win 1st National Flying Club at 700 miles and fly Barcelona with the International. If the National Flying Club took a lead and decided to join in with the International and send to Barcelona I would send. I look at it like this. The National Flying Club is there to provide extra-long distance races for fanciers in the UK. What is really required is for members of southern sections to stretch themselves in races at a greater distance than they now fly. If pigeons were to be entered in the International Barcelona by the National Flying Club, providing these pigeons were of top NFC quality, such as pigeons that had already flown Pau, then UK fanciers would have a really good chance of making a name in a big prestigious International race.

At first the numbers might not be high, but as soon as those on the South Coast, who would be flying about 1,060km (660 miles), were to realize that there was prestige to be had they would soon join in and be keen to send. Not only that, but if the likes of me were to time in and get pigeons from Barcelona, we too would become household names, not only in Britain but throughout Europe and possibly the world. We may not win but our pigeons, because of the feats they performed, would be famous. Not only that but it would renew the National Flying Club, which had introduced the conditions to make it possible. The National Flying Club would then start to regain the status it had once held because it was prepared to provide a challenge to every fancier in the sport.

Inspiration

These days pigeon racing needs inspiration. If I have any reputation at all, and I am not saying I have, it is because I have flown well from an inferior position. If the National Flying Club were to compete from Barcelona it would soon enjoy a similar situation to my own. National Flying Club pigeons would gain respect because they were doing well Internationally from an unfavourable position. Every good fancier in the UK would be challenged to compete and good ones could expect a real chance of success. In time many NFC fanciers would do well. The NFC as a whole would gain respect and become stronger because of it. 'Challenge' is at the heart of long-distance pigeon racing. If the sport were easy and everyone could do it there would be nothing to accomplish. The role of the NFC depends on providing circumstances for challenging races. The foundation of the National Flying Club was built on precepts like this.

CONCLUSION

Brian Denney is the type of fancier who has pursued quality for so long that anything less offends him. He literally can't stand to have anything less than the quality he strives for. But things are not as simple as that. Beauty is in the eye of the beholder, so pigeon quality in Brian's eye is not just physical or how a pigeon looks, although that may be a starting point; it is also behaviour around the loft, behaviour at exercise and eventually its mature behaviour in flying great distances.

If at any stage a pigeon does not look or act like a marathon pigeon in the making, it is certainly suspect. I suppose you could sum up his attitude by describing pigeons in Brian's hands as being athletic performers from the start. They have to look and feel athletically capable. They have to be pigeons that, even as young birds, inspire confidence by the way they act and feel. They have to be pigeons that take exercise easily and enjoy doing it. Lame ducks or pigeons that are reluctant to fly are not encouraged. Pigeons that have to be sustained with medicine have no place in a loft that has an apple tree growing through its centre.

Quality is everywhere, even in the loft that is ideally constructed for cultivating long-distance pigeons. Brian, I feel, would be equally offended by a loft that was also not an ideal place for pigeons. He would certainly see it by the results.

The Challenge

There is another aspect to the Denney life: Brian Denney lives for a challenge. The nature of long distance racing includes a challenge as part of what it is. Without it the sport would not exist. No one can guarantee they are going to be 100 per cent successful all the time. All they can say is that they are going to be more successful than most and achieve a greater proportion of pigeons that eventually achieve success in long races than most. Very long races even have an extra degree of difficulty. Brian Denney has succeeded in increasing the number of successful long-distance pigeons he breeds to a point where his success can be measured as a high proportion of those originally bred. Even much larger lofts do not always achieve this and often fail, for long-distance racing the Denney way is not just a matter of size and money, it is also a matter of the application of high standards.

Brian does not have a huge loft and does not want one. This is a significant move. What Brian can say is that because of his insistence on quality in a small loft he can expect to breed a greater proportion of pigeons that will eventually fly the distance required.

Nevertheless there is always danger lurking ready to pounce should the loft go down the wrong track. The whole loft could as easily slip back to the point where the colony no longer produced long-distance pigeons. Instead, in Brian's hands the loft has gradually moved forward to produce a greater proportion of good pigeons over the years. This is no accident. Any long-distance loft is always balanced on a knife-edge where things could go either way. That is why the Brian Denney story is that of a lifetime of continual testing of what is produced.

A Household Name

Gradually things have got better, breeding and performances have improved. Brian is now a household name and rightly so. No one who has put a lifetime into building a successful strain of pigeons should be dismissed and his efforts taken for granted. In today's sport we all too often take what is achieved for granted. Unfortunately we tend to take the likes of Brian Denney for granted. The sport today tends to undervalue long-distance achievements because they don't necessarily impress immediately with a lot of quick money. What they certainly do, though, is to produce magic moments the sport remembers for a long time.

A Touch of Magic Every Year

Because of the distances from which Brian competes, more often than not he is timing pigeons in the quiet hours late at night on the second day. Out of the dusk the flash of a pigeon suddenly appears as if by magic, wanting only to get into the loft where it was born. This sort of thing is likely to happen most years in the garden of the Denney home. The loft is known for it, but the magic produced every year is still as powerful and compelling as ever. It is this sort of magic, rather than the prize money or the sums earned by buying and selling pigeons, that is at the heart of pigeon racing. We should be grateful that Brian Denney has stuck to his guns over the years and maintained the quality of his family of pigeons. If he had not done so the sport as a whole would be much the poorer. He provides the magic, we should provide the praise.

Conclusion

The Journey

It has been a long but enjoyable journey visiting all the fanciers in this book and hearing ideas about long-distance pigeons from some of the best and boldest exponents of the sport. For the most part they have achieved the greatest success in the most difficult races, though not always against a background of perfectly blessed personal circumstances.

The journey from loft to loft, from one set of ideas to the next, can truly be said to have been a mental journey as well as a physical one. Yet despite everything said and everything done, not one of the fanciers in this book ever claimed to know it all. Indeed most were at pains to point out they are all still groping their way forward towards a more complete understanding of pigeon racing from the long distance. None has yet reached his goal. This is heart-warming, since for the true fancier it places the subject of long-distance pigeon racing right up there with Douglas Adams's *Hitchhiker's Guide to the Galaxy* in the search for the meaning of life, the universe and everything, where anyone without a sense of proportion unwisely claiming to know the size of the problem is automatically suspect. For these reasons long-distance pigeon racing can be a test of finding not only the honest reliable pigeon but also the honest reliable fancier. At its highest level the sport can be pretty heady stuff.

All Home

In the world of long-distance pigeon racing contentment comes from having all your pigeons home in good time from a long race. Personal contentment, as so defined, can be more important than winning first prizes. The elation of actually winning is the reward for the other side of the coin, the competitive side of the sport. Regardless of which side we take, however, the 'all home' feeling of contentment and satisfaction is very powerful. This is certainly true for all the fanciers in this book, especially perhaps in places like Ireland, where the pigeons have to cross two stretches of water to get home. Fanciers who play the long distance strive for the 'all home' feeling all of the time. Nevertheless, even those with high levels of success only ever achieve 'all home' from time to time. Most are happy to settle for a high percentage in good time.

The proportion of returns may vary from loft to loft or from race to race. In extreme cases nothing gets back, while in a few cases everything gets home in good time. Percentage returns are usually high but hardly ever 100 per cent.

Monitoring Success

All good fanciers monitor their degree of success against the ideal of 'all home'. A fancier's standing in long-distance pigeon racing may be judged in terms of percentage returns. Percentage measurement is now at the heart of the sport. As well as the race returns themselves, percentages can be used to monitor success in breeding, by comparing the number bred with those that eventually succeed in long races. This kind of statistic can be a challenge to our thinking. It is essentially what this book is all about. We ask how each fancier can improve his level of breeding success and reliability as measured in percentage terms. Every fancier has his own views but the question still remains. The fanciers interviewed in this book have some answers based on their vast experience. Some are still perplexed, while some are ready to admit they are still trying to find answers. All, regardless of their opinion, will have done a valuable service to the sport of long-distance pigeon racing if they provoke discussion.

If that happens the sport will continue to thrive and the rest of us will continue to be amazed by the feats these small birds achieve. All we have to do is to try to understand how and why it happens and, perhaps more to the point, gain a better all-round understanding of the world of long-distance pigeons.

Continuous Experiment

What every fancier who tackles the problem of long-distance racing is in fact doing is conducting a continuous experiment throughout his pigeon career. Breeding and testing go hand in hand, but unfortunately the experiment is not always conducted under exactly the same conditions every time. Indeed, conditions can vary so much that in one race a good pigeon with obvious ability is at the front with the highest velocity, while the following year the same pigeon with the same level of fitness may be halfway down the field or even a week late.

The direction of the wind and the distance flown may account for some of the anomalies, but pigeons certainly do not fly in an exact straight line as the proverbial crow is supposed to do. They adapt their flight continuously according to the conditions and the hazards they meet.

Nevertheless, long-distance pigeon fanciers continue with their practical experiments of breeding and testing, year after year, according to the ideal they cherish of 'all home' or 'flying faster' every time they send to a race.

The way these inconclusive home experiments are conducted fall broadly into two categories, both of which have a loose scientific basis: 'line breeding' with related pigeons of proven excellence, and 'cross breeding' with unrelated pigeons, also of proven excellence.

The first method attempts to improve the breed by conserving known good ancestral related genes and then further testing the offspring. The second method attempts to improve the breed by statistically identifying from a study of results unrelated quality pigeons and then breeding and testing the offspring produced. Both methods acknowledge that breeding animals and birds in order to improve performance is far from certain. Breeding for performance can indeed be called hazardous, but people still do it. These life experiments, although never conclusive, continue in every loft attempting to improve performance. The conditions where and how both forms of experiment can be practised also vary. For the second one to succeed the sample has to be large. For the first one to succeed the time allowed before improvement has to be long. Both, however, regardless of their merit, must continually test the offspring to find out. We expect to find consistency of performance but even this can be interpreted in different ways.

'Gold Medal' Versus 'Super Ben'

Would 'Super Ben', the wonder pigeon from Calais, still be a super pigeon if flying into Ireland from France? Would a NIPA Gold Medal pigeon still be a super pigeon if it had flown to Calais in International races such as Barcelona and Perpignan? I admit that these are hypothetical questions, but they deserve our attention, since merely posing them is enough to make us think on a broader scale. We are in fact questioning qualities and how we should judge value. The truth is that both the Irish 'Gold Medal' winner and 'Super Ben' were excellent pigeons in their own environment when set against the competition among which they found themselves. There is almost certainly some basic quality common to both that could be of immense value for the future of pigeons everywhere. I hope this is so and that fanciers everywhere can find a fair answer without prejudice, given the common bond of searching for excellence that fanciers share with each other.

Final Summing Up

The title of this section may leave some readers perplexed, but I hope it will draw together the threads that have already been laid out and also persuade some to reread the interviews in a new light. That is part of the problem with new ideas, especially complex ideas concerning pigeons. Not everything new is appreciated first time around. It generally takes two or three takes and a bit of actual practice to appreciate new ideas fully. In my experience pigeon fanciers like to see everything demonstrated before they believe it can happen.

Conventional thinking about feeding, training and how a pigeon should look tends to be understood straight away. Simple but new ideas that point to a new departure in the way we think might take a little longer. Geoff Cooper, in a telephone conversation after I had interviewed him, related to me his thoughts on the subject of new ideas: 'If I had a complete novice who was prepared to follow

Monty Roberts, the Californian horse trainer famous for his 'Join-Up' method of confidence-building with horses.

my advice I could get him to succeed at the top level of competition within three years; a person with a lot of experience, a person who had already achieved some level of success, would take much longer, perhaps never.' He is clearly of the opinion that old ideas have to be dislodged before new ideas can be put in their place.

Monty Roberts, the famous Californian horse trainer, had a similar experience when he first attempted to introduce his revolutionary 'Join-Up' method of training wild horses. Old hands just could not take it. They tried to prove him wrong by getting him to saddle the wildest horses they could find. Their strategy of attempting to trip him up failed, but it took a long time before the majority were converted to his way of thinking.

What's It All About?

During the course of writing this book I have visited many lofts, all different, but there are similarities when it comes to essentials. They are certainly the same in their objective to breed and train pigeons to fly huge distances. This is not easily achieved, especially at the speed of today's competition. Only a small percentage of pigeons that are originally bred manage to eventually fly long distances, still less to win top prizes.

This is the same in all sports in which animals and birds are required to perform mentally and athletically. Horse racing, greyhound racing, sheepdog trials, show jumping and many other sports have this in common with pigeon racing. Far more are bred than actually make it to the top. This fact is often overlooked or not fully appreciated by pigeon fanciers as they start out trying to establish a loft of long-distance pigeons. Almost all are over-optimistic; almost all are filled with a sense of future glory, sure in their minds they will eventually triumph.

Few Will Succeed

A very high proportion of new starters believe that most of what they breed will eventually succeed. This is not so. Failure is always high. Even limited success, if it eventually arrives, will be accompanied by a whole series of failures on the way. It is at this time – the time of failure, disillusionment and discontent – that the whole process is likely to become tiresome and new starters may choose to give up the whole quest and move down to a lesser and easier distance. Others, however, resolve to think more deeply and try harder: there are fanciers in Ireland, for example, who have been trying their entire lives to breed and train a pigeon to fly from France to Ireland. Many have yet to succeed. That is a measure of the task.

All the fanciers in this book have resolved, at one time or another in their pigeon career, to think more deeply and try harder to come to grips with the problems of long-distance pigeon racing. This is not easy, particularly if the initial intent was to arrive at a position where a good measure of reliability is to be achieved.

Reliability

Reliability is the key word, for that is the only way by which long-distance pigeons and their lofts can really be measured. A lone win or the odd poor performance is the same when it comes to the sport, representing only part of a much bigger picture. Any pigeon can be lucky or unlucky, as the case may be. Once a pigeon is released it has to depend on its own resources. The owner has lost any form of control he thought he might have. Any pigeon on a long flight may drop to the ground and have a drink from contaminated water. Any pigeon may receive a minor bump that affects its performance or it might benefit from such quirks of good luck as roosting on a ship travelling in the right direction.

A collection of more than one good or bad performance, either by the loft or by the individual pigeon, largely eliminates this degree of chance. Assessing the overall sample in percentage terms is better than assessing a part. After a run of performances we can make choices based on better information. Good long-distance pigeon men are making these judgements all the time based on consistency rather than the occasional super performance. Consistency and regular results confirm the good. Failure to achieve consistency confirms the bad. That is why Alan Darragh's NIPA Gold Medal pigeon, Robet Ben's 'Super Ben' and the Hagens Brothers' 'Sarina' are examples of good pigeons: they signify consistent quality. The fact that they also represent a rare event underlines this finding.

Line Breeding

That is also why all of the fanciers interviewed agree that it is necessary to have very good blood if one is to have even a small chance. Good blood, as defined by good fanciers, is blood that consistently produces good pigeons time and time again in racing, in breeding or in both.

The importance of having good blood lies at the heart of this book, but each loft slightly differs in how it arrives at this objective. Some, like Bernard Deweerdt, Geoff Cooper, Alan Darragh and Brian Denney, have concentrated on building a basic family of related birds bred off outstanding individual birds, and a cross is only introduced into this basic good blood from time to time. These occasional crosses are preferably from a similarly related family. The cross is introduced to avoid the decline that is likely to come from inbreeding. In the case of the men I have just mentioned, the cross is allowed only in minute quantities so as not to dilute existing established quality, but rather to boost it. A successful cross can also take place on a larger scale. The Hagens Brothers introduced whole teams to provide an extraordinary boost, but in their case whole teams are tested for suitability by racing them first. The chance of actually breeding an extraordinary champion pigeon, though, is still remote.

Such chances are likely to arrive only once or twice in a lifetime, but because they can and do happen they are a sign of what is possible. Successful line breeders always have a fall back position though, that of being able to produce a good quantity of very good pigeons without producing the totally exceptional. If the exceptional occurs it is special, regardless of which breeding method is used, but line breeders expect to produce good pigeons from within their own family without the expense of having to buy introductions on a regular basis.

Cross Breeding

Pigeon breeding in the area covered by International racing is in a privileged position. Its privilege is derived from the huge numbers, perhaps twenty or thirty thousand, who take part in the really big races every year. Statistically pigeon fanciers, if they are so inclined, can undertake to perform a meaningful analysis from this huge sample. Most fanciers in England are not so inclined and think any kind of statistical research involving results is unnecessary and largely a waste of time. Nevertheless a few enlightened fanciers use statistics derived from results to make their assessments.

Readily available race statistics can be highly valuable if properly understood. They can undoubtedly be of enormous benefit when it comes to deciding on stock. The best cross-breeders of long-distance pigeons take advantage of this huge resource of information, covering approximately 80,000 pigeons each year in international races alone. This reduces to 20,000 records of individual pigeons that have actually flown the distance in good time. These results tell the distances flown, the speed at which individuals fly and the competitive position in the race.

The International Barcelona Liberation. Every year between 24,000 and 30,000 pigeons are liberated from Barcelona to fly back to northern Europe. This huge race, covering many hundreds of miles, is the annual highlight of long-distance racing for more than 7,000 pigeon fanciers. Photo: © Copyright Peter van Raamsdonk

This is an enormous boon to the diligent fancier who is prepared to analyse 20,000 individual results from approximately 7,000 lofts to find the best and most consistent pigeons over a period of years. No other sport can boast such a huge sample from as many countries. Robert Ben of Calais, a cross-breeder *par excellence* who has consistently introduced high-quality imports to his stock loft, studies International results over three years in order to make his stock choices statistically viable. Robert tells us that 'results, results, results' are at the centre of his buying policy. They are a way of getting to his 'objective'. He is right, of course, since his racing results underline the fact that the breeding performance of his stock loft is far better than most other lofts. His initial research was the basis of his breeding policy. He has used the advantage of high competing numbers in long-distance International pigeon races to work to his advantage. Most have yet to recognize fully the huge information resource that pigeon racing provides for free.

The method employed by Robert Ben of Calais and, to some degree, Mark Gilbert of Windsor can be called 'cross breeding'. More often than not introductions are unrelated, but as with the related method the quality of the original birds has to be exceptionally high for it to succeed. It is for this reason buying also has to be good for the whole process to succeed. Buying and selling of pigeons should be a two-way sympathetic process between the buyer and the seller.

Enormous Odds

The cross-breeding man understands the enormous inbuilt odds against breeding really good birds; his method tries to readjust these odds downwards. He attempts to shorten the odds by improving his initial selection of stock birds, either by doing detailed research before he buys or buying known champions. The latter course tends to be more expensive, but both paths require a steady drip-feed of introductions that continually update the stock of a cross-breeding loft with good imported genes.

Robert Ben travels by train to the Netherlands every year to buy pigeons for the purpose of updating his stock with more high-quality genes. Fanciers who can afford to pay more buy actual champions.

The jury is still out on whether the 'cross breeding' or the 'line breeding' method is likely to produce the better results, although on the face of it cross breeding seems likely to get a good result more quickly, provided diligent selection using the results method is adopted in the first place.

Good Pigeons Are Still Cheap

Nevertheless, good pigeons can still be cheap, since despite what has been written and published over the years, despite the detailed information available from results, pedigrees, written reports in the fancy press and from the Internet, most fanciers do not investigate as much as they should. Some hardly investigate at all; those that do may be able to home in on a relatively cheap deal.

Considering the work that has gone into the creation of a team of long-distance pigeons it is still possible to buy from very good pigeons relatively cheaply. The fact remains, however, that no one can expect to buy something absolutely ready made. Work has still to be done after the purchase. This comes in the form of further selection. Herman Brinkman tells the story of 'Brinkie Boy', whose Vertelman sire had a brother bred in exactly the same way, but whereas the brother was almost worthless at stock, the sire of 'Brinkie Boy' was a goldmine. Sorting the wheat from the chaff is work. Evaluating the stock once it has been introduced is an additional, but necessary, task.

Good Taste in Pigeons

There is such a thing as good taste in pigeons. Good taste in this context is not entirely visual, it is also mental. Good taste is informed taste, and the more informed the better the taste. It is all about quality of research and the quality by which performance is assessed. Open races, for example, are always better than restricted radius races. International races are better than national races and difficult races are better than easy races. Lack of research is bad taste; it allows all sorts of mumbo-jumbo to cloud judgement. Judgement based on anything from eyes at one end to vents at the other can thus be mighty dangerous. Judgement based on races restricted to a small area can be equally dangerous. Judgement based on races where there was a following wind and judgement based on races where a clear advantage to a particular area can easily be seen are all dangerous and have to be taken into account.

Genuine pigeon men appreciate visitors to their lofts who already know a little about these things and who know a little about their pigeons. Visitors of this quality are usually more than welcome. Genuine pigeon men almost always want their pigeons to do well in other lofts and welcome visitors with good taste.

Long-distance fanciers are interested in their place in history. They really want to help. All the fanciers interviewed in this book fall into this category. This kind of man is not affronted by extra knowledge; on the contrary, they appreciate it. Research and good taste almost always build a respect between buyer and seller. This rapport is an essential element to a productive and worthwhile deal. This is intelligent bargain hunting. Good buying is based on results before a family of pigeons has become a 'strain' and a 'brand name' When a family of pigeons gets universally popular and 'brand named' it is almost always past its best.

Training and Racing

The next problem we all have to come to grips with is the training, racing and conditioning of the 'long-distance pigeon'. Here again nervous jokes abound. Quite a few fanciers interviewed, when asked about a particular policy of feeding and racing or whether they are giving baths frequently or feeding well-known supplements prior to a big race, have said, 'I should do it but I am too lazy' or 'I don't have the time to do such things.' Many joke more about what they don't feed than what they do. They all seem to think potions and magic liquids in the drinking water may not only be too expensive for their value but may also be counter-productive to real condition.

Most long-distance fanciers see 'top condition' more as resulting from the loft as a whole than from the care of individual pigeons. That is one of the reasons almost all fanciers see ventilation and temperature as a prime source of both fitness and condition. For most long-distance lofts, fresh air must enter from above the pigeons and outgoing stale air be exhaled even higher through the roof. It's all a matter of comfort and efficiency, comfort without draughts and an efficient exchange of air at the same time. Jelle Outhuyse, Herman Brinkman, Geoff Cooper, Alan Darragh and Bernard Deweerdt have all worked hard on the construction of their lofts in an attempt to achieve an ideal exchange of air. Alan Darragh even points out that a well-ventilated loft he once sold brought success for another fancier. This is probably going a bit far, but all of them stress that local conditions close to the loft, such as other buildings and trees, affect the performance of the loft as a whole.

The Natural Cycle

The natural cycle of pigeons is almost certainly connected with the breeding cycle. For most lofts, absolute top condition cannot be achieved the whole year round. There are cycles in every location where a particular loft is naturally in better form at one time of the year than others. A lot of this is to do with temperature; some lofts, even in the same garden, may be warmer and therefore better attuned to getting good condition early in the year than others. Robert Ben points out his new loft can sometimes have five or six pigeons arrive before any from his old loft, but he is not prepared to alter the old loft because that too has its own advantages. The fact that the pigeons like it is vital, but undoubtedly temperature and condition are linked. It seems that trial and error in location is the secret. It is impossible to state categorical rules without examining and knowing the surroundings at the local end.

To Scrape or Not to Scrape

That is the question ... and a good question it is. Scraping every day, or even twice a day, is often thought of as being the ideal way to success. After all, it's hygienic and should prevent the spread of disease. Yet we have seen that many of the most successful long-distance lofts do not scrape from one year to the next – at most, all they do is to scrape the perches. The floor is left to accumulate droppings. There is one vital proviso in that the loft must be completely dry. The droppings must be allowed to become dry. There are several ideas behind this policy. The first is that an accumulation of droppings helps to generate natural immunity and is therefore healthier in the long run. Geoff Cooper cites *The Pigeon*, Wendel Levi's account of the commercial production of pigeons for food. Where health is of vital importance for commercial reasons, dry droppings have been shown to produce the best overall health. The dry dropping method may also be preferred since, by keeping cleaning to a minimum, there is more time to observe the pigeons, which also seem happier and more content in a loft where they can pick around for whatever pigeons pick around for.

Herman Brinkman believes in the less labour-intensive approach and so does Jelle Outhuyse. These are both working fanciers in the sense that they still have full-time jobs and just do not have the time for constant cleaning on a daily basis.

There is a high chance that when either retires their pigeons would have to adjust to a retired owner and possibly might not perform so well during the change.

Pigeons that have to make an effort to adjust to their owner are at a disadvantage. Most owners don't think in these terms: they demand adjustment from their pigeons rather than the reverse. As pigeons are such an adaptable species there is usually no problem, but it is still the case that the less adjustment the pigeon has to make the better. Alan Darragh, for instance, manages wild pigeons within his team ('I have wild pigeons that would cut the face off you'), yet he manages them by accommodating himself to their likes and dislikes. Condition and performance therefore are likely to improve the more the pigeons are left alone. All the fanciers in this book note that the loft is the pigeon's home and as such must be respected. It is we the fanciers who are the intruders, not the pigeons. A dry droppings loft helps to keep the inevitable intrusion of basketing, feeding and training to an absolute minimum. For that reason alone it has to be a good policy. Pigeons should always associate the intrusion of the owner into their territory with something pleasant, such as being fed. Bernard Deweerdt, after his experience with the German fancier who wore the Bavarian hat with a feather, does not allow visitors into his upstairs racing loft any more; the Hagens Brothers do likewise, but for reasons of security. It is essential for pigeons to feel mentally safe at all times if they are expected to suffer the pain and expend the enormous physical effort required to get home from long flights. Happiness may be a prime motivator with pigeons, but contentment is the basis of it all. Anything that adds to contentment must be good. This may be why the Hagens Brothers have made the huge decision to race only on the nest (Natural) system in 2007, but there are other reasons as well. Bold decisions from good fanciers should never be dismissed. They always deserve our careful consideration.

Medicine

All the fanciers in this book use medicine in one form or another. All are sparing in its use. For them the worst thing that could happen is for their colony of pigeons to become medicine dependent. All of them vaccinate against paramyxo and a few also against paratyphoid. Bernard Deweerdt administers each vaccine separately because he believes combined vaccines can sometimes be less effective. Nevertheless some use the combined dose and have no problem with it. Northern Ireland, where Alan Darragh lives, is the odd one out because, being surrounded by the sea, some of the well-known conditions common in the rest of Europe have not yet reached Ireland.

Most of the fanciers treat, albeit sparingly, for the various strains of trichomoniasis or canker, as it is more commonly called. Alan Darragh thinks canker is the root cause of a lot of other conditions, so he treats more often than most. The majority treat prior to the racing season or to mating, and again before the longest races in order to reduce the count of the protozoa. A reduction in anything living off the pigeon, whether virus, bacteria, protozoa or parasite, is likely to induce form, but natural resistance is likely to last longer and show in the breeding of future generations. Brian Denney and Bernard Deweerdt are both strong in this belief.

There is another form-inducing treatment that a few recommend, including Herman Brinkman, who uses Linco Septrin (co-trimoxazole), a mild antibiotic treatment for the respiratory tract, three weeks before his special candidates are due to go to Barcelona. The three-week gap before the event is essential in order to allow time for the pigeons to regain form. He only ever uses this once a year.

Every fancier stresses that young birds should not be treated in the year of their birth. Any constitutional weakness has to be discovered as early as possible in the life of every bird. All pigeons must acquire a strong natural immunity as early as possible. All good long-distance fanciers treat the young bird stage as an essential trial period. This trial is also an indication of how well the breeding loft is performing. Ideally in a good long-distance loft not a single young bird should be lost in the year of its birth. This never happens. It is an ideal not even found in nature. Nevertheless losses must count as a better measurement of failure than should prizes as a measure of success. Young birds should not be expected to win prizes but only to survive their infancy intact. Some of the very best old birds were poor as young birds. Robert Ben even goes so far as to claim that some of those that became his best old birds were not raced at all during their infancy. Alan Darragh, on the other hand, tests his young birds by entering them in races from the English or Welsh mainland. In his opinion it is essential to have pigeons that have the inbuilt mental ability to cross a cold Irish Sea, since this is one of the main tenets of his selection process.

Food and Feeding

Geoff Cooper always feeds a proportion of barley in his mixture. He uses this small proportion because barley is the least-liked grain as far as pigeons are concerned. Thus barley is always eaten last and acts as a kind of control of the amount fed. Geoff likes his pigeons slim and athletic without any extra weight. That is why he feeds barley. There are firm reasons for this kind of thinking. Weight is a vital consideration with pigeons because they fly. There has to be a relationship between weight and flying.

Geoff was not sure I had taken in this vital message, so to make doubly sure he asked me how much I thought a seagull weighed. Of course I did not know, but I guessed about three-quarters of a pound. 'Wrong', he exclaimed, 'six ounces, and the one I weighed had a full crop at the time'. His argument was won. His message was that 'weight is the enemy of flight provided strength is not compromised'.

The subject of peanuts and the feeding of various seeds came into many of the interviews. The traditional thinking behind peanuts is that pigeons being prepared for a vital long-distance race should be gradually brought to a peak of fitness by increasing the fatty energy-giving food in stages until just before basketing, when they are given as much as they can eat. Alan Darragh does something different called 'carbohydrate loading.' Five days before basketing he feeds depurative for two days. At this stage the pigeons are almost as fit as they can be; they are not working, they are just resting. During the final three days they are fed as much carbohydrate as they can eat. This does not necessarily mean peanuts. Alan thinks deeply about pigeons and feels his method encourages the pigeon to continue eating in the basket and gaining form while being transported to the race. Most pigeons eat very little in the basket and lose form; his birds gain form because they eat.

It appears there are many methods of feeding, but most are based on the idea of a gradual build-up to the final event by increasing the percentage of strong energy food in stages. Not everyone interviewed was in favour of peanuts as a necessary food for final conditioning. Some were even opposed to their use. Similarly not everyone was in favour of barley and some were opposed to its use, but again Alan Darragh, who has thought as much about feeding as anyone, maintains that barley is great for feather quality.

Buying Pigeons

Many of the fanciers interviewed related stories about their stock and how they acquired them. Herman Brinkman got his original Van der Wegen pigeons when he bought furniture for his new marital home from Hans Eijerkamp, a well-known fancier and furniture dealer. Both Geoff Cooper and Mark Gilbert have visited and bought pigeons from the Deweerdt family. They have bought the best pigeons they could afford at the time or have had to save up to buy them. Everyone wanted good pigeons, but most could not tell at the start if they had them. Geoff Cooper and Herman Brinkman were disappointed. They were wrong. The proof was because they eventually became good pigeons. What was once thought bad became good, especially after they started producing reliable long-distance birds, although Geoff continued to make mistakes for a long time before the penny dropped. Long-distance birds do not necessarily look the part, as Robert Ben, Herman Brinkman, Geoff Cooper, Bernard Deweerdt and Mark Gilbert all testify. Brian Denney feels he can identify class, but even he, along with most of the others, has been disillusioned at one time or another, or has been led down a false path based on how a pigeon should look or what its performances were, only to be proved wrong when the birds have started to breed good pigeons.

I have earlier used the phrase 'good taste in pigeons', meaning informed taste as a result of research done by the buyer. Robert Ben certainly does his research before he buys pigeons, based, so he tells us, on 'results and nothing but results'. We have to believe him, for his own results confirm that he is no ordinary fellow arriving at a loft with a lot of cash ready to throw about. He has decided what he wants before he even gets on the train. That was when the hard work was done, not at the loft where he intends to buy.

The International Results

Every year approximately 80,000 pigeons race in international races, of which about 20,000 individual results, including ring numbers and times, are published in book form as International results. In recent times these have also been posted on the Internet. Collectively this is a tremendous resource of vital importance, but the overwhelming quantity of information has put many of us off. Few are inclined to wade and sift through 20,000 results looking for consistent pigeons. The task is far too

Examples of International results printed in book form. Every result is posted to competitors after each race.

big, but there is a way to eliminate some of the work involved and achieve nearly the same result with less effort.

Part of every entry in International results is a column that tells the number of pigeons sent and the preference order the loft expects the pigeons to arrive in the race. Of course each loft puts its best pigeon as first preference and so on down the list. For a pigeon to be considered the best of any particular loft it usually has known previous form. As an example of how this works, Jelle Outhuyse of Harlingen in the Netherlands (see Chapter 2) has a pigeon that was 216th in the International Barcelona of 2006 flying 1,344km (835 miles). His entry in the 2006 Barcelona race is shown at the bottom of this page.

The (4 1) in the fourth column signifies he sent four pigeons to the race and 1147976.00 was his first choice. As it happens, as previous results reveal, this pigeon does have exceptional form: 1147976.00 was 219th in the Barcelona race of 2004. So here we have a consistent pigeon that has flown 835 miles twice and obtained a high position on each occasion, beating many thousands of birds. Surely this pigeon must be classed as a very good bird worth breeding off. The same might apply to other 'first selected' pigeons from other lofts that are not immediately at the very top of the result but nevertheless are, above all, consistent in good competition.

Jelle Outhuyse from Harlingen, Friesland, whose pigeons regularly fly 1,344km (835 miles) from Barcelona.

Late-bred pigeons purchased of birds such as this can be bought relatively cheaply. Because they are hardly known and have received little publicity, they are just the type of pigeon that would help to start a stock loft from scratch. All we are doing is using the published international results to evaluate consistent performance by using the thoughts and assessment of the pigeon's owner.

This short cut to evaluating results is an alternative to the tedious business of checking them one by one. By concentrating on 'first marked' pigeons that are likely to have previous performances, we can do it much quicker. Other evaluation methods will come to light as familiarity with International results grows, but whatever method or group of methods is used it must be based on the consistency of either loft or pigeon.

If the process is repeated over and over again, year after year, anyone who cares to take the trouble can soon acquire a stock loft composed of birds bred out of the best consistent International

Pos	Name	Town	Sel	Ring Number	Velocity
216	Jelle Outhuyse	Harlingen	4 1	1147976.00	967.19

performance birds. A stock loft built in this way will have statistically a much better chance of breeding good pigeons than its competitors who are not prepared to do similar research. It will certainly help in getting good tested blood for reasonable money. It may result in the breeding of an occasional exceptional pigeon for the race team. It will without doubt improve the odds of breeding quality pigeons that are themselves likely to score in long-distance events.

The Cheapest Way

There is another aspect of this selection analysis method in that eventually a good pair of exceptional breeders might also be found. If very lucky, two pairs of exceptional breeders might be found. Any loft holding two pairs of exceptional breeders will certainly be a champion loft in a very short time. What I have outlined is by far the cheapest and quickest way of getting to the top of long-distance racing. I know it is a new approach and may take some understanding, but the method is based on known data worked out by the buyer not the seller. This puts the buyer in charge. The 'line-bred' method of breeding a team of pigeons takes much longer and requires greater knowledge and skill. Cross breeding based on statistical analysis of the initial stock and progeny testing of what is produced is a good alternative.

Which Method is the Better?

This question is impossible to answer, for in truth the probability is that both the 'line-breeding' method and the 'cross-breeding' method need exponents of each system operating at the same time in order to work at their best. The cross-breeding man needs the products of a line-bred family to use as a cross and the line-breeding man needs the occasional cross from an excellent but rare inbred cross. That being so, modern developments may have a direct bearing on the undoubted difficulty of breeding performance animals and birds through the unique ability of the computer to sift and analyse vast quantities of data and the availability of individual DNA results to confirm parentage. When it comes to pigeons and pigeon racing, 'results' are generally at the heart of everything, just as they have always been, but the computerized statistical analysis of 'results', particularly of International events, backed by DNA verification, will be of great significance in influencing future breeding for the better.

The founding fathers of Belgian pigeon racing were incredibly far-sighted when they introduced the basic *miezen* or '1 in 4' pool as the basic level of their pools. No doubt they realized at the time that all pigeon results based on velocity are imprecise owing to the way wind and distance differences affect results compiled on the single criteria of velocity or metres per minute. They were, of course, left with little or no choice since other systems of working results are equally flawed or perhaps worse.

This realization of the flaw in the system was probably why they introduced the *miezen* pool in an attempt to iron out anomalies of the velocity system by making the results so comprehensive, with everyone in this basic pool earning the same reward. It is this system that enables the Belgians to stage large International races of huge importance over huge areas. Little did they realize, long before the introduction of computers, how this large basic

Line Breeding

Cross Breeding

proportion and the extensive results generated by it could be used statistically in future times to further help in breeding better pigeons.

Huge databases containing the details of thousands of capable pigeons, all of which have flown a minimum distance in good time, are thus now readily available. We can find out where these pigeons are and who owns them. Once the computer has crunched through many races and years of competition, we can also identify consistency of performance by individual pigeons that by definition must have good genes or they would not be there. Consistent performance must be the basis of everything and, as so often happens in pigeon racing, when it comes to producing future champions good consistency and average consistency are often reversed. The averagely consistent pigeon often breeds far better birds than its better-performing cousin. It is for this reason we need a big sample to work on. The *miezen* pool and the numbers it generates is therefore ideal source material for finding good genes.

We are now fully in the information age; by using the information tools available, better-informed breeding of long-distance pigeons is bound to emerge.

Racing Hens

The Hagens Brothers have a speciality in that they are very successful with hens, especially in the extra-long races. By specializing in the 'natural' system, which utilizes hens as well as cocks, their success rate has increased. When widowhood became the standard convenient system of racing pigeons, the racing of nest hens as a consequence was devalued and the contribution hens might have made to the overall success of the loft was overlooked. The truth of the matter is that hens are wasted by the widowhood method. Widowhood became popular because it was simple, seductive and successful for the average fancier. It fitted easily into the life of the busy man, but if time is not a problem there are other methods equally as good. The nest system for long races is one of these.

The Sport Itself

The sport of long-distance pigeon racing constantly changes, yet the mystery of the long-distance pigeon remains. The role of the flock is probably one of the least understood aspects of pigeon life. How pigeons communicate within the flock is still not known. It is known, however, that a racing flock cannot exceed a certain size; above this size it appears that individuals can no longer communicate with each other effectively. Pigeons liberated from Barcelona, for example, quickly break up into smaller groups within the first 12 miles of their journey home, but this aspect of pigeon life is still hardly understood, since it is difficult to scrutinize minute changes in the air when the target is moving. Nevertheless, it is a civilizing thing to speculate about pigeons and how they get home. Even to speculate on the subject and fall short of understanding is civilizing. To breed a lone pigeon that can home late at night after a hard fly of 500 or 600 miles is a challenge, but to understand how it manages to do it is another. The search for why the hair stands up on the back of our neck every time we see it happen is possibly our reason for trying.

APPENDIX

International Races

Historically there are five main International races each year. These races are organized by four Belgian clubs or associations. The countries that take part every year are France, Belgium, Germany, the Netherlands, Luxembourg and the United Kingdom. Poland, Hungary and the Czech Republic occasionally enter the Barcelona race.

CLUB DE FOND WALLONIE FLEURUS
Secretary
Daniel Stoclet
Rue du Geradot 17
B-6180 Courcelles
Belgium
E-mail: clubfondwallonie@skynet.be
Main race: Marseilles, held at the end of July each year.
Average entry: 15,000 birds

CUREGHEM CENTRE, BRUSSELS
Secretary
Alex Rans
Populierenweg 18
B-3020 Herent
Belgium
E-mail: info@cureghem-centre.be
Main race: Barcelona, held at the beginning of July each year
Average entry: 25,000 birds

ASSOCIATION COLOMBE JOYEUSE, BRUSSELS
Secretary
Pierre De Rijst
Heuvelstraat 121
B-9500 Moerbeke
Belgium
Telephone: 054/41.40.52
Main race: Pau, held in the third week of June each year
Average entry: 9,000 birds

ENTENTE BELGE / BELGISCHE VERSTANDHOUDING
Secretary
Yvan Eeckhout
Beekstraat 37
B-9600 Ronse
Belgium
E-mail: yvan.eeckhout@bbri.be
Office
Mme Violette Goditiabois
Planche 8
B-7860 Flobecq
Belgium
E-mail: giverleyen@belgacom.net
Main races: Dax, held on the second Saturday in July each year
Average entry: 18,000 birds
Perpignan, held on the first Saturday in August each year
Average entry: 17,000 birds

Index